AMERICA

Winter 2011/12

THE RACONTEUR

9b Dogo Street, Cardiff, CF11 9JJ

www. theraconteur.info

PARTHIAN

The Old Surgery, Napier Street, Cardigan, SA43 1ED

www.parthianbooks.com

First published 2011

ISBN 978-1-9080-6964-1

Printed and bound by Gwasg Gomer

The Raconteur gratefully acknowledges the financial support of the Welsh Books Council.

A cataloguing record for this volume is available from the British Library.

THE RACONTEUR

9b Dogo Street, Cardiff, CF11 9JJ
www.theraconteur.info

in association with

PARTHIAN

THE RACONTEUR

CONTENTS

THE RACONTEUR

THE RACONTEUR

THE RACONTEUR

A-Z
of American Literature

A

All writers are influenced by the place from which they come, but, arguably, few nations have produced literature so dominated by the very idea of that place. From the Plymouth brethren to Jonathan Franzen, American writers of all eras have indulged in an almost obsessive attempt to define the nature of the vast, constantly evolving experiment that has become known as AMERICA.

The complexities involved in the make-up of a country of such diversity, a country of 50 self-governing states, covering nearly 4 million square miles, and home to 310 million people, makes for a deep well of inspiration. Since the early twentieth century American writers have used this source, and have consequently dominated not only the global market, but often have dominated the conversation. Americanisms have proved a powerful, intoxicating hegemony; the British Isles, certainly, have proven more susceptible than most to the swagger, the glamour, the danger of the American experience.

And all this, arguably, has come from America's perpetual need to discover itself, to define itself, and to offer those explanations to the watching world. Conservative America has looked to its novelists to reaffirm the glory of the American Dream, and the country's liberals have looked to the novel for the truth in the nation's often brutal shortcomings. The American Dream itself is swallowed by its own abstractness as soon as it is touched, devoured by its own hypocrisies. America's role as 'world police', adopted after the threat of apocalyptic conflicts in Europe ended centuries of pseudo-utopian isolationism, has more recently threatened to end the world's love affair with Uncle Sam's Hollywood show. But at the heart of America's difficulties lies a bare, if tarnished, fact: that it truly is the land of opportunity, as much as any land can be.

The truth is that ever since the birth of Hollywood, America has been doing what it does best; selling itself. And the salespeople have been its writers, its painters, its poets. And we have bought the product with the guile of addicts.

B

Malcolm Bradbury called Saul BELLOW the greatest American novelist of the twentieth century. Bellow's impeccable style, wit and intellectualism marked him as the goliath of American fiction for the 56 years he was writing novels. During his career he won a Nobel Prize, a Pulitzer (*Humboldt's Gift*, 1976), a National Medal of the Arts, and remains the only writer to have won three National Book Awards (*The Adventures of Augie March*, 1954; *Herzog*, 1965; *Mr Sammler's Planet*, 1971). He remains the touchstone between the realists, the postmodernists and the modern, smart breed of American writer. Outside his adopted shores (Bellow was born in Quebec but is most definitely a son of Chicago) Bellow's influence is just as significant. Martin Amis, to name just one of his most vocal fans, has called him America's greatest ever writer.

Bellow's work is often dense, picaresque, but is always marked with a stark philosophical intelligence and striking wit. Between 1953 and 1975 Bellow wrote a series of novels of such depth and genius that it is unlikely a creative period of this quality will ever be repeated. Without Bellow the novels of Roth, DeLillo, Toni Morrison, Updike and Franzen (to name just the big-hitters) would be very different creatures. And on top of this Bellow was the first to translate Hebrew writer I.B. Singer into English (Singer

Saul Bellow

himself went on to win the Nobel prize in 1978).

Likewise it is difficult to think of Tom Wolfe's debut novel *BONFIRE OF THE VANITIES* (1987) being quite the same without the shadow of Bellow and his mastery of the tragi-comic. *Vanities* is the story of the fall of wealthy Wall Street mover Sherman McCoy after his mistress hits and kills a black man with her car. It is a novel about the complex corruptions that go into a city structure like New York, and also into a decade like the 1980s. Wolfe explores the press, City Hall, Black Rights, and the American middle-classes in this enormous but highly readable novel. It is the ultimate comment on Wall Street capitalism, and although Wolfe's politics are somewhat dubious at times for even some conservative tastes, the work has often been compared to the novels of Dickens and Thackeray for the way it deliciously portrays the city in which it is set. *Bonfire of the Vanities* is the New York novel of the modern age. Although nearly 25 years since its publication, has proven to be timeless in its portrayal of the rulers of the capitalist machine.

C

Founded in 1953 by poet Lawrence Ferlinghetti and Peter D. Martin, the three-floor independent CITY LIGHTS BOOKSTORE was a renowned beatnik hub frequented by Jack Kerouac, Alan Ginsberg and Bob Dylan. The literary landmark has been a North Beach meeting place for writers, thinkers and readers ever since and hosted the National Book Critics Circle Awards in 2008, which our Associate Editor attended. In 1955, Ferlinghetti launched City Lights Publishers and the much-loved Pocket Poets Series, which can be read in the Poetry Room.

Raymond CARVER once said, 'Writers don't need tricks or gimmicks or even necessarily need to be the smartest fellows on the block. At the risk of appearing foolish, a writer sometimes needs to be able to just stand and gape at this or that thing – a sunset or an old shoe – in absolute and simple amazement.'

Carver was a major player in short form fiction, describing himself as 'inclined toward brevity and intensity', and rarely wrote anything over 10 pages. Influenced by Chekhov, Hemingway and Richard Yates, Carver's first collection of stories *Will You Please Be Quiet, Please?* was published in 1976, while his most revered collection *What We Talk About When We Talk About Love* (1981) was republished as *Beginners* in 2009. The more recent version featured the stories as Carver had originally written them and revealed the heavy edits they had originally succumbed to at the hands of Gordon Lish who changed titles, endings, murders and motives, but rarely touched his trademark opening lines: 'A man without hands came to the door to sell me a photograph of my house'. Edits aside, Carver's is a brand of dirty realism, where minutiae depict the sadness and struggle of ordinary lives and the blue collar every day. In this repsect, his writing is similar to contemporaries Tobias Wolff and Richard Ford.

After a battle with drink Carver eventually managed to quit alcohol only to be diagnosed with lung cancer, which prematurely edited him out of the game in 1988. Luckily for the rest of us, The Great American Short Story still has plenty of life left in it.

D

D is for Dick, Philip K. DICK, the late American novelist, essayist, mystic and short story writer with a huge science fiction fanbase. Literary critic Fredric Jameson dubbed him the 'Shakespeare of Science Fiction' and yet Dick is probably best known for the string of posthumous popular films his books have inspired from *Blade Runner* to *Paycheck* to *A Scanner Darkly*. In fact, Dick's influence spreads even further, to *The Matrix* and *The Truman Show* – films that bring over $2 million dollars apiece to his estate, but in his lifetime only earned the impoverished cult writer $200 pulp magazine dollars per short story. Still, at the time that appeared to be enough to keep him in speed and other drugs; he claimed to take up to a thousand methedrine pills a week.

His novel *The Man in the High Castle* won the prestigious Hugo Award in 1963, yet most of the accolades the author has been anointed with came after the grave – the award-winning novelist was the first Sci-Fi writer to be included in the Library of America in 2007. In 2005 *Time* magazine named *Ubik* (1969) one of the one hundred greatest English-language novels published since 1923 and Michel Gondry has been talking about adapting the novel for the big screen for the last couple of years.

One half of a set of twins born prematurely, Dick far outlived his six-week-old sister Jane, the phantom twin motif coming to haunt many of his works. He was a man of idiosyncrasies, an agoraphobic who managed to marry five times in a pre-internet dating era. Or managed to lose five wives may be more correct; between the drugs, the visions and the psychological conditions he was far from the easiest man to live with. When he was not battling the realities of his own reality, his writing was prolific and insightful but his prose often suffered, becoming incoherent from his excesses. Like Orwell and H.G. Wells before him, Dick's books written and set in the twentieth century are incredibly resonant three decades after his death. Perhaps the surge in popularity of his stories in the sphere of Hollywood is down to the fact that audiences are more open to his futuristic visions and prophetic anxieties now:

> 'We live in a society in which spurious realities are manufactured by the media, by governments, by big corporations, by religious groups, political groups. I ask, in my writing, What is real? Because unceasingly we are bombarded with pseudo-realities manufactured by very sophisticated people using very sophisticated electronic mechanisms. I do not

> distrust their motives. I distrust their power. It is an astonishing power: that of creating whole universes, universes of the mind. I ought to know. I do the same thing.'

These are words Dick wrote in a 1978 essay, and yet they could easily apply to the twittering state of play today. A clever dick, indeed.

E

America has a powerful relationship with its own relatively short history, and the iconic figures who populate the story. A look at the EARLY LITERATURE of the United States can give us an interesting insight into the national psyche as it stands now. The adventurous documentations of settlers such as Captain John Smith (founder of Jamestown and lover of Pocahontas) enlivened Europe's thirst for exotic dawns and encouraged the first influx of speculators and explorers to the New World. The puritan writings have proved the importance of Protestantism to American society from the start (there have only been two Catholic presidents; Kennedy and Obama), their dependence on scripture for guidance, and the power of the religious right in modern society (like the oldest family on the block). But there are also poets of extraordinary beauty and emotion such as Anne Bradstreet and Edward Taylor, who managed to purvey the true hardships of life in a new world. It is from the written word that we have the finest impressions of men of true genius such as Benjamin Franklin and Thomas Jefferson, men who still have a hold over the nation they helped to build to this day. But perhaps the most endearing and enduring collection of writings we have are the letters of John and Abigail Adams. These letters portray a strong and doting marriage, a family bond that became the totemic aspiration of all middle-America, with John as the archetype of the man of duty and Abigail as the mother, wife and pillar of the community. But these letters are also of great historical importance: not only was Adams a chief architect of the Declaration of Independence and the US Constitution, he was first vice-president and third president of the former colonies, and oversaw the building of the White House.

The process of turning books into bytes began in America with Project Gutenberg at the University of Illinois. Founded in 1971 by utopian idealist Michael Hart, Project Gutenberg became the first and largest single collection of free electronic books, or E-BOOKS, in the world and continues to support the creation and distribution of e-books today. It is also the oldest digital library, and now offers over 36,000 free e-books to download to your PC, Kindle, Android, or other portable device. The rise in popularity has been relatively slow. In 1999 American publisher Simon & Schuster introduced their new imprint i-books featuring authors Arthur C Clarke and Raymond Chandler. Yet it was not until July 2010 that online bookseller Amazon.com reported that sales of Kindle e-books outnumbered sales of hardback books for the first time – it sold 140 e-books for every 100 hardback books.

The future for bricks-and-mortar bookstores in 2011 has looked bleak, with Borders liquidating in the US and both Borders and high-street chain Angus & Robertson going under in Australia. By January 2011 e-book sales at Amazon had exceeded its paperback sales. Does this mean the book as we know it is dead? Does reading in electronic form remove the pleasure? Or does having a library in your pocket rekindle a lost interest in reading? If you look to sales, physical book sales may be in decline, but overall book sales are up. In 2001 162m books were sold in Britain, a decade later 229m. You don't need to be much of a mathematician to tell that is a rise, a 42% rise in fact.

The e-book may increase your shelf space, or your post-pub one-click shopping habit, yet the concept of bookless rooms isn't any easy one to really come to terms with. Then again being able to walk around with access to classic, searchable texts in an instant, without breaking your back carrying them about your

FREEDOM
A NOVEL
JONATHAN
FRANZEN
THE CORRECTIONS

person is appealing – useful, convenient, and ever on hand to bluff your way to brilliance. Still the e-book experience is currently rather clinical. What happened to loving books as objects? They never appeared to object. Those of you who see digitalisation as the bastardisation of books are clearly not going to love new immersive reading innovations like Booktrack.com (soundtracks for books). Then again, reading beautifully bound books is a pretty immersive, tactile experience and the increase in bibliophile porn in the form of beautiful reissues of classic books should cheer you up some.

F

In an age when the very existence of the book as a physical entity is questioned on what feels like a daily basis, the publication of Jonathan Franzen's latest novel *FREEDOM* in 2010 was a reminder of what a literary event used to feel like. The long-awaited novel had a reputation before ever being in the public domain – it was promised to be epic, Tolstoyan, and a contender for the title of Great American Novel. Hype? Certainly. But Freedom is a towering achievement, nonetheless. America needs literary big-hitters, as much as it needs Hollywood and the Lincoln Memorial, and without Franzen its milieu seems to be only full of potential or full of writers in the twilight of their career. And, of course, the role needs to be filled by a man; (the title of Great American novelist is apparently a kingship, after all). In the UK the release of the novel made headlines outside the scope of literary interest. Franzen had his spectacles stolen at an event in London. And this was shortly after he discovered that the version in his hand was not the final version of the book. Thousands of copies were recalled at massive cost. It had been a long time since the life of a book was extended beyond the book itself.

Freedom, almost consciously, ticks all the boxes that make up the Great Novel. It is epic, it is a microcosm of wider, far-reaching issues, and it wears its heavyweight forebears proudly. It is physically big, and it is stylistically impressive. Franzen himself is a confident, literary presence, a man who seems to have spent the decade between his previous novel and this, perhaps, preparing himself for the robes of office. The first 50 pages of *Freedom* is astonishing in its panoramic fireworks, a real tour de force. Following that the novel is strident, swaggering, less virtuoso than its opening, more respectful of the town elders who made Franzen's art possible. What Franzen has tried to do is further his ongoing project of defining the American experience. What surrounded the release of the book is just as much a part of the novel as the words on the page.

As far as literary events go, sometimes the aftermath has much more impact than the pre-marketing hype. Erica Jong's 1973 novel *FEAR OF FLYING* now seems the obvious feminist zeitgeist book, written and published in an America still adjusting to Jane Fonda TV interviews and the second generation of counter-culture ideas leading to a 'second-feminism'. It is a novel about female sexual freedom, sure, and it is a frank exploration of these ideas for the time, but at its heart is a character in Isadora Wing who belies the stock-simplicity suggested by the 12.5 million sales. Wing is never truly satisfied by her travels and her experiences, and it turns out a 'zip-fuck' is not what she was looking for, after all. Even though Jong claimed that over a thousand women wrote to her claiming that *Fear of Flying* had given them the courage to leave their husbands, it is ultimately a book that advocates freedom and using that freedom to find a new kind of peace rather than social revolution.

G

One of the most significant female writers of the twentieth century, it is difficult to overestimate the impact Martha GELLHORN had on the generations that followed. Essayist, excellent novelist and short story writer, Gellhorn is widely regarded as one of the finest war correspondents of her era. It is no exaggeration to state that in a 60 year career she covered virtually every major conflict across the globe. From the Spanish Civil War (where she travelled with her husband Ernest Hemingway) to Vietnam and beyond, she carved out a distinguished career in the most male-dominated of fields.

But her focus did not solely cover martial conflict. Her reports from the decrepit heartlands of the American Depression earned her recognition in the highest echelons and the lifelong friendship of Eleanor Roosevelt. Her novel, *The Lowest Trees Have Tops* (1967), is a biting satirical comment on the influence of Joe McCarthy. In her seventies she was reporting on Reagan's wars and genocides in Central and South America, a virulent critic of the US right wing foreign agenda. Today the Martha Gellhorn Prize is awarded each year to journalists who have 'told an unpalatable truth'. 2011's winner was Julian Assange.

The Unites States, of course, always liking to think itself a meritocracy and not a plutocracy, is no stranger the establishment of awards. The most significant, perhaps, is the GOLD MEDAL from the American Academy of Arts and Letters, established in 1916. Recipients read like a who's who of American artistic achievement, as it recognises the fields of fiction, criticism, drama, sculpture, poetry, music, history, graphic art and painting.

H

There is a popular volume of Ernest HEMINGWAY's work available entitled *The Essential Hemingway*. It includes his short debut novel *Fiesta* and extracts from three other novels – *A Farewell to Arms*, *To Have and Have Not* and *For Whom the Bell Tolls* – as well as many of the short stories on which his legacy as master of the clipped sentence and pared-back style has come to rest. Even a brief

Martha Gellhorn and Ernest Hemingway

survey of the titles of some of these stories gives some insight into the breadth of Hemingway's oeuvre and life experiences, from 'The Snows of Kilimanjaro' to the 'Big Two-Hearted River' and from 'The Revolutionist' to 'The Killers'.

He was a journalist in Kansas City, an ambulance driver on the Italian front in World War I, a foreign correspondent and expat artist in 1920s Paris; he was in Europe throughout the turbulence of the Spanish Civil War, D-Day and the liberation of Paris; later he became a resident in both Cuba and Key West, Florida, leaving for Idaho after the revolution. He had four wives, authored ten novels, ten collections of stories and five non-fiction works; he had a near-death experience when his plane crashed on safari in east Africa and had countless scrapes with mortality as a war correspondent. His life was ended by a self-inflicted gunshot wound to the head, the combined risk factors of bipolar disorder, alcohol dependence and a physical brain injury finally taking their toll on the winner of the 1954 Nobel Prize for Literature.

The debt owed by twentieth-century American letters to Ernest Hemingway is such that there is now not only an annual lookalike contest at Sloppy Joe's bar in Key West, but an International Imitation Hemingway Competition for a 'really good page of really bad Hemingway', with the winner flown to Harry's Bar, Papa's favourite Venetian watering hole. Despite his many imitators over the years, the supposed simplicity of his prose style continues to be deceptive. There is only one Ernest Hemingway – man's man and writer's writer – and all his works are essential.

William S. Burroughs once wrote that, 'HOLLYWOOD is still the image of the capital of the world, which is to say, the world centre for time travel.' The place, the industry, has tempted many great writers to go and try their hand forcing their stories into the hands of image makers, those with the keys to the time travel. It is obvious to suggest that the heavy pay cheques drew many writers to the weatherless air of L.A. but many writers genuinely sought to achieve something in the relatively new medium early on.

Read Christopher Isherwood's excellent novel on the process of writing for Hollywood, *Prater Violet*, or Evelyn Waugh's satire of the Hollywood scene, *Loved Ones*, to see the world some great writers found themselves in during the early part of the twentieth century. Raymond Chandler once asked the question, 'Why do film stories always have to have this element of the grotesque?' Grotesque or not, great art often possesses a central darkness, and Hollywood even saw the pens of true greats such as Graham Greene and William Faulkner set to work for them.

Essentially, Hollywood is little different now from any other creative industry, churning out trash on a massive scale while important, moving work seeps through out of a long forgotten crack in the woodwork – just as lowbrow fiction, celebrity biography and cookbooks dominate bookshops; just as musical theatre and regurgitated classics dominate the West End. But it is important to remember the time when it attracted some of the world's greatest writers.

I

'I GREET YOU AT THE BEGINNING OF A GREAT CAREER, which must yet have had a long foreground somewhere, for such a start' is perhaps the most famous line in an American letter, a phrase that connects two of the greatest American minds of the nineteenth century. When you imagine that the great essayist Ralph Waldo Emerson had just read 'Song of Myself', that epic poem which owes more to Homer and the Bible than to anything in its own time, in retrospect his remark seems like something of an understatement.

But the remark does come in the context of a gushing five-sided letter which fully captures the enthusiasm of Emerson for 37-year-old Walt Whitman. The poet had sent one of the first batch of 795 copies of *Leaves of Grass* to the man who had acted as a kind of by-proxy mentor when writing his essay 'The Poet', published eleven years earlier. The article had been a public call in the wilderness for a new prophetic poet to step forward as the voice of the newly independent, democratic and multiracial America. Emerson had lamented that '[o]ur logrolling, our stumps and their politics, our fisheries, our Negroes, and Indians, our boasts, and our repudiations, the wrath of rogues, and the pusillanimity of honest men, the northern trade, the southern planting, the western clearing, Oregon, and Texas, are yet unsung.'

One can only imagine the great leap inside his heart as he read Whitman's verses: 'I celebrate myself, and sing myself, / And what I assume you shall assume, / For every atom belonging to me as good belongs to you. / I loafe and invite my soul, / I lean and loafe at my ease observing a spear of summer grass.' These were words that would set American culture ablaze with possibility. 'Walt Whitman, an American, one of the roughs, a kosmos...' was a poet of America for America, just like Emerson had prophesied.

The book's recipient admitted to having 'rubbed my eyes a little to see if this sunbeam were no illusion; but the solid sense of the book is a sober certainty.' He 'felt much like striking [his] tasks, and visiting New York to pay [Whitman his] respects.' Whitman was to have Emerson's phrase embossed in gold across the green cloth of subsequent editions and the joy for all of us is that we can still share in Emerson's sense of wonder by opening *Leaves of Grass* today. It is still, quite possibly – as the letter described it back in 1855 – 'the most extraordinary piece of wit and wisdom that America has yet contributed'.

'In a completely sane world, madness is the only freedom!' wrote J.G. Ballard. You do not need to answer the repeatedly asked chicken and egg question does the 'madness' cause the creativity or vice versa to know that there are numerous men and women of American letters who have experienced instances of INSANITY to varying crazy degrees. Men like Pulitzer-prize-winning bipolar poets Theodore Roethke and Robert Lowell (both sectioned more

Walt Whitman

than once) and the modernist poet Hart Crane, who threw himself off the Brooklyn Bridge when he was 32. The King of instability, Edgar Allan Poe deserves a mention, obviously. In fact this sort of thing was particularly prevalent amongst poets, it seems. See more on both Poe and Sylvia Plath under 'P'. Innovative and influential *Infinite Jest* author David Foster Wallace is one of our more recent American Literature tragedies, committing suicide in 2008 after suffering depressive episodes for over twenty years, through which medication had helped to keep him productive. His unfinished manuscript *The Pale King* was released earlier this year.

For a long time, female insanity was seen as an affliction of the gender, and any behaviour that was seen to be unladylike or disagreeable or vaguely promiscuous could get one sectioned for a string of time in an asylum, as Zelda Fitzgerald well knew. All it needed was a husband's or a father's signature, which makes Charlotte Perkins Gilman's classic short story 'The Yellow Wall-paper', detailing the author's enforced rest cure of isolation and feeding for her free-thinking ways, such a brave and extraordinary piece (see 'Y'). In more recent times, the misery memoir has made a bunch of people bestsellers for printing their tear-stained manu-scripts – a trend that developed following the publication in 1994 of Elizabeth Wurtzel's *Prozac Nation (Young and Depressed in America: A Memoir)*, a 90s' grunge version of Sylvia Plath's *The Bell Jar*. Wurtzel and Plath each document the depressive episodes of bright young girls in different eras of America. Similarly, Susanna Kaysen's memoir *Girl, Interrupted* recounts her two-year stint in the late 1960s on a teenage psychiatric ward at McLean Hospital. The private hospital is the largest psychiatric facility of Harvard Medical School, and its clientèle has also included David Foster Wallace, Plath and Lowell. In 2011 the insane artist story has been updated again through the releases of *Paradoxical Undressing* about Throwing Muses lead singer Kristin Hirsh's experience of schizophrenia, and *Your Voice in My Head*, in which US-based British journalist Emma Forrest details her struggle with depression.

Other American writers and books that should be mentioned in this section include Kate Chopin and *The Awakening*, Edith Wharton and *The House of Mirth*, the depression and suicide attempts of Dorothy Parker and representations of insanity in Ken Kesey's *One Flew Over The Cuckoo's Nest*, Vladimir Nabokov's *Lolita* and the books of William Burroughs and J.G. Ballard.

J

The American experience, as seen through the eyes of its literary figures, can be broken into the different aspects of the ingredients that make the United States the stew that it is. Arguably the most prominent taste to some of the greatest literature the twentieth century has seen has been the workings of the American Jewish community. Two of America's ten Nobel Literature Laureates have been proponents of JEWISH LITERATURE; one of them, Isaac Bashevis Singer, wrote entirely in Hebrew, leaving it to the other, Saul Bellow, to translate him for the English-speaking world. Jewish literature, certainly in post-war America, has dominated the landscape. A slew of big-hitters have been classed first and foremost as Jewish writers, most prominently, perhaps, in the guise of Philip Roth. Roth's preoccupation with the importance of sex and death to life has given the middle-class Jewish novel a perhaps unfair reputation as being dour, misogynistic and with an over-reliance on self-analysis; a stereotype that other prominent Jewish artists such as Woody Allen have done nothing to dissuade. The truth is some way off that. Important female writers such as Allegra Goodman have tackled Jewish issues with a fresh intellectual outlook. There is, certainly, a central angst to the Jewish novel that is entwined with the cultural history of the people, but this angst needs to be put into perspective when comparing Jewish literature to say, the protestant self-aggrandisement of John Updike and his skin-problems. I.B. Singer's novels are grand in a way that Updike's efforts at the epic could never be.

The Jewish tradition is central to an understanding of the American psyche, a psyche that is constantly wrestling with ideas of identity. The Jews were nomads long before America was envisioned as the New World, a home for all the dispossessed, and they have often been the most authoritative voices on matters that mean the most to the battle for America's soul.

> To the red country and part of the grey country of Oklahoma the last rains came gently and the men came out of their houses and looked at the ruined corn and then they sat in the doorways of their houses, thinking and figuring. And then out of John Steinbeck's panoramic description of the landscape and the way 'the dust hung like fog' and the way 'the sun was as ripe as new blood', we see a huge red truck standing in front of a little roadside restaurant.
>
> Into this American tableau walks a man with cheap, new clothes and hobnail boots. In the restaurant, the truck driver plays the slot machine and gossips about a murder with the waitress. As he rolls his gum under his tongue and walks back to the truck, the hitchhiker says:
>
> 'Could ya give me a lift mister?'
>
> 'Didn't you see the *No Riders* sticker on the win'shield?'
>
> 'Sure I seen it,' the man fires back, 'but sometimes a guy'll be a good guy even if some rich bastard makes him carry a sticker.'

In this way, Steinbeck introduces Tom JOAD, one of the most enduring figures in American literature, hero of *The Grapes of Wrath* and emblem of the politicised working man during the Great Depression. Relaying the epic, quasi-biblical story of Joad and his family migrating west to the false promised land of California by means of a novel laced with documentary 'inter-chapters', Steinbeck not only imbues the Joads with all of the hope

Henry Fonda as Tom Joad
The Grapes of Wrath – Twentieth Century-Fox

and shame of the dispossessed but also bestows upon the American experience a universality that reaches out across continents and generations.

Just by itself, Joad's opening gambit is a devastating analysis of post-Crash America and since: a country, in Joad's eyes, divided into 'good guys' and 'rich bastards'. Steinbeck's hero stands for human dignity in the face of inhuman economics. It is no wonder that songwriters including Woody Guthrie and Bruce Springsteen, as well as generations of ordinary Americans, have been 'sittin' down here in the campfire light / Waitin' on the ghost of Tom Joad.'

K

Jack KEROUAC was born in Lowell, Massachusetts in 1922 to Catholic French Canadian parents, a tight working-class community. He was a star school football player – an athletic career cut short by thrombosis – and was someway toward the all-American hero. Handsome. Well-read. Clean. He died in 1969 from internal haemorrhaging caused by alcohol abuse.

Kerouac the man was a complex figure; his myth less so. Ask any Kerouac devotee what he means to them and it all boils down to an interpretation of his work as a manifesto for freedom. Kerouac was the duke, the lieutenant of the beat movement; the true maverick, the cad. He, apparently, coined the name 'Beat' – a nod to his vivacious, if complicated relationship with his childhood Catholicism. To be in a state of Beatification. But to many of his followers he was the figurehead of the counterculture. His masterwork, *On the Road*, a book that has passed into folklore and is now a rite of passage for teenagers the world over, is the story of a spiritual journey as well as the physical ride across country. But his later published works are much more focussed on realms of spiritual discovery.

Kerouac was never a great writer; perhaps he was an important

JACK KEROUAC

I SAW THAT MY LIFE
WAS A VAST GLOWING
EMPTY PAGE AND I COULD DO
WHAT I WANTED

thinker, but his value lies in the symbolism he gave to the generation who were breaking free from the shackles of conservatism. It is strange that so many see him as a standard-bearer when Kerouac himself was just recreating the adventurousness of his heroes, such as Whitman and Jack London. But way before his unpleasant and tragic demise, Kerouac had been adopted by the counter-culture; as Lester Bangs wrote in his *Rolling Stone* obituary, 'Jack... was one of the first artists to broadcast to the world the sensibility adorning (the 50s and 60s)'. Kerouac, as broadcaster, wrote about a fascinating generation of thinkers and adventurers, people who read widely and deeply, and began to ask questions about the rules surrounding them. 'The hipsters,' he wrote, 'whose music was bop, they looked like criminals, but they kept talking about things I liked, long outlines of personal experience, and vision, nightlong confession full of hope that had become illicit and repressed by War, stirring, rumblings of a new soul (that same old human soul).'

Eric Ehrmann wrote of Kerouac's importance, 'He was fearless in running the gauntlet of self-censorship imposed by publishers during the dark days of the McCarthy era. Finally, in 1957, he made it. James Dean had already shocked America in *Rebel Without a Cause*, but he was acting. In *On the Road*, Kerouac was a rebel without a cause and he had all the guts to tell the world.'

Perhaps in a similar vein to how Kerouac shook up the literary scene of the fifties, Tony KUSHNER's seven-hour epic *Angels in America: A Gay Fantasia on National Themes* changed the way Americans viewed their theatre. For some decades Broadway had not changed, had not stepped outside the parameters established by the revolutions of Eugene O'Neill in the twenties and thirties. Kushner not only created a dazzling 'event' but he did it whilst addressing society's attitude to AIDS. It was daring, but the play is also everything theatre should be: fantastical, relevant, shocking, poetic, engrossing. Kushner, famous for the long gestation periods of his projects, is far from prolific, but as a modern, serious, powerful voice in theatre, there are few louder.

L

> 'Lolita, light of my life, fire of my loins. My sin, my soul. Lo-lee-ta: the tip of the tongue taking a trip of three steps down the palate to tap, at three, on the teeth. Lo. Lee. Ta. She was Lo, plain Lo, in the morning, standing four feet ten in one sock. She was Lola in slacks. She was Dolly at school. She was Dolores on the dotted line. But in my arms she was always Lolita.'

Vladimir Nabokov's controversial cult classic *LOLITA* was first published in Paris in 1955, and then New York in 1958 taking its place in the American literary canon. One of *Time*'s list of the '100 best English-language novels from 1923 to 2005', middle-aged protagonist and unreliable narrator Humbert Humbert recounts a story of his obsessive love for and sexual relationship with 12-year-old nymphet Dolores Haze, who he nicknames Lolita. While initially gaining readers and reputation for being an erotic book, today Lolita is regarded as one of the great literary novels combining irony, cultural commentary, tragedy, cruelty and evocative dancing wordplay. A tale about the pathos of the sexual deviant, it is also a book that nearly never was. Choosing to write in English, rather than his native Russian tongue, the novel took Nabokov five years to write, and upon completion publishers did not rush to take the manuscript off his hands. He was turned down by Simon & Schuster, New Directions, Viking, Doubleday, and Strauss before trying his luck in France.

After publication responses continued to be mixed. Despite a multitude of typographic errors, Graham Greene, writing in the *Sunday Times*, declared *Lolita* 'one of the three best books of 1955'. *Sunday Express* editor at the time, however, John Gordon did not agree, believing it to be 'the filthiest book' he had ever red, full of 'sheer unrestrained pornography.' A scufuffle ensued during which British Customs Officials seized any copies entering the UK and

France's Minister of the Interior banned the novel. Upon publication in America in 1958, *Lolita* became the first book since *Gone With The Wind* to sell 100,000 copies in the first three weeks of publication.

M

MOBY DICK may not be the greatest of all American novels, but it is the first Great American Novel, a concept that has built and built in importance since *The Whale*'s publication in 1851 to regular national debate. Great American Novels have certain criteria; they must be epic, contain themes that respond to the national zeitgeist, and they are always written by men. In many ways *Moby Dick* set the precedent for what all Great American Novels that followed needed to be.

The book itself has had a peculiar life. Immovable as it is now from the annals of greatness, the epic story of one sea-captain's obsessive quest for the monster of the sea who took his leg was originally received with unfavourable reviews. *Southern Quarterly Review*, for instance, suggested a 'writ *de lunatico*' should be issued against Herman Melville and his characters. Melville himself, who had written to his friend Nathaniel Hawthorne claiming that it was time for American writers to step up and achieve a greatness akin to Shakespeare, was no stranger to either outer or inner turmoil. What he tried to address in his novels (*Moby Dick* being his masterpiece) were the same themes all those great writers with which he felt a tight spiritual bond had written of: democracy, the failure of Christianity, fate versus free will, providence, immortality. Aside from these existential concerns, Melville spent much of his literary career deeply in debt, torn between the popular successes of his early seafaring tales and, from the 1850s on, his desire to write 'great literature' that would last through the ages. As he wrote to Hawthorne during the seventeen month composition of his

MOBY
DICK
MOBY
DICK
MOBY
DICK
MOBY
DICK
MOBY
DICK
MOBY
DICK

'whaling book', 'What I feel most moved to write, that is banned – it will not pay. Yet, altogether, write the other way I cannot. So the product is a final hash, and all my books are botches.'

Moby Dick (or *The Whale*) is a sweeping, intense adventure, specked with essays on whaling, and with some of the most memorable characters in the whole of literature. Melville was regarded for much of his later life and after his death as a writer of the second order (and certainly out of fashion if not altogether an eccentric oddity) however a revival and re-evaluation came with the hundredth anniversary of his death in 1919. His work was now being read by an audience removed from the brutality of Melville's age, but who could not resist the questions he asked and the characters with which he tried to answer them. Within just a few years of Melville's centenary celebrations, Moby-Dick could be found in comic book form, in cartoons, as the name of myriad seafood restaurants across the globe, as well as on Federal stamps and Hollywood films.

It is now as difficult to imagine the American literary landscape without Ahab and Moby-Dick as it is to imagine the English one without Dickens. The book, indeed, has come to dominate the American canon just as the whale came to dominate the captain. Writing of his toils with the book to Hawthorne in June 1851 Melville said: 'I was talking about the "Whale"... I'm going to take him by the jaw, however, before long, and finish him up in some fashion or other. What's the use of elaborating what, in its very essence, is so short-lived as a modern book?'

Famous writers who date other writers have always been a subject of gossip and fascination. The fact that some writers pair up should not be so unusual – brought together by shared passions and friends – and love and the breakdown of love are both great muses. Logically two artists paired together should bring an understanding of the creative temperament and the social isolation necessary to get any work done, much like A-Lister film stars who can't date outside the Hollywood top earners. However these love stories do not always have happy endings. From stealing lovers' lines for their own characters to overlapping influences and harsh but fair editing, literary MARRIAGES can be the best and worst hotbeds for new writing and rarely run smoothly. Often such affairs of the heart prove tumultuous, and yet it is in such a passionate clashing of egos that our own fascination grows – the relationships riddled with jealousy, rivalries, and the temptation to win arguments lost in life on the printed page instead.

In the past wooing writers were celebrity couples – Sophia Amelia Peabody and Nathaniel Hawthorne, Martha Gellhorn and Ernest Hemingway, Allen Ginsberg and Peter Orlovsky, Anais Nin and Henry Miller, and F. Scott Fitzgerald and Zelda Sayre. For others, the pairings may not have grabbed them much more limelight outside the bookish sphere, yet within it readers and critics have found themselves unable to avoid seeking nuggets of autobiographical scraps of gossip amongst the fiction. This can be seen as a shifting attitude across time from friends' disapproval of Robert Lowell's description of the collapse of his marriage to Elizabeth Hardwick in *The Dolphin* – to which he replied: 'My story is both a composition and alas, a rather grinding autobiography, though of course one neither does nor should tell the literal or ultimate truth. Poetry lies.' – to a *New York Observer* writer's analysis of Siri Hustvedt's *What I Loved* (2003) as a novel about her husband Paul Auster's ex-wife Lydia Davies.

These details of the literary love triangle or artistic affair often get in the way of critical debate, hungry as we are for the newly discovered lustful poem or the next biting collision that will rival the one between Ted Hughes and Sylvia Plath. The break-up of quick-burning literary pairing David Foster Wallace and Mary Carr came close, disintegrating in a cluster of arguments and broken furniture. More often than not, today, these outbursts take place behind closed doors or not at all. Unfortunately for the reader, the modern great American literary couple appears to have little time for slamming doors and histrionics. Instead they are smart, serious, career-minded people: Nicole Krauss and Jonathan Safron Foer, Dave Eggers and Vendela Vida, and the New York dwellers Zadie Smith and Nick Laird.

N

Our emblematic cities are always atypical. NEW YORK is no more America than London is Britain or Paris is France. But there is something in their size, their symbolism, the extraordinary power they exert over our hearts and minds. They resonate. Even if we have never visited them, they evoke. And this is why, while the President sits in Washington, the nation's literary capital is over two hundred miles north-east, on the Hudson river.

Home not only to *The New Yorker*, the *New York Quarterly* and New *York Review of Books*, but also to *The Paris Review* and countless other literary magazines and journals, the Big Apple is the place to make it as a writer just as it is the gateway to America, a city where dreams are broken and made.

New York was where freed slaves headed in the Great Migration and where the Harlem Renaissance flowered. New York is the home of Broadway, off-Broadway and Tin Pan Alley, the New York Intellectuals and the Beat Poets and host to the PEN American Center. Its hotels and bars and jazz clubs have invented and reinvented American culture for generations. At the Algonquin, ten years of boozy literary lunches gave birth to *The New Yorker* and at the Chelsea, Bob Dylan married folk music with rock music and reconnected popular music with poetry. Each new wave of immigrants makes the place its own and the city's cultural history is a narrative of style-fusion, from abstract expressionism to pop art to street graffiti, by African-Americans and Jewish-Americans and Nuyoricans (New York Puerto Ricans). To dip one's toes in the waters of New York's literature can seem like paddling in the wellspring that created the modern world, for all its ills. From

Washington Square and *The Age of Innocence*, through *Invisible Man* and *The Thin Man* to *Breakfast at Tiffany's* and *Atlas Shrugged*; from *The Bell Jar* to *The Godfather*, *Mr Sammler's Planet* and *Sophie's Choice*; from *Bright Lights, Big City* and *The Bonfire of the Vanities* to *The New York Trilogy* and *Underworld*; from *Sex and the City* to *Exit Ghost*, it can sometimes seem, like in all of the big world cities, that these 300 square miles have somehow swallowed the world.

And like all great world cities, it is a place where you can be not necessarily from but can gravitate to, knowing that because the city belongs to no one it also belongs to us all.

O

It may be difficult to understand the size of the impact the dramas of Eugene O'NEILL had on American theatre almost a century after the Provincetown Players first performed *Bound East for Cardiff* in July 1916. With the company's move from Provincetown to MacDougal Street in Greenwich Village (to a theatre O'Neill named The Playwright's Theatre) O'Neill spent eight seasons between 1916 and 1922 with full artistic scope for his daring and experimental dramas. His first recognised success, *The Emperor Jones*, in 1920, was not only considerably shorter than most Broadway productions, but had an African-American as the lead role. Despite O'Neill's almost provocative experimentalism in form and content *The Emperor Jones* proved irresistible to both public and critics alike, moving to Broadway for an unlimited run, and winning its author the first of four Pulitzer Prizes.

O'Neill had spent much of his career up until this point drawing on his experiences of a tragic family life (his brother was an alcoholic, his mother a morphine-addict, his father a travelling actor who moved his family from hotel to hotel), and his life as a young merchant seaman when he would spend months on land in drunken hazes amongst the bars and brothels of New

York's Hell's Kitchen. By 1922, at the age of 23, he was the sole surviving member of his original family, leaving him free to explore the darker side of sibling relationships and family bonds. His work is at its strongest when starkly autobiographical, be it the masterful family dramas of *Moon for the Misbegotten* or *Long Day's Journey into Night*, or the epic tale of barroom wastrels *The Iceman Cometh*.

For such a successful and famous playwright O'Neill never stopped pushing the boundaries of American theatre. He incorporated expressionism (*The Hairy Ape*), modernised Greek-tragedy (*Mourning Becomes Electra*), used schematic set locations (*Beyond the Horizon*), modernised the use of the aside (*Strange Interlude*), tested audience endurance with four and five-hour plays, and created an ambitious play-cycle detailing a critical history of America through the story of one family in *A Tale of Possessors Self-Dispossessed*.

For all this, and a Nobel Prize in 1936, by the end of his life O'Neill was regarded as somewhat of a has-been. From 1943 he was unable to write due to hand-tremors brought on by a very rare degenerative disease. This, along with constant refusal to sanction productions of his work due to a lack of faith in the companies that wished to perform them, meant that O'Neill's work went largely forgotten until posthumous productions of *Long Day's Journey into Night* and *The Iceman Cometh* in 1956 helped remind the world of his genius.

Far removed, it seems, from the heady days of O'Neill's experimental theatre, the American literary scene is now dominated in a way never seen before by one figure. OPRAH Winfrey's Book Club guarantees bestseller status for any novelist. But perhaps the importance of the club is that Oprah (unlike British attempts at a similar venture with Richard and Judy) has never been afraid – or dumbfounded – by literary fiction. Oprah has promoted serious literature, not supermarket paperbacks, and whereas Richard and Judy are guilty of mistaking middle-brow for literature, Oprah has continually promoted the works of Toni Morrison, Andre Dubus III and Isabel Allende to name just three important literary

Edgar Allan Poe

novelists. Along with a much needed vociferousness on the significance of the modern literary novel, she has also worked to turn new generations toward the works of Carson McCullers, and has reminded young Americans that Faulkner, Dickens and Tolstoy are not just to be studied for English lit. term papers. As Oprah retires this year, and her Book Club retires with her, it will be interesting to see just what an impact she had on the American market place for quality novels in the years after the void left by her absence is felt.

P

As Hershel Parker notes in the opening of his introductory essay on Edgar Allan POE, 'The life of Poe is the most melodramatic of any of the major American writers of his generation.' This could even be an understatement. Poe, a writer and visionary for whom the word genius is wholly fitting, experienced a life defined by tragedy, death, and madness.

Even so, it has been only relatively recently that an accurate picture of the man's life has been established. Two days after Edgar Allan Poe's death, his supposed friend and anthologiser, Rufus Griswold, set about composing a series of letters in Poe's name, ultimately rewriting his lifetime's correspondence, portraying the late author to his friends as little more than a treacherous, petty, paranoid back-stabber. For years after these forgeries tainted Poe in the eyes of every biographer who approached the subject of his troubled life. His reputation has never fully recovered.

His dark gothic tales and poetry have often suggested insanity and a certain type of inhumanity that careful analysis of the facts of his life do not bear out. Poe may have been an alcoholic for most of his adult life, but he was, in better times, a dedicated husband, and a passionate man of letters. He was first a critic for various magazines in the burgeoning publishing discourse of the young America, making a name for himself as a hatchet man in

THE BELL JAR
SYLVIA PLATH
THE BELL JAR
SYLVIA PLATH
THE BELL JAR
SYLVIA PLATH
THE BELL JAR
SYLVIA PLATH
THE BELL JAR
SYLVIA PLATH
THE BELL JAR
SYLVIA PLATH

the old English vein. His poetry in his early period, although well-remembered now, is little more than extremely capable pastiches of the European Romantic tradition. But it is testament to his skill as a craftsman that he has always been widely popular even outside the realms of the poetic-classes. His macabre tales are even more popular. Perfect tales such as 'The Tell-Tale Heart' and 'The Black Cat' are given as examples of the highest achievements in the art form in creative writing classes across the globe. Poe's genius is still hotly debated by critics in America, but the truth is that, with the possible exception of Mark Twain, he is the most highly regarded writer of his century in the minds of both readers and writers alike.

Sylvia PLATH has become the cult poster girl for geeky teenage angst, a writer who is constantly and unfairly defined by the man of her life and her death more than she is for her work. She famously ended her own life in 1963 by sticking her head in a gas oven at the age of 30. Her husband Ted Hughes had not long left her for another woman. These facts, along with her own battle with depression are the most talked about and picked over aspects of Plath's life. Ted Hughes was later to become Poet Laureate, but Plath was also a fine poet responsible for painful confessionals from 'Daddy' to 'Lady Lazarus' and she wrote angrily and eloquently about women's victimisation.

Plath was a bright spark of course. She penned her first poem aged eight, in the same year that her father died, and then gained straight As throughout school, and entered Smith College on a scholarship in 1950. A stint as student 'guest editor' for *Mademoiselle* in New York City during the summer of her junior year was followed by the sleeping-pill suicide attempt described in her 1963 autobiographical novel *The Bell Jar*. Upon resuming her studies Plath graduated from Smith in 1955, landing a Fullbright scholarship to study at Cambridge University. She married Ted Hughes in 1956, and *The Colossus*, her first book was published in 1960. Others, including both versions of *Ariel* were released after her death, and Plath was awarded a posthumous Pulitzer Prize for the *Collected Poems*.

Much has been written about Plath, and there has been plenty of buck-passing and blame exchanged her devotees and commentators loyal to Hughes. The publication of the majority of her journals in 2000 (except for the last two, one of which was burnt by Hughes), allowed the poet to finally speak for herself. Despite this, her legacy of cult fascination will long continue and Cambridge University Press has recently published a new book *Representing Sylvia Plath* in the UK. Edited by Tracy Brain and Sally Bayley, it is available in America this autumn.

Q

Writers can be a prickly, confrontational breed. It comes from being part of a community of recluses, the strain of such a contradiction forcing just as many QUARRELS as it has done iron-cast bonds. The eccentricities of great minds, coinciding with the American love affair with celebrity drama has often resulted in deliciously barbed opines from one writer goaded into giving criticising another. But even before the birth of television, some could not help but offer their views on their contemporaries. Henry James commented that 'An enthusiasm for Poe is the mark of a decidedly primitive stage of reflection' as long ago as 1876. But it was after the war, coinciding with what has been identified as a strident masculinity in American literature from the pens of some of the veterans of the conflict, that some rivalries became entertainingly vicious.

There is a famous episode of *The Dick Cavett Show* in which Gore Vidal and Norman Mailer lock horns. Norman Mailer asks Cavett to just get on and ask him one of those questions off his piece of paper. 'How about I fold it four ways and stick it where the sun doesn't shine?' is the chatshow host's response. Vidal, a big man, hides his silent joy behind his hand.

Gore Vidal himself, once described as America's 'self-appointed hazer-in-chief' has been no stranger to literary spats. He famously penned a very long essay, 'Rabbit's Own Burrow', in the *New York Review of Books* laying bare every aspect of John Updike that he felt needed addressing. Vidal attacks, with superior wit, Updike's style, his politics, his personality and his philosophy. This, claims Vidal, is a retort to Updike's own writing in *The New Yorker*, where, in 'super-patriot mode' Updike had begun to take potshots at the 'whittlers and belittlers' – figures, according to Updike, like Vidal – who nowadays 'set the cultural tone'. By the end of 'Rabbit's Own Burrow' one gets the impression that the arrogant naivety that Vidal seems to accuse Updike of in his philosophies and politics is exactly what drove him to foolishly pick a fight with Gore Vidal.

Of much lesser significance, but just as entertaining, was the fairly recent feud that developed on a Canadian book programme between journalist-turned novelist Tom Wolfe and Pulitzer prize-winner John Irving. On the show Irving compared Wolfe to John Grisham saying, 'I can't read him because he's such a bad writer.' Wolfe had recently called Updike and Mailer 'a pile of old bones' and Irving had decided to wade in. What did Irving think of the 'war' between Mailer and Updike and Wolfe? 'I wouldn't call it a war,' he said. 'You can't really have a war between a pawn and a king.'

R

According to Thomas Pynchon 'RECLUSE is a code word generated by journalists meaning "doesn't like to talk to reporters"'. In our society, saturated as it is by a media obsessed with so-called celebrities, it seems only right that there is a certain sort of novelist who eschews the trappings of fame. But in America, which provides the apotheosis of media meaninglessness, there is also a certain sort of novelist who not only avoids journalists, but doesn't actually publish anymore.

Two of the most famous American novels of the twentieth century – *To Kill a Mockingbird* and *The Catcher in the Rye* – precipitated their authors' disappearance from public view. Arch-recluse J.D. Salinger said: 'There is a marvellous peace in not publishing. It's peaceful. Still. Publishing is a terrible invasion of my privacy. I like to write. I love to write. But I write just for myself and my own pleasure. I pay for this kind of attitude. I'm known as a strange, aloof kind of man.' There is a purity in the strangeness of Salinger. He was, by his own admission, 'in this world but not of it', something that seems clear in the famous fist-shaking photo following his ambush by a photographer in New Hampshire.

The photograph perhaps tells us as much about American culture as Salinger's writing itself, merely by dint of the fact that it is an image. Certainly, more people will know Thomas Pynchon as the reclusive author who appeared on *The Simpsons* with a paper bag over his head than have read and made sense of *Gravity's Rainbow*. It is not surprising therefore that the ultimate novel about a reclusive author who chooses not to publish borrows its title from an Andy Warhol painting concerned with the relationship between images and power.

In Don DeLillo's *Mao II*, Bill Gray works endlessly on a novel he chooses not to finish, lamenting the demise of the novelist in a culture which terrorism can jolt and twist, making 'raids on our consciousness'. DeLillo completed the novel two years after the Ayatollah Khomeini issued a fatwa calling for the death of the British novelist Salman Rushdie following publication of *The Satanic Verses*. But tellingly, *Mao II*'s mining of the American psyche did not, in the end, hinge on the person of the novelist but rather, rightly, on his words. Most presciently, DeLillo's recluse predicts that in the future 'the major work involves mid-air explosions and crumbling buildings'.

In the United States Public Broadcast Service TV gives the public a chance to produce and/or watch televisions programmes that would not otherwise be made by mainstream providers. In the UK the BBC is constantly fighting battles against the ignorant right who would like to see publicly-funded television filled with reality shows and cheap product-placement-laden costume dramas with Lady Gaga soundtracks. *The Charlie Rose Show* is an excellent example of intelligent television that would never exist in a world filled with commercial stations. Funded by private donations, the show has run since 1991 and ROSE himself, with the trademark round table set and thick black backdrop, has interviewed everyone from Leonardo di Caprio to Mahmoud Ahmadinejad. It is the conversations with the great cultural figures of the twentieth century that the show has had some of its most intriguing moments. An ageing Norman Mailer talking about Hitler's childhood, Fran Leibowitz revealing how she has a *chaise lounges* she reclines on for her daily seven-hour reading sessions, Salman Rushdie discussing his fatwa; Rose's personable manner, and the between-worlds atmosphere to the studio (only Rose and his guest inhabit the room, the cameras operated by specially developed robotics) means that his guests are often more candid than they might otherwise be.

Rose suffered serious health problems in 2006 but has fought off death to return to the screen. The free online archive of the Rose interviews is a remarkable collection, and one of the easiest places to lose a few days browsing on the internet.

S

The dedication in *Beloved*, for many critics the masterpiece of America's most important post-war novelist Toni Morrison, is made to 'Sixty million and more.' It is an understated reference to those innumerable victims of the transatlantic slave trade, who endured the Middle Passage after they were sold in West Africa to work on plantations in the New World – those whose eyes, in the words of Zora Neale Hurston's earlier title, were 'watching God'.

Toni Morrison

Beloved is not the only American novel to deal with SLAVERY; indeed, it is not the only one of Morrison's books to explore the deep-rootedness and importance of ancestry to the African-American psyche. But the 1988 Pulitzer Prize winning work of fiction did crystallize some long-repressed memories of slavery, not only in the lives of individuals – both black and white – but something deep in the national experience of America.

Morrison is the author of a long string of novels documenting the African-American experience, including *The Bluest Eye* and *Song of Solomon*, the *Beloved-Jazz-Paradise* trilogy and later works like *Love*, but she is also an intellectual. As a critic, she is acutely aware of how the canon of American literature is, in her phrase, 'studiously white'. In the wake of *Beloved*, a whole cottage industry sprung up in academic studies of Morrison's work. The rush of cultural criticism may at times have been riddled with post-structuralist jargon, but resulted in the positive effect that many readers – black, white, American and non-American – now know a canon of literature that stretches back from relative newcomers like ZZ Packer through Maya Angelou and Alice Walker to include James Baldwin and Ralph Ellison, Nella Larsen, Langston Hughes and W.E.B. Du Bois to a classic of American letters whose mere subject matter means it can never, ever afford to be ignored.

The Narrative of the Life of Frederick Douglass, an American Slave is not only what you would assume from its title, but also an abolitionist tract. It is only the most famous of a number of such memoirs that became fashionable as the clamour grew in mid-nineteenth century America for the end of one of the most despicable chapters in the history of humanity. But, as Morrison's dedication implies, however many books there are, we can never know the whole story – or the depths of the horror.

The very fact that Houghton Mifflin's 'The Best American' series features an annual collection of the Best American SPORTS WRITING, in which a guest editor is invited to pick around twenty-five articles from a long-list of 100, tells you all you need to know about just how seriously Americans take not only their sport but also their longform journalism.

American sportswriters are as exceptional as American sports. Baseball and the American variety of football are part of US national identity precisely because the rest of the world has never caught on. In Britain, we eat burgers and shop at malls and do a hundred and one other everyday things that originated in America, but where sport is concerned we still prefer to be beaten at cricket and rugby by former colonies while resting on the laurels of having invented 'the beautiful game', a global obsession so popular that some Americans have even heard of it, even if they get its name wrong.

But the British fixation with the hubris of calling a national championship the 'World Series' does not cover up the fact that when it comes to sports journalism, America can easily lay claim to the field. Far from churning out back page filler, writers like Gary Smith, a master of the human interest story, can truly be spoken of in the same breath as poets and novelists. Smith specialises in long-form essays – eight-, ten- or twelve-thousand words – uncovering the conflicts that drive the sporting greats.

Refreshingly, the great American sportswriters do not see their role in the culture as restricted. They trawl far and wide in search of a story. Smith even came to Wales to interview rugby's Gareth Thomas, national captain and only openly gay athlete in a male team sport in the world so far as the American writer could ascertain. 'Wot butt?' Smith quotes Thomas as saying. 'You come to this tiny village in this tiny country and tell me I'm the only gay man in a major team sport who's out of the closet? All the diversity in America, and no one there has done this? America's the pioneer, butt! Am I right? America's at the top of the table in everything! So why...?'

Smith goes on to use Thomas – and Wales – to explore America's own attitudes, to sport and to sexuality. And if we are to disagree with Thomas that America is the 'pioneer... in everything', we do see how, at least in sportswriting, America is Muhammad Ali, Babe Ruth and Michael Jordan rolled into one.

T

Ten years on – and in the year that Osama Bin Laden was finally tracked down and killed by American Special Forces – we still don't quite know just how significant 9/11 will turn out to be in the history of the world. The fateful Tuesday morning on which the TWIN TOWERS were attacked was, of course, immediately hailed as a turning point. It was certainly an iconic moment, one that captured the pure hatred with which America's global hegemony was perceived in large parts of the Muslim world and the complacency of the world's only superpower which at the time simply failed to comprehend how or why it had been attacked.

We are all now living in a post-9/11 world. The fact that the attack happened in 2001 means our young century has been defined by a world supposedly divided along a face-off between Islam and the West. Extremists on both sides would certainly have us see it that way. But these ten years later, which must seem much shorter and much longer to those directly affected on the day, the world is a very different place. The day when millions marched against the idea of invading Iraq, to be met with the deaf ears and blind eyes of Tony Blair and the majority of Britain's elected representatives, while George W. Bush made America the nation the rest of the world loved to hate, seem very remote.

There is now a man in the White House who grew up partly in Indonesia, the most populous Muslim country on earth. And while America's 'hawks' continue to repaint the simplistic pictures of the twentieth century as if 'reds' had simply been replaced by 'terrorists' as the ubiquitous 'enemy', Middle Eastern youth has staged its own revolution to demand democracy, far removed from the hateful ideology of Al Qaeda's unhinged minority.

The world, as we should always have known, is a complicated place. The destruction of the Twin Towers on Tuesday 11th September 2001 has produced fertile ground for writers of fiction and non-fiction, to incite, to condemn and – hopefully – to try to understand. Because it is only real understanding that will mean deeds follow words and some kind of healing process can begin.

U

Such was the incredible popularity of Harriet Beecher Stowe's anti-slavery novel *UNCLE TOM'S CABIN*, that kennels were established across America specifically for the training of bloodhounds that were to appear in its proliferating stage adaptations. Many actors spent their entire working lives touring 'Tom' shows across America, playing, in succession, the young George Shelby, before maturing into the role of brutal slave-owner Simon Legree and finally playing George's kindly old father Arthur. It is estimated that over three million people saw a 'Tom' show in the last four decades of the 19th century, far more than ever read the novel. The impact and influence of the novel is due as much to its cultural mutations as Beecher-Stowe's polemic. *Uncle Tom's Cabin* (subtitled *Life among the Lowly*) was not just a publishing sensation - the biggest-selling novel in North America until the publication of *Ben Hur* in 1880) - it was, and remains, a pop culture phenomenon. Among multiple film versions are *Mickey's Mellerdrammer* - in which Disney's famous mouse appears dressed in 'blackface' replete with exaggerated, orange lips and bushy, white side-whiskers made out of cotton – and a 1987 TV miniseries starring Samuel L. Jackson. Scorcese's *Gangs of New York* features a staging of a 'Tom' show with Abraham Lincoln played, somewhat incongruously, by John Sessions.

All racial stereotypes are present and politically incorrect in the novel, from the impossibly saintly (and arguably docile) eponymous Uncle Tom, to the tragic mulatto Eliza and the 'ragamuffin' slave girl Tipsy. This makes *Uncle Tom's Cabin* strange reading in our current 'post-racial' historical moment, combining, as it does, casual racial stereotyping with impassioned abolitionist outrage.

'Uncle Tom' has long been an expression of contempt between African-Americans, often deployed by those who have not read the book, usually denoting some form of collusion with the 'white man' - witness the offence caused to the boxer Joe Frazier when Muhammad Ali used the term against him in the run-up to their Heavyweight Championship fight. The slur has had the unfortunate effect of crudely oversimplifying the discourse of Beecher-Stowe's novel, which, for all its obvious faults, provided multiple narratives of the tremendous human suffering caused by slavery. It accounted for the moral cost of slavery, to both slave and slave owner, for a reading public, particularly in the Northern states, that knew very little, and understood even less, about the conditions endured by black slaves throughout the South.

Beecher-Stowe shares much with her near-contemporary Charles Dickens, who admired *Uncle Tom's Cabin* for the 'generous feeling' it inspired in him, in that both writers could veer from excoriating social critique to vulgar sentimentality within a single paragraph. Perhaps, though, it is this very sentimentality that explains the widespread popularity of Beecher-Stowe's novel, and therefore the efficacy of its anti-slavery message. Certainly, there are not many writers who can boast that their work has had such a directly shattering effect on the history of their country. On being introduced to Beecher-Stowe, at the height of the Civil War, President Abraham Lincoln was reported to observe, 'So this is the little woman who made this great war.'

V

Having taken some centuries for America to become comfortable with its cessation from Europe, a turbulent period of founding, a civil war, a few presidential assassinations, America seemed to move back toward a more European, VICTORIAN attitude toward society and moral cohesion. Widely regarded as America's greatest of all novelists, Henry James found a fruitful preoccupation in the difficulties of the values his society found itself adhering to that were established, primarily, two thousand miles across a sea most American's had braved under the promise of a new chance. It is perhaps no surprise, then, that his finest work is, in essence, a tragedy unveiling a young girl's lost dreams and curtailed innocence. *The Portrait of a Lady* (1881) could be perhaps the Great American Novel, and not only because it is as vast, heavy, and as flawed as it is impressive, admirable and beautiful. The lady of the title, Isabel Archer, is America, beautiful, naïve, young, and her suitors, older, pragmatic, cultured, are the Europe that America forsake in its doomed quest for 'freedom'.

Some of James' greatest achievements focus on the 'American' abroad, placing his characters in, often, melodramatic consternations that are played out with enduring subtlety and insight. For all of James' great works, however, from *The Wings of a Dove*, *The Bostonians*, *The Turn of the Screw*, *The Ambassadors*, it is one of his lesser-known masterpieces that captures the genius of the man. *What Maisie Knew* is the story of a young girl, 'disposed of in a manner worthy of the judgement seat of Solomon' when her divorcing parents decide to possess her for six months at a time. The story of a collapsing marriage through the eyes of a child, James also manages to portray the sexual and financial mores of the age through the uncluttered perceptions of a not-so-naïve young girl.

W

Walden Pond, near Concord, Massachusetts was the place chosen by Henry David Thoreau for his experiment in living which tapped into the ancient tradition of hermit-philosopher but that was also a deeply American experience. Thoreau claims it was an 'accident' that his two years of 'Life in the Woods' began on the 4th of July, but

Independence Day 1845 seems a fitting date to have begun a great American adventure. As Verlyn Klinkenborg has noted, *WALDEN* is not only the story of a man who goes to live in the woods, 'it is also the story of a man who built a house.'

For here is not – as the book is often billed – an account of a man giving up on society, or even rebelling against it. Thoreau comes across as a thinker who believes deeply in a balance between company and solitude. He is also a master of the extended metaphor: 'Time is but the stream I go a-fishing in. I drink at it; but while I drink I see the sandy bottom and detect how shallow it is. Its thin current slides away, but eternity remains. I would drink deeper; fish in the sky, whose bottom is pebbly with stars.' Thoreau believed in the intellect as 'a cleaver' and his head as 'an organ for burrowing... a divining rod' and Walden was the place he chose to 'mine'.

He believed in education too, and in books. Perhaps surprisingly for a man who has gone to live in the woods, his concern is with worthwhile reading material as much as it is with catching fish. As much as anything, Thoreau went to Walden so that he could concentrate on Plato without the distraction of newspapers. A broadband connection would probably not have been on his list of basic requirements if he were to repeat the experiment today.

What Thoreau realised was that so much of life is a distraction from what really matters. He wanted to live, to approach the essence of things. Modern America, using Thoreau as a touchstone, would do well to remember his own points of reference throughout the work, which frequently include Confucius and the *Bhagavad Gita*. But also his defence of 'we Americans and moderns generally'. He attacks those who are 'dinning in our ears' that Americans – being the population of a young country – are 'intellectual dwarfs compared to the ancients, or even the Elizabethan[s]' by making the very American claim that 'a living dog is better than a dead lion.'

Thoreau is a champion of life and the living. And yes, he is a champion of the individual: 'If a man does not keep pace with his

companions, maybe it is because he hears a different drummer.' America's mid-nineteenth century transcendentalists are full of such wisdom, much of it drawn from the waters of Walden, which Thoreau calls 'my well ready dug'.

The United States, born from a mixture of religious vehemence and high-minded libertarianism, was also born from the smoke of unavoidable WAR. America's relationship with conflict has been complex ever since. In the early days, writers, quite often a left-leaning bunch, were always more likely to muse upon the horrors of war rather than write lurching bestsellers with a battlefield backdrop. Margaret Mitchell's *Gone with the Wind* marked a change in that. It is a brash, populist epic, and is the second biggest selling American novel of all time (after Lew Wallace's *Ben Hur*). But the civil war that disrupts Scarlet O'Hara's love affair with Rhett Butler is never really treated as anything more than a device to create drama, to raise the stakes. It was the war that was to come to Europe as the film version of Mitchell's book hit the picture houses that would create America's greatest conflict fiction. The first was Norman Mailer's *The Naked and the Dead*, published in 1948; his hefty account of his own war in the South Pacific. It was a massive bestseller in a country thirsty for first-hand knowledge of the war. As a straight, visceral, adventure story it is a remarkable book that broke taboos of language and content and redefined what a best-seller could be.

For other ground-breaking novelists it took longer for their experiences to find a home on the page. Joseph Heller's *Catch-22* was not published until 1961 whereas Kurt Vonnegut's *Slaughter-house 5* came out in 1969. The three books together represent not only how differently war can effect great minds, but in Mailer's realist tome, Heller's snappy satire, and Vonnegut's dazzling science fiction, we can see a development of how a country was learning to deal with its own dark corners. Just as writers such as Toni Morrison, Ralph Ellison and Charles Johnson were tackling other difficult elements of the American truth in starkly contrasting ways,

Mailer, Heller and Vonnegut gave America an insight into what was soon to be regarded as the nation's most internationally-defining preoccupation.

X

To borrow a technique from the popular American game show *Jeopardy!*, to which question is the answer '*The Adventures of Huckleberry Finn*, *Catch-22*, *The Catcher in the Rye* and *The Color Purple*'? Is it 'What are the greatest ever American novels?' Guess again, contestant number one. The real question, and the one they don't want you to ponder, is 'Which classics have American censors banned?' X-RATED. Whether for political, pornographic or puritanical reasons, the US censors sure do like to *blank* the *blank* out of pretty much *blanking* everything worth reading.

The Bill of Rights set out by the rebellious forefathers was intended to protect fundamental civil liberties and its First Amendment (1791) brought freedom of speech to the fore. What happened when words were written down and published, however, was a slightly different matter. The actions of the review boards can seem like a brought-to-life *Fahrenheit 451*. At times, they've even gone as far as Bradbury's book-burners, setting fire to 500 first-edition copies of *Ulysses* at the New York customs offices when Joyce's publisher attempted to ship them in from France in 1923.

Until the 1960s, American anti-obscenity legislation, like that in the old country, was based on the Catholic Church's Index of the late nineteenth century and reflected a reaction against the forces of urbanisation, industrialisation, immigration and accompanying social changes. From Anthony Comstock's New York Society for the Suppression of Vice to jumpy moms putting the squeeze on librarians to take books off shelves, via McCarthyism, there are plenty of morally outraged groups with the power to veto the public's right to read. There's even Orwellian talk of re-edited versions of staples such as *Tom Sawyer* to suit today's sanitised times.

They're all missing the point - great literature can be a time capsule, a teaching aid and often deals with troubling subjects. Revising history reeks.

Y

In 1929 William Faulkner wrote his second novel *Sartoris*, the story of the decay of a southern aristocratic family. It is an excellent novel, and may have proved a highlight in a lesser writer's career, written with tight flourishes and with the hand of a mature craftsmen. By 1949, however, when William Faulkner collected his Nobel Prize, the significance of the novel lay largely in the fact it was the author's first work to be set in his 'apocryphal county' of YOKNAPATAWPHA, the place where most of Faulkner's stories would take place, and all of his masterpieces. A year after *Sartoris* he had written *The Sound and the Fury*, and the year after that *As I lay Dying*, and the world would never be the same again.

What Faulkner had found was the perfect canvas on which to splash his portraits. Many of his characters were based upon people he knew, and the county itself was based upon the place where he grew up, Lafayette County in Mississippi. Using this vehicle he was able to set himself free with his experimentation, a radical and swift progression from the dynamism of *Ulysses* in 1922. For all of Joyce's fireworks, Faulkner, learning and building upon the Irishman's accomplishments, was always a consummate storyteller and could never be mistaken for a charlatan or a vulgarian (as was the opinions of, among others, Virginia Woolf and Bernard Shaw of Joyce). Faulkner, although sometimes complex and dazzling, is highly readable and involving in ways that high art often cannot be.

William Faulkner, 1954
Carl Van Vechten

Yoknapatawpha County itself is luminously exact in its construction, and many of the characters in Faulkner's novels have cross-textual existences as they wander from town to town, intruding on someone else's story. Also, by using this county Faulkner could raise themes and tackle difficult questions that he otherwise may have found difficulty in approaching (such as the questions of peonage slavery in *Absalom! Absalom!*). Yoknapatawpha County set Faulkner free, in the same way that theatre released Beckett, and in the same way that the room of one's own released Woolf.

'THE YELLOW WALLPAPER' is a classic gothic autobiographical short story by the crusading feminist journalist and intellectual Charlotte Perkins Gilman that was originally thought shocking and unprintable in 1892 California. Gilman, whose work focused on the inequality of women in marriage, here wrote a lucid honest horror story with nods to Edgar Allen Poe as well as the stream-of-consciousness writing that would go on to mark the books of Virginia Woolf and James Joyce. Initially 'The Yellow Wallpaper' appears to be about the mental unravelling of an imaginative young woman, yet through the interventions of her husband, a doctor, it also passes symbolic social comment on a woman who is unable to live the free-thinking life of self-expression she so desires: 'Personally, I disagree with their ideas. \ Personally, I believe that congenial work, with excitement and change, would do me good. \ But what is one to do?'

The short story is based on Gilman's own experience of depression shortly after the birth of her first daughter in 1886. Her 1935 autobiography *The Living of Charlotte Perkins Gilman* tells of how the writer was referred to a leading specialist in nervous disorders, Dr S. Weir Mitchell, who prescribed a 'rest cure' of forced inactivity. The ever-so insightful Mitchell was a man who believed that female depression was simply the result of too much mental activity and not enough time and attention given to their domestic lives. For Gilman, his 'treatment' was a disaster, and kept from her work she went on to have a nervous breakdown. In the story the narrator becomes the creeping woman trapped behind the yellow patterned wallpaper of her isolated room, the faint figure who 'seemed to shake the pattern, just as if she wanted to get out.' Gilman did get out, abandoning the 'rest cure', her first husband and first child. She went on to have a successful career as a journalist and academic.

Z

ZELDA SAYRE. Writer, ballet dancer and, according to her husband, 'the first American flapper'. Icon of the Jazz Age, the Roaring Twenties and the Lost Generation, Zelda had it all. Young, rich and beautiful, alcoholic, schizophrenic and one half of the original celebrity on-off relationship, her place in American letters is further cemented by her marriage to fellow alcoholic author F Scott Fitzgerald.

Her novel *Save Me the Waltz*, entirely written during a two-month incarceration at the Johns Hopkins Hospital in Baltimore, was a semi-autobiographical account of their marriage. Scott was furious at Zelda's depiction of Alabama Beggs, an aspiring ballet dancer who marries a painter and struggles to cope with her husband's fame, battling to allow her own creative spirit to shine from under his shadow. This was all a bit rich coming from a man who had lifted whole sections of his wife's diary for *This Side of Paradise* and based several of his most important heroines – including Daisy Buchanan in *The Great Gatsby* – on Zelda. When Daisy wishes her child grows up to be 'a beautiful little fool', he is merely repeating what Zelda had said under anaesthesia after giving birth to their daughter Frances 'Scottie'.

When one considers what modern American culture values – wealth, fame and a shallow kind of beauty - and how its most venerated pop culture icons often end up – in a tangle of broken promises and broken dreams, failed marriages, substance abuse and insanity – it is somehow poetic to see Zelda not only as the first American flapper, but as the first American little girl lost, precursor to Marilyn and a million wannabes since. And these rare spirits who live too fast and die too young show us only that every generation is lost. Like Zelda, America herself is both beautiful and damned.

FICTION

IS THIS A DIRTY WORD IN DORCHESTER?

Russell Celyn Jones

When Picton's ex-wife returned to America with their daughter, she settled in a dry town outside Boston. This was the first thing he noticed: no bars or liquor stores. They were expecting him tomorrow, but he first wanted to take a look at the place they now called home and drove straight from the airport in his rented Chevrolet. What greeted him was a pristine nexus of clothing boutiques, beauty parlours, realtors, antique furniture shops, book-ended by cathedral-sized clapboard churches. To one of these churches Josephine took Rosa every Sunday.

It was six in the evening and the bistros and restaurants were bustling, although by eight they'd be closed, he was soon to learn, and by nine everyone in this dry town would be in bed. After London everything seemed – he struggled to put a name to it: ready-limed; waiting for celestial instructions. A thin and frail-looking woman in red tracksuit jogged slowly along the sidewalk, disappearing every few seconds behind huge piles of old snow. Balanced in her hand was a paper coffee cup. Cars shuddered to a halt to let her cross the street. She mesmerised him. He heard himself wondering where the local A&E was.

He'd not seen his daughter or his ex-wife in two years and with just twelve hours away from being re-united, his nerve endings were singing with dread. What he saw of where they lived was not at all comforting. He drove through the town and joined Route 9 and then I-95, coming off at Westwood, out of a dry county into a wet one. He crept past the illuminated bars along the strip, looking for his B&B.

The house was easier to find than its owners. After knocking on the screen door for several minutes he let himself into a lounge where a TV was flickering in the dark, the sound muted. On every surface and windowsill were photographs of children, grandchildren and antique toys: the clutter of a long life. A few moments later two old people emerged from different ends of the house, wearing matching frayed plaid dressing gowns. The man was tall and gallant, blinking heavily. The woman looked shrunken, but had the bigger voice, greeting him and telling him where to find his room.

Stunned by jet-lag he went straight to bed and coasted through six hours of sleep. A metal radiator clicking as it expanded woke him at five-thirty and he heard the old couple moving around downstairs. In the old days he'd have begun drinking by now, with the night still cloying to the sky.

He showered in a yellow bathroom under the gaze of strangers staring out of family portraits on the wall. In the dining room he found the landlord, who looked startled to see Picton there.

The old man began to shake as he spoke: 'Had an MRI this week. Numb in the lips. Doctor said I might have a blocked carotid.' Picton noticed the table was bare. There was not even any coffee brewing. 'It's this shadow on my brain that....' He broke off and rubbed his forehead.

He'd been put in charge of the breakfast by his wife, he explained, while she was talking to another of their guests upstairs. When a phone rang in a distant room Picton saw him react, noticed his agitation.

'Could be my neurosurgeon now,' he said.

'Then why don't you take the call? I'll make the breakfast.'

The old man lurched away in the direction of the ringing phone and Picton went into the kitchen to see what he could do about getting some breakfast. He found some pineapple and melon in the fridge and put them on the table; made some coffee in the filter machine.

The landlady appeared as he was laying the table and sat down to watch him. 'Geez, you should get her to tell you her stories,' she said of their other guest. 'They're incredible. Grew up as a sharecropper, married a wonderful man, then he and their three kids drove down to North Carolina and were all killed in a road accident.'

Picton served her coffee, silently offered the fresh fruit. When her husband joined them, he served him too.

'So what did the surgeon say, hon?' she asked.

'That was his secretary. He's going to call me later today.'

She turned to Picton. 'Are you seeing your daughter today?' He'd emailed the purpose of his visit to her when he'd made the reservation. In reply she offered to give him a 'Norman Rockwell experience'. 'Must be difficult to have her live so far away from you,' she continued. 'But at least she's not dead.'

His daughter was not dead, but after two years absence he was having difficulty picturing her in his mind's eye. In several hours time he'd be picking her up from school, and now began to worry about the reception he might receive. He stood up and excused himself. It was barely eight, but he had to get out of that house.

He drove back along I-95 and Route 9. Another four inches of snow had fallen during the night and the ploughs were out in convoy. Sparks flew around their steel buckets like fireflies. In the small town of Wellesley he left the car on a meter, bought a New York Times and a latte and found a bench at a four-way junction in order to smoke. He sipped the weak coffee and read an article on why some mothers had supported George W Bush. He'd protected their children, was the basic idea, from nasty terrorists. He wondered if his ex-wife felt that way too. Her return to America had coincided with the invasion of Iraq, and he was finding it difficult not to take everything, even the war, personally.

The only other people smoking that he could see were sitting in cars. One or two swigged from bottles in brown paper bags. In these dry suburbs, the car was the new pub. The condition

Josephine set before allowing access to their daughter was his total abstinence, and he'd not touched a drink in a year and a half. But his thoughts were never far away from it.

He stubbed out his cigarette and threw the pack of Camels in a bin. He didn't want to be greeting his little girl for the first time in two years with smoky breath.

Since Josephine had been called to New York on business he'd arranged with her to pick up Rosa at school after her soccer match – a gentle start for them both. The school was half a mile outside town and he decided to leave the car on the meter and walk. He crunched snow underfoot. His frozen breath steamed up his glasses. Where the sidewalk ended, surveillance began. A patrol car crept up alongside him and an officer peeled down his window to ask if everything was okay.

'Okay? Yes I think so.'

'Walking somewhere?' the policeman sounded doubtful.

'To my daughter's school,' he said and felt proud to be saying so after so long a time.

In the playing field twenty girls warmed up in the bitter air. From the touchline he failed to recognise which one was Rosa. A woman skated past on roller blades, pushing a three-wheeled baby buggy. A lull in movement, then a fleet of SUVs drove into the school grounds like an invading army. Soon the field was flooded with mothers. Standing to one side with hands in pockets, Picton watched the two teams move the ball around the pitch, tackling one another with a politeness he'd believed obsolete. After forty-five minutes the coach sprung the girls loose and he watched them run to their mothers on the touchline. An ache grew in his bones.

A girl with long black hair tied up in a French plait was hovering nearby. 'Hi dad,' she said.

Something inside his head stretched so taut his vision became blurred. His title he'd so dishonoured was still ringing in the air. He made to shift his feet to get a better view of her but his shoes were cemented to the frozen ground. She moved position to stand in front of him. He looked down at the dried blood on her dirty knees. Then he fell headlong into her eyes.

'Did you win?' he managed to say. 'I couldn't work out the score.'

'Four-two.'

'Not bad.' This waif of a girl in an oversized Arsenal soccer kit had her mother's high cheekbones and his dark brown eyes. He wondered if she'd had to re-familiarise herself with him from old photographs.

'Mom said you can take me to Starbucks if you like.'

'Okay. Where is it?'

'I'll show you.'

His decision to leave the car in town began to assert its negative effect, as Rosa stumbled along the sidewalk on studded boots and shivered in her football kit. The same SUVs he'd watched arriving at school were now overtaking and made the road swing. Behind their windows he glimpsed children sitting in the warmth. He and Rosa did not talk, and the silence he filled with a memory of walking the two miles home from school, through docklands in a city of industry. But that was his history of childhood – in Port Talbot, Wales – and almost unreachable now.

In Starbucks he ordered her a caramel frappuccino and went to sit among teenagers with their laptops open on the tables. She didn't say anything, more interested in her drink than talking, and he could certainly identify with that.

'How is school?' he asked finally.

'Okay I guess.'

'You have friends?'

'Of course I do.'

She stirred her frappuccino with a straw. All ten of her fingernails had been nibbled and there were traces of eczema on the knuckles. Despite running around for an hour, her soccer kit retained the scent of detergent.

'You looked good out there today.'

'We have to play one sport each semester. I didn't want to do hockey.'

'Is that field or ice hockey?'

'That's what hockey is. Ice hockey.'

He heard her frustration with his lack of understanding of the terms of her life. Two years and she was already a strident citizen of the United States, with all traces of England undetectable.

They drove to her house with Rosa giving directions. As he parked in the drive the front door swung open. Rosa's black Labrador bounded out, swishing its tail and licking her outstretched hands. Picton envied their familiarity. A young woman with rosy cheeks and a vague, promiscuous smile emerged from the doorway and handed him a cordless phone. 'It's Josephine,' she explained. Alarmed by the timing of her call he couldn't control his hand sufficiently to take the handset. 'She wants to talk to you?'

Picton pressed the handset to the side of his face and the first and only thing she said was he should take Rosa out tomorrow for the day. She did not care to swap platitudes with him. He handed the phone back to the nanny. Behind her head he caught a glimpse of the wide open plains of the house before she ushered Rosa inside and gently folded the door shut.

He took her into the city on Saturday and began the day where yesterday it had ended – in Starbucks. A man coming out as they were going in greeted Rosa, and gave Picton a hair-triggered look. 'Is this your dad?' he asked.

'Yes,' she replied, her face averted, as though she wasn't quite sure.

'Pleased to meet you, sir, I'm Rosa's IT teacher. Have a nice day.'

As they explored Boston Common the simple cadence of walking helped to make him feel all things were possible. But Rosa got tired of walking and from Beacon Street they joined a 'Duck' tour – a drive in a converted Marine amphibian landing craft through the historic parts of the city. Rosa pointed out the Sheridan

Hotel where she'd been to a birthday party the previous Saturday. Six girls in two adjoining rooms, movies on demand, room service... he couldn't imagine that any more than he could see of the city through the scratched plastic windows. The guide's commentary was glib and intrusive, and his constant habit of reminding passengers how the British had been defeated here grated on Picton. 'It's like we're inside a radio,' Rosa said at one point and that seemed about right to him too.

They went for lunch on the top floor of the Providential Building and ordered pizza. Dusk was slowly gathering outside, turning the Charles River a gun-metal grey.

Picton suddenly asked, 'Would you like to come back to London with me for a week or so?'

'Okay.'

After all this time, it was as simple as that … Okay.

'We'll have to ask your mother, of course.'

'She might say no.'

'You think so?'

'I don't know. She might.'

'But is that okay with you?'

'I already said it was.'

He was boring her. He had a fear of being boring, because drunks were bores of the highest order, and if he couldn't captivate his own daughter just a little it would suggest he had some way yet to go.

He watched her toy with the ice cubes in her glass of coke. 'What do you remember about London?'

'Lots of things. Hampstead Heath. The Odeon Holloway Road...'

Now he'd got his reply he was unable to recall what they'd done in those places: who'd accompanied them on Hampstead Heath, what films they'd seen in the Odeon.

Then Rosa asked, 'Are you still sick? Mom said that's why we had to leave you.'

'I was sick, but I'm better now.'

'That's good.'

'Yes, it is good.'

The pizza was covered in raw zucchini and snow peas. Far too ambitious for a simple pizza and it defeated them both. A waiter swooped down on them and said, 'You guys still working on that?'

'No,' Picton replied. 'You can take it.'

'Shall I box it for you?'

'Why is it when you order lunch here they also give you your dinner?' he whispered to Rosa as the waiter receded, and made her laugh. And because he'd made her laugh it suddenly got lighter outside.

It was snowing by the time they left the building and Rosa scooped snow from the hood of a car, made a snowball and threw it at him. She called him dad frequently now, reprising the word with some relish, he sensed.

He was aiming to return her at the time agreed with Josephine, but took the wrong exit off Soldier's Avenue – towards Arlington and the Mystic River. Beside him in the car Rosa chanted the television programmes she liked. America's Next Top Model. American Idol. Her absolute favourite was CSI Miami. So silent this morning, nothing could stop her talking now. He made another wrong turn off the Mass Pike and felt the pressure building; the heat of failure.

When they finally got to the house, forty-minutes late, there was a light shining in Josephine's bedroom.

'Your mum's in,' he said.

'Mom's still in New York,' Rosa replied. 'She's not here.'

'Then why's the light on?'

'It's Frank, I guess.'

'Who's Frank?'

'Mom's boyfriend.'

'Does Frank live with you?'

'Most of the time.'

'Is he nice, nice to you?'

She shrugged. 'Sure.'

He stalled the car and stepped out onto the drive, his legs barely able to hold his weight. He shook hands with Rosa and waited while she rang the doorbell and disappeared into the house. Whoever opened the door did not show his face.

A mile out of town he pulled off at a gas station and bought a pack of Camels. Out front of a Dunkin' Donuts he sat in the car smoking one cigarette after another as people came and went with their coffees and cakes, and imagined Rosa at the house, watching CSI Miami with Frank.

Everyone at the B&B was already in bed. He sat in a rocking chair in the darkened lounge and called Josephine's cell phone.

When she answered he stood up. 'Is this a bad time to call?'

'It's okay. Not brilliant, but okay. How are things going?'

'Can I take Rosa back with me to London... for a week or so?'

In the silence he shook from the recoil of his own words.

'She's in school, Picton.'

'I can wait 'til she's finished school,' he said in another big rush.

'I've got an open return. I'm allowed to stay for up to ninety days.'

'What about your business?'

'I've left my partner in charge. He knows what to do.'

'I'll have to give it some thought,' she said finally.

She had not dismissed the idea out of hand. That was something to clutch onto.

'If you want her to stay with you while you're here, in your B&B...'

'I can't change the past,' he said suddenly. 'But I am trying to do the right thing now.' This sudden retreat into history, however brief, he knew instantly to be a bad idea.

'I'm glad you're off the booze, Picton,' she said after a pause, 'but you can't expect me to congratulate you.' She'd once said it was worse than having a sexual predator in the family, because a drunk never takes a day off.

The phone went dead. She'd hung up on him. He sat down again in the dark, trying to remember the times when he might have made her happy.

On Sunday, Rosa had other commitments: church and a church brunch. So he stayed in his room all day dozing and reading a collection of Fitzgerald's short stories he'd found on a bookshelf. His concentration was finally broken by the sound of his hosts arguing downstairs. He heard the old man say, in a voice gravelly with frustration, that he wanted to go to his swing band rehearsal. She was pleading with him to rest, reminding him of his recent and inconclusive MRI scan. Moments later, they were both outside Picton's door, inviting him to supper.

At the table the old man kept offering him beer, wine, whisky, while apologising for their argument earlier. 'I guess you heard us,' he said. 'Seems crazy to be disagreeing, after fifty-six years of marriage...'

'Fifty-five years, actually,' his wife corrected him. 'But it feels like fifty-six! And stop inviting him to drink, John.'

'Why not, we're having us a nice time here...'

Picton felt her rough dry hand land on the back of his wrist. 'Call it feminine intuition, but I can't help but see the effort you're making.'

The next day he picked up Rosa from school and drove her back to the B&B past the now familiar big-box stores and multiplex cinemas on Route 9, the snow drifting into the fetch between cars, tyres moaning on the tarmac. With her overnight bag on her lap, Rosa flicked through radio stations.

As he introduced Rosa to the landlady he felt his daughter's fingers pushing into his hand. The landlady was wearing a baseball cap with a bicycle light clipped to its brim. 'Would you like a tour of my house?' she asked in an egg-shell voice. 'It was once a station on the Underground Railway.' She ushered Rosa forward while shining the light on her cap into crevices in wall panels and floorboards and behind a fake chimney breast. 'Runaway slaves used to hide in there. Incredible, isn't it?' She showed Rosa the nook underneath the stairs big enough to hide a family of four. 'Sometimes they were re-captured, you know?' She clenched both her hands into fists. 'Then they were lynched in Dedham Square.'

Later, in their room, Rosa lay in the other single bed insisting on keeping the overhead light on to ward off the ghosts of slaves wrenched from their hiding places. He maintained a watch until she fell asleep. Rosa asleep had yet another impact upon him, like that of a ballad. He slept that night more soundly than he had in years.

They woke the following morning to the smell of baking. For once the landlady came through with breakfast: eggs and mozzarella cheese baked on a tortilla. She sat between them and told Rosa about the night a fugitive from justice had knocked on their door, asking for a ride back to Dorchester. 'As soon as I opened the door the hairs came up on the back of my neck,' she said. 'I knew I was in trouble with this young man. Luckily my rape training taught me how to humour him and I would have gotten rid of him too if John hadn't come along saying "Hi! Welcome to Westwood" and offering the guy a lift to a bus stop. So now we're all in the car. John is telling him about his knee surgery, and I don't know who I want to kill the most. When this guy sees a liquor store he's out of the car before we've even had a chance to stop. Then he gives us the finger!' She made the gesture to illustrate. 'The police told us later he'd hijacked a car at gunpoint and ran out of gas along a-ways from our house. "Old couple help armed robber to escape" is how the *Westwood Gazette* wrote it up. We were not popular for a long while round these parts.'

Rosa was making the finger gesture herself now, in all innocence, until the landlady took her hand and pushed it gently under the table. 'Don't do that, hon, that's a dirty word in Dorchester.'

He dropped her off at school and a few hours later, pulled over at a bar that was still lit up like a beacon from the night before. He was a dry-drunk, but the atmosphere of bars still had a tremendous pull on him – like the grave of a loved one. In the darkened room, there were a few men sitting in booths nursing half-empty glasses. He sat on a stool and ordered a cranberry juice. The barman asked him what British people thought of the wars in Iraq and Afghanistan. Picton said he had no opinion either way, and ordered a refill. He still liked to say: 'Give me another of those.'

The barman's name was Len, and because he was now on first name terms, became confessional. In Picton's experience, it was the barman's job to listen to confessions, not make them. But nothing could stop Len now he'd found someone sober to tell his story to, about his tour of duty in Iraq with the National Guard. Picton had never been to war but he'd been a drunk, and saw the similarities. In both cases, men went out and came back ghosted, or never came back at all.

He returned to the B&B early afternoon to discover the old couple bumping into one another in the kitchen. They were pale and drawn. The neurosurgeon had called to tell the old man that it was urgent he came into hospital right away. This was an hour ago, and they seemed incapable of making the next move. Picton offered to drive them to the hospital.

The old man sat in the front, saying nothing, staring out of the window at the virgin snow on a golf course. His wife leaned forward between the seats and said to Picton, 'Will you be all right to fend for yourself till we return?'

'I'll be fine,' he said, 'you just look after him.'

After dropping them off at Beth Israel he lit out for Rosa's school. She was waiting for him in reception, wearing black patent leather shoes with a three inch heel, black Lycra tights, pink tutu and maroon tee shirt – her dancing costume. A couple of secretaries whispering into phones covertly watched them leave.

In the B&B he sat Rosa down at the old couple's computer while he made supper: pasta with salmon and asparagus, and felt momentarily unshackled from his unhappiness – a delicate state of mind for sure, and a light flashing on the telephone to indicate a message was enough to deflate it. He gave some thought to the old couple and what hell they were facing. Or it could be a message from Josephine, about his taking Rosa back to London.

He tried to play the message back by pressing a white button with a red cross and in less than three minutes, a police car raced into the drive.

He told Rosa to go hide under the stairs, in the old slave nook the landlady had shown them.

He opened the door to the policeman, a big Hispanic guy. 'Was it you who dialled nine-one-one?' Without an invitation the cop entered the lounge, looking up at the oak beams in the ceiling. 'Gee, old place. This your house?'

'No, I'm a guest.'

'Where're the owners?'

'This is a B&B.'

'And they left you here?'

'Well yes, they had to go to the hospital.'

The voice of the policeman plunged into cold command. 'Okay, sir. Some ID please.'

Picton hooked his wallet out of his back pocket and produced a UK driving licence. The policeman had clearly not seen one of these before and called through the details on his short wave radio. 'Picton Hughes, that your name?'

There was a loud thump from under the stairs, like a broom falling over. The cop's eyes moved in that direction. 'Is there anyone else here with you?'

Picton looked away quickly, towards the stairs. 'Well, my daughter's here.'

'Let me see her.'

Picton called, 'Come out here, Rosa.'

She tumbled out of the dark recess beneath the stairs in her high heel shoes, Lycra tights and pink tutu.

'So she's staying here with you, correct?'

'No... yes. She lives here. In the US, I mean.'

The cop asked Rosa: 'Is this your dad?'

'Yes,' said Rosa.

'What's his address?'

Rosa didn't know Picton's address.

'What's his date of birth?'

Rosa didn't know that either.

The cop got back on his short wave radio, called in a four letter code, then asked in a softer brogue, 'How long you visiting for?'

'A week or two, up to ninety days.'

'A week or two...' He was repeating Picton as though measuring his words for their honesty. Then he said, 'I'm not satisfied you're telling the whole truth.'

'I can phone the owners for you,' Picton said, then realised he didn't have their cell number. The only number he had in the whole of the United States was that of his ex-wife. 'Look, officer...' he began to whisper hoarsely. 'I'm just trying to do the right thing here.'

Rosa cried as they travelled in the police car. The door-locks shunting, the steel mesh screen between the front and back seats were blunt and menacing. When they got to the police station, Picton was allowed to call Josephine. He squatted at a table with the cop standing over him, eye level with a holstered weapon and waited for Josephine to answer.

She was travelling in a cab, heading out to La Guardia on Grand Central Parkway, coming home. 'It's real cold here,' she began. 'I'm passing the lake in Flushing Meadow and it's all frozen over.'

He told her the facts of what had happened. When she replied, with calm understanding, 'They seemed to have over-reacted,' his relief went all around the world.

They would have to wait until Josephine could get there to vouch for him and over the next few hours he helped Rosa with her

English homework. She was studying Romeo and Juliet and they read all the parts out loud to an audience of police.

By the time his ex-wife arrived and cleared his name, Rosa was wan and pale from fatigue. They walked in single file from the police station to the parking lot. Outside her car, Josephine's pale blue eyes that rarely betrayed feelings of doubt, could now not meet his. This incident, he realised, was too reminiscent of another near the end of their marriage, when he'd called her from a police station in Cardiff, a hundred miles from where they lived. She drove all the way from London and found him in a cell, naked, covered in mud and blood and unable to account for how he'd got there.

It was Rosa who broke the silence. She nudged her mother to get her full attention, and then gave her the fuck-you finger.

'Is this a dirty word in Dorchester?' she asked.

Josephine crushed Rosa's erect middle finger inside her fist. She lowered her head to whisper in Rosa's ear. 'Go say goodbye to your father.'

Rosa snapped off from her and came to a stuttering standstill inches short of him. 'Goodbye daddy,' she said. He kissed her lightly on the forehead before she turned and sprinted away.

He watched Rosa climb into her mother's Land Cruiser and disappear behind its smoked glass windows. 'I don't suppose it's worth much, but I didn't teach her that little trick.'

'It happened on your watch,' Josephine replied, 'which amounts to the same thing.'

Josephine had changed in two years, he thought, back into the person she was before marrying him. 'What about tomorrow?' he asked.

'You're not ready for this, Picton.'

He struggled to control his breathing. The air was freezing going into his lungs. 'I've spent eighteen months getting ready for this. Please understand...'

She cut him off by slashing her hand through the night. 'I'm not interested in understanding you any more.'

'I'm not a perfect father.'

'I don't expect you to be a perfect father.'

'What do you expect? Can you please tell me that?'

'Safe,' she said. 'Come back in six months. We'll see how you are then.'

He returned to his B&B thinking that if he left early enough in the morning he might make the first flight out. He wanted to alert the owners that he wouldn't require breakfast and to pay the bill, but no one was in. The house was silent and dark. He left the money on the kitchen counter and carried on upstairs.

He slept fitfully until around 5am, then dressed, washed and packed. Downstairs he encountered the landlady in the twilit lounge, all buttoned up in a blue overcoat, rocking back and forth in the rocking chair.

'How long have you been there?' he asked, then added: 'Where's John?'

'In surgery as we speak.' Her voice was small and remote. 'He's going to be there another twelve hours, they said, all on his own.'

'Can I do anything?'

'What could you do? My daughter's on her way down from Maine. My son's flying in from Seattle.'

'I'm leaving now,' he said. 'Thanks for having me.'

'We've never been apart longer than a couple of hours, in fifty-five years of marriage.' She looked up and saw him meditating on the near-full bottle of Jack Daniels on the counter. 'Take that with you, if you want.'

He scooped up the bottle and pocketed it in his coat. He allowed no thought on the matter. 'Good luck then. I hope it works out for John.' But she never replied, being too far out in the fields of her own concerns to hear.

The Mass Pike was swollen with orderly lines of vehicles going into the city, slipping over the old snow. He was heading for the airport, but when he saw signs for Cambridge, took a detour. Minutes later he was parked alongside the Charles River, as the sun was coming up in an aubergine sky.

He sat on a bench near the river overlooking the Harvard towers on the other side, his whisky on the bench beside him. He reached out now and again to touch the cold bottle. He kept pulling the cork to hear that pop, but replaced it each time into the neck. The river looked stunned from three months of winter. If he lifted that bottle to his lips now he'd drink and never stop.

Along the river path, a regular succession of early-morning joggers passed by. Harvard students, he guessed, no more than six years older than Rosa, who gave him not so much as a glance. A middle-aged man, he was as good as dead in their eyes. But he was no more dead than that sleeping river.

The thought made him laugh, and because he laughed, knew he'd made it through. The wind had begun to rise now and he stood up. He left the whisky on the bench and followed the students along the path. Fresh and young in their tracksuits and trainers, they already owned the future as a glittering prize for their abstinence.

THE RACONTEUR INTERVIEW

ALLEGRA GOODMAN

Allegra Goodman is author of six novels and a regular fixture on the New York Times *bestseller list. Her latest,* The Cookbook Collector, *seems to have cemented Goodman's reputation with the critics as an author of big, important American books. GARY RAYMOND spoke with Ms Goodman as she spent the summer in Israel, away from her family home of Cambridge, Massachusetts...*

America seems to have an obsession with defining itself, discovering itself, explaining itself through its literature. And, from a cultural perspective, America has a deeply mythologized, almost sacred view of the family unit. Do you think your work is an ongoing attempt to achieve the former through an exploration of the latter?
I think all cultures mythologize the family, and the novel is well suited to an exploration of the relationships and rivalries within families. In my novels I look at nuclear families, extended families, ruling families – for example, the rabbinical family in *Kaaterskill Falls* and work families like the lab in *Intuition* and the start-up companies in *The Cookbook Collector*.

When I think of the sort of middle-class Thanksgiving 'rituals', or even the gatherings of Yom Kippur – the way everyone has a role and a place – I find myself thinking that the family is a microcosm of America...
There's certainly a rich tradition of American literature about the family, both extended and nuclear. Eudora Welty wrote the extended family so well. John Updike wrote beautifully about the nuclear family, and what I love is the slight sense of loneliness in his nuclear families, the modern sense of separation from grandparents, aunts and uncles. However, I do not think that writing about family is particularly American. Family and familial rituals are natural subjects for novelists in every country.

Do you think, perhaps, Harry Angstrom is the true American hero – that lonely figure in the centre of the vastness of American life? And do you think,

in a way, he's the typical *American, in some ways?*
No, I don't think he's typical at all. The true American hero is necessarily atypical.

There are often subdued conflicts in your novels: science versus religion or art, creativity versus capitalism. Do you think America as it exists today is somehow born of the left right divide?
One of the pleasures of writing fiction is that you get to sidestep simple dichotomies, whether academic, political, or religious. I enjoy exploring moral ambiguity and individual contradictions. The left right divide is real in our country; the issues are important, but much of the discourse surrounding it is boring. I think good fiction provides an alternative.

In what ways does it provide an alternative?
Fiction provides perspective from the inside. After all, what can a novel do that an Op-ed can't? Dramatize thoughts and motives as well as action, and explore the gap between the two. Fiction thrives in irony, while political debate stamps irony out.

Is that what you see in America now? A lack of irony? I suppose there is a tendency to see other people's political processes as somewhat comical. But there seems to be something profoundly disturbing about the nature of leading Republican candidates at the moment, such as Michelle Bachmann and Newt Gingrich.
I live in the People's Republic of Cambridge, but I'm aware that the United States is a really big country.

Jewish literature has played such a significant role in the evolution of American letters. How important is it for you to be part of that tradition?
The Jewish tradition is important to me not only as a literary heritage, but as a subject. I've written about Jewish identity (*Paradise Park* and *The Cookbook Collector*), the Jewish American family (*The Family Markowitz*), Jewish secularism (*Intuition*) and Jewish

separatism (*Kaaterskill Falls*). That said, I feel I'm part of a second tradition as well—the rich tradition of English and American novelists. I admire and study Defoe, Swift, Austen, Dickens, Eliot, James, Orwell, and many others.

There's a non-attributed quote on the sleeve to The Family Markowitz *that invites the reader to 'imagine a kinder, gentler Philip Roth.' Were you happy with that suggestion, and would you be now?*
I thought it was funny at the time. I didn't take it seriously.

How did The Family Markowitz *come about? Did it start out as a series of short stories?*
Very early, when I was just 19, I wrote a one act play called *Oral History* which was based on the funny dialogue between a pixelated elderly lady named Rose Markowitz and an earnest graduate student who is trying to record her oral history. I converted that play into a short story and began writing other stories about Rose and her family—her sons, Ed and Henry, and her grandchildren. Robert Gottlieb was the editor of *The New Yorker* at the time, and he published many of the Markowitz stories. His interest and support spurred me on. I never envisioned the stories as chapters of a novel, but after several years I did collect and arrange them so that you can trace a gentle narrative arc through the series. When FSG published the book, people read it as a novel, but it wasn't written that way. In a sense *The Family Markowitz* was the perfect transition for me between the shorter and longer form. My first proper novel, which I wrote at the same time, is *Kaaterskill Falls*.

It seems that the literary heavyweights today spend a great deal of time evoking the spirit of Tolstoy (for obvious reasons).
Oh, I look back to Defoe and Swift, and I think many others do too. Mark Twain owes a lot to Swift, in my opinion. Charlotte Brontë writes in the psychological, confessional tradition of Defoe.

What is it specifically about Defoe and Swift? You're going back to the earliest novelists.
Defoe pioneers a confessional psychological tradition, and Swift pioneers a satirical tradition. In my own literary gallery, Defoe is the portrait and Swift the landscape. They are equally important to me.

Are there modern writers you look to for inspiration, also?
Recent novels I've loved include *Room* by Emma Donoghue, *Never Let Me Go* by Kazuo Ishiguro, *Wolf Hall* by Hilary Mantel (please finish that sequel ASAP!) and *Imperfect Birds* by Anne Lamott.

How far do you think the novel can go?
Of course the answer depends on your conception of the novel. My kind of novel studies human behaviour, which is infinitely complex – so one thing I can say for sure – I'll never run out of material.

I was very interested in a certain interpretation I found myself playing with when reading Intuition, *and how you may have been talking about something to do with the nature of craft when examining the nature of scientists. The character of Robin, especially, who goes through a series of situations that could be allegorical to the emotions experienced in novel writing – passion, self-doubt, drive in the face of adversity, loneliness, vindication. What is your experience of novel-writing?*
Yes, you put your finger on it. Dramatizing scientific work – and scientific doubt – I was struck by the commonalities in creative work in many disciplines. As so often with novel writing, I could enter into my characters' minds and hearts and even their work by drawing upon my own experience. My own experience of novel writing varies with each book, but generally, I'd say I'm a slow starter. I spend a lot of time trying out ideas and writing notes before I begin to see a narrative emerge. I'll try out voices as well, writing sample pages and trying dozens of beginnings. After many months, I'll finally hit upon a paragraph that works, an idea that

seems interesting, or even just a detail that intrigues me. This will become my starting place. I'll build the novel from there.

Interestingly, though, a major difference is the lack of a 'family' for a writer when you do lift your head from the page/microscope, like the ones portrayed in Intuition. *How do you balance your role as a family member, and a community member, and that solitude of the writer?*
One of the things that drew me to scientists as a subject was my fascination with their collaborative work. I've always been a little envious, since, as you say, writing is solitary. Of course, working with other people has its own difficulties – as I describe in *Intuition*! Generally I like the balance family and friends provide. Since I have four children, I get a natural break from solitary work – whether I like it or not! There are times when I don't have enough quiet time to write, and that's difficult. I have found, however, that if I keep working steadily, I can get the job done, even if I can only manage a few hours of work a day. I tell myself that it's good to work slowly and that I wouldn't do well with huge blocks of uninterrupted time. This may be rationalization! Someday I'll try the experiment with more time, and let you know.

What drove you to the themes in The Cookbook Collector? *There seems a real exploration in there of people who exist outside of things, observing life rather than experiencing it. You've said it's a novel about hunger.*
I was interested in framing the hunger I see in the world. I wanted to dramatize the way that people substitute words for deeds, and virtual or vicarious reality for the real thing.

Everyone in the book seems slightly reticent about having a true, relaxed relationship with anyone else. It's a novel populated by very tense people, I think. Do you think there's something 'unsatisfiable' about them all?
I'd rephrase that. I don't think the characters are 'unsatisfiable.' I think they are dissatisfied. That's certainly true of George. Jess is not reticent at all, but she has to grow up enough to have a true relationship.

Do your characters ever do things you don't expect? Was there ever a different plan for them from the way things turn out in the book?
I always have a plan, but my plans evolve. For me, writing is a constant interplay between structure and improvisation. I work out plot and social structure, and teach myself as much as I can about my characters so that I'd know what they would do or say in a given situation, and then I improvise, particularly in dialogue, and with the interplay of different points of view. It's fun to think of characters escaping or rebelling, changing the direction of a book, but in my experience the real surprises come at a point where I realize I must think more deeply about motivation and write in a more nuanced way.

The Cookbook Collector *has been a very successful book, both with the critics and in terms of sales. I get the impression it has moved you a rung up the ladder in the eyes of the critics. You're now so often paired with Jonathan Franzen in discussions about American literature, and he seems to have become the sort of President Elect of American Letters in recent years. Do you feel anything has changed? Have the stakes gone up?*
I avoid thinking too much about ladders (so narrow and precarious!) and focus instead on the work at hand. My goal is to try to do justice to the world, and the fascinating people in it. To dramatize a discovery, to show a girl growing up, a young man's ambition, a scientist's jealousy, an old woman's delusions, a father refusing to forgive his son, an emotional recluse starting to fall in love, to write in an authentic way about these and so many other circumstances is my life's work. The stakes can't get higher.

It seems to me that your research, mostly, feels complete, but is always worn lightly.
One of the joys of writing novels is exploring other people's experience and perceptions. Creating a character means thinking about what that person might do or want or enjoy. This requires a certain amount of research and imagination, all of which I love. I

understand the adage write what you know – but I think most novelists would agree that at some point you have to explore what you don't know if you want to write more than one book. That said, what you know best and what you are watermarks each page; you can never disappear entirely as an author. That's the beauty of fiction. Your work can be deeply personal without being autobiographical.

Your body of work is certainly amounting to an ongoing exploration of something important to you, but common thought dictates to get on those bestseller lists something of that has to be diluted or compromised.
An ongoing exploration of something important to me. That is exactly right. I start there and not with any thought about bestseller lists. I do think of my readers – but only with the greatest respect. I owe readers three things: good stories, fully realised characters, and my best undiluted thoughts about the world. I try to appeal to the highest common denominator.

But does being that successful literary novelist bring another set of responsibilities or does it give you that little bit more freedom? What if you turned round to your publishers and handed them an experimental novel?
I don't mean this in a glib way, but I think all my novels are experimental. They aren't experiments in form—so they aren't traditionally experimental, but they do experiment with ideas and with character. I test my characters like a chemist to see what they're made of!

A great deal has been made about the debt The Cookbook Collector *owes to Jane Austen, but I think your body of work looks much more to Tolstoy, and to Flaubert. Do you think that's fair?'*
Well, I admire Tolstoy tremendously, and what I love most is exactly what you say – the great scenes, the gatherings, the places where the novelist illuminates individual lives in the greater social and

political context. That's been a goal of mine since I first read Tolstoy at 16.

To have a shadow over your creative urges (as I think most writers probably do) from such an early age, has Tolstoy always been a positive influence?
I've never thought of great writers like Tolstoy as shadowing me. I prefer to think of them as shading me! They're the redwoods of the forest, and I love to work under and along with them. My idea of the literary tradition is ecological, more than anything else. I think we'll know what lasts over time, that artists rise and fall and regenerate eventually, and that the best, like those redwoods, seed new life around them, even in their crowns.

Yes – sorry – 'shadow' is a word with darker connotations than I intended. And that is a beautiful metaphor for your creative life.

Do you think that now writing – creative writing – is seen as an industry, something that can be taught and recreated; do you think there is a danger that legions of postgrad students are being corralled into 'ways of thinking' when it comes to the novel?
I think the teaching of creative writing is becoming an industry, and perhaps an academic discipline, but making art never can be. The danger of the workshop approach, in my opinion, has less to do with instructors imposing ways of thinking and more to do with too many cooks in the kitchen. Workshops get dangerous when every student becomes a critic and every voice is valid and the student writer loses sight of his or her own objectives. The best students and the ones who have the best chance to survive as artists are neither the most receptive, nor the most resistant to critique. They are those who can discriminate between critical voices, and know how to take what they need.

Are you part of a 'writing community', do you have people you show your work to in progress? Writers who show their work to you?

I'm pretty shy about showing my work while in progress, and try to avoid it whenever possible. I do have one or two early readers. One is my amazing editor, Susan Kamil.

This issue of The Raconteur *is looking into the creative relationship between America and the UK. You lived over here when you were younger; what influence did that experience have on your creative development?*
I lived in the UK as a baby and then for a year after college – so I can't claim enough exposure to show a real influence. The true influence I've had has been through English literature. I studied seventeenth-century poets in college, and Shakespeare in graduate school. I love American literature, and Jewish literature, but I feel as close to Austen as to Aleichem.

This again puts you into a Jewish-American tradition that uses the European masters as guides rather than the Americans. Why is it, do you think, that may be the case?
I think American novelists – and Jewish American novelists – draw freely upon the European masters. We aren't slavish, but the American tradition is young, and we know a good thing when we see it.

But the American-Jewish tradition seems to have avoided the influence of those voices that one could identify as particularly 'American', such as Faulkner. Even the great Jewish-American novelists such as Bellow are themselves drawing largely on the Europeans. Do you think it's fair to say Jewish-American writing is 'traditional' in that sense? Is it more 'old world' literature? Family sagas? The hero's journey?
I think this may be a generational phenomenon. People identify with the books they read. I'd be interested to know if Bellow read Faulkner, and what he thought of him.

I think Bellow respected Faulkner greatly. But their acquaintance suffered a pretty-much fatal blow when Bellow took exception to Faulkner's defence of

Pound in the mid-Fifties. I think Faulkner's biggest influence on Bellow, in the end, was to be a totemic figure of the degradation of the American arts. Bellow viewed Faulkner's late-life eccentricities as the great example of everything going wrong. And of course novels such as Mr Sammler's Planet, Herzog *etc were his reactions to this eventually.*
Interesting!

Of course, within all that, is that (somewhat nostalgic-feeling) community of yesterday's great writers. Bellow writing to Faulkner, Bishop and Lowell, the famous photo of Vonnegut, Mailer and Gore Vidal. Do you think that kind of 'community' has gone? Did it ever exist? Do you have experiences of that kind of thing?
I do believe in a community of writers – and readers too. That doesn't mean we're all on the same page, or in the same picture. It means that we're in conversation, through our work. One of the best things about art is that the conversation isn't limited to the living. It includes the dead.

This is a huge question, but I came across a quaotation recently that has made my temptation to ask too great. What are your thoughts on "that unknowable place from where our books come"?
My books come from my imagination, my memories, and my experience. The mystery is the way the three mix. That's what I can't explain. In some ways, writing fiction is like dreaming, where your mind dramatizes and displaces the elements of your everyday life, worries, and desires. To imagine writing a novel, take that experience of dreaming and extend it: imagine writing other people's dreams.

THE RACONTEUR

ESSAY

GREEN-CARD BLUES

POETRY

DO NOT LEAN ON DOOR

lloyd robson

my wife lives in the land of my longing. no, not quite. my wife *is* the land of my longing. need pays no heed to lines on a map and cannot be satisfied by sensations by skype. my wife is american, my wife lives in queens. surrounded by bengalis, latinos and seasons of city extremes, she lives alone in our apartment, part-filled by some of my favourite things, an emergency clarks pie in the freezer and my slippers in the closet. i am stranded in cardiff. i cannot currently live with my wife so i rent my flat from a previous existence. out of date and dissatisfactory. our marriage is the plenum ideal, our life together a vacuum. we cannot afford an a/c unit. our love is ever so hot and ever so lonely. our bodies are aching and ageing. life is fleeting and the fleet is accelerating. we both feel it. we are both waiting. on the paperwork.

we wait on my green-card. we were told 'three months' almost a year ago. i visit when our finances afford it. meantime, we spend many hours with sweaty ears pressed to receivers. the telephone is no communicator of emotion or nuance, no defuser of despair and confusion. great love for each other is lost in interference; great love for each other but nowhere to put it. so we shout down the cable; argue to force each other's engagement; to demand the attention we miss in the morning, at lunchtime, the evenings. the night times. the long, lonely night times. so we argue by phone; engage each other for hours over meaningless misunderstandings and moot points turned to poison. we argue because it's the nearest our animals can come to expressing how their greedy needs grow urgent. she does for rationality what I do for sobriety.

euphoria is saddened by solitude. we have nowhere to love but our hearts, and our hearts are explosive.

the telephone is a heartless shit and misinterprets our different english. she takes 'don't throw your toys out of your pram' as being far more dismissive than it actually is; i'm on the verge of phoning the police when she screams 'charlie horse! charlie horse!' as if being murdered. we argue because soft words cannot express the intensity of our emotions. we create crises to prove our devotion. we drive each other to tears because we're too old and tough to cry over the actions of beaurocrats and immigration officials.

people presume our welsh-american marriage means liberal use of that 'special relationship' between our nations – free entry to the uk for her and america for me – but those days are long gone, since the right-wing papers convinced the rulers it was foreigners ruining our once 'great' nations. we must prove it's a real marriage; must prove our earnings. it is, but I have so little income. i'm letting her down.

my wife no longer risks visiting my kingdom. a four-hour interrogation and humiliation at gatwick did for her. the warning stamped in her passport her own personal star of david. she is excluded because she visited her husband too often. my family and friends ask 'when will catherine be over?' and my heart slumps into straightjacketed, moronic rocking. this is love not allowed to be; this is devotion tripped up by red tape; this is life delayed, a genuine tragedy – the romance is not lost on us, but it does not make us warm to our circumstances.

i sit up all night because i cannot face the empty bed with only a marriage certificate and a photo of us kissing to remind me of my wife and life in waiting. we are both forced to dampen our existence. it is a crime against passion.

oh to while a smile away with my catherine, over sushi in fort greene; over sex in the bedroom; over a trip to jones beach; over where to put the bookshelf or whose turn it is to be in when fresh direct come a'calling; whose turn to answer the door on a sunday to the christians seeking a spanish-speaking congregation; whose turn it is to sit back-to-the-taps; whose turn it is to be pampered for no other reason than to give or receive; whose turn it is to have a crisis; whose turn it is to burn the almighty; whose turn it is to be the adult; whose turn it is to be artistic; whose turn it is to write. we do not take turns because we do not have the opportunity. old problems rise to the surface because we do not have the daily cleansing of living in the same apartment, the same city, the same continent, the same breath and same moment – every second is five hours apart and every breath in frustration.

as a rule i do not write of this because I do not want to give it life, but it will insist on punching my guts from the inside. i feel it. i am feeling it now. feeling the distance. the wire that travels under the sea; deep, brown, empty yet busy, purple sea – empty if you're drowning, busy if you're a little fish – and up, out of the chesapeake into your mom's kitchen and its speakerphone and i cannot say it. i can tell you 'i love you', oh i can tell you 'i love you' a million times over and i do, i do love you a million times over and i tell you all the time or i think i do, i mean to do – i do, don't i? i tell you 'i love you' and if i don't then well, i'm sorry, i thought i had that one pretty much covered but that's not it, i can say 'i love you' and mean it to my marrow but i cannot speak on behalf of my eyes when they catch you dreaming in a free-stroke moment; or what my hand would tell your hip as we sleep; or what my unrequested coat can say in the rain as it drapes from your shoulders – for we are both believers, that some of the old ways should continue to exist. hence, we got married. you allow me to be a gentlemen without it threatening your contemporary existence as woman. you allow me to be man, animal and husband. you accept i am not exactly evolution's pinnacle and still a work in progress. you have accepted what little I have to offer, you just never thought you'd have to wait this long. five and a half years together; three and a half of marriage; time together spent three months at a time on a tourist visa or six months in cardiff spent climbing the walls. it's no way to live; it's no way to love; it's no way to build for the future.

i miss the odour of you, catherine; the colours that fold the air in your presence; the gentle precision of your touch. i love you and can tell you til i'm blue in the face but i cannot show you i cannot show my dedication to home-building and daily support i cannot conclude tasks i cannot show you i am capable of concluding tasks until i am with you on a permanent basis, not just concept but in form. i cannot give you your daily dose and i cannot receive mine in return. the wait is cruelty; the wait is starving.

we both agree, saying 'i love you' gets boring fast but trite words on the phone are, some days, all we have. those lonely days with nothing to say but plenty to feel. those lonely days when we don't want our reticence to be mistaken for rejection and all we want is a wordless *cwtsh* to keep us going. a small caring act, a minute generosity, a soft touch or a shoulder to lean on. the phone cannot show you, skype cannot show you, so i cannot show you and this retards our existence. catherine, your uxorial love is my saviour. no beaurocrat can keep me from sharing your existence but blue is the colour of our marriage so far, blue as the ocean, the big lonely ocean between coastlines and cities and bedrooms and that small soft touch that oils relations. neither love nor us deserve such distance. neither us nor our love deserve to be apart.

notes:

charlie horse is american slang for cramp;

fresh direct is a food store offering home delivery.

Do not lean on door

the decal instructs, and some pay attention

Don – the spanish landowner
ono – the japanese artist
Donot – the french existentialist
notle – the english gentleman
tlean – the irish barman
ean – the scottish student
anon – it could be anyone
nondo – the brazilian forward
doo – the korean dogwalker
ndoor – the senegalise musician

all sit and keep me company, before
bursting out of the subway
up stairs
past tourists
through barriers
carrying fresh pressed formal wear, hockey sticks, flowers
until then, we wait
read listen gaze study shoes and faces
adjust our grip on the chrome handrail
and rearrange our shopping.
we try to ignore our enforced hiatus
travel with no more than a slide and vibration
wait for the return of the upstairs action

until then, be patient
find ourselves a squeeze-in space
try not to rub against the jam of the pack
that gentleman's hand
that woman's backside
read the signs:

Do not lean on door

Don – are you listening?
notle – cut that out
doo – get back to williamsburg or
quit your posing

can't you read the sign?

Do not lean on door

for it might open
and the rumble and tumble of subway hoards
will not thank you for
not heeding the city's warning for
not standing clear of the closing doors for
here in new york there are doors aplenty and plenty to fall
the trick, if trick there be
is to avoid being pushed against your will
to avoid being squashed to the pane
to step your timing and step with the crowd
while remaining free of the mass...

all are welcome – two dollars a ride
come, become
one of us come
find yourself and shed your skin but

Do not
leave it behind on the subway seats
Do not
travel between cars
Do not
ignore the warning signs
Do not
think you won't be fined
Do not
presume you're importance has precedence over
closing doors
Do not
slow this city down
Do not
slow this city down
Do not
slow this city down

sure, squeeze between the irish barman and the japanese artist
the korean dogwalker and the scottish student
give a dollar to the senegalise musician
check out the beautiful anon – they could be anyone
just bide the advice of the french existentialist and

Do not lean on door

Dizzy Gillespie talking to fans, Buffalo, N.Y.
© Tom Marcello

REFLECTION

FROM HAVANA TO HARLEM: AFRO-CUBAN/LATIN JAZZ – AN AMERICAN ART FORM

Bobby Sanabria

On April 6, 2011 the National Academy of Recording Arts and Sciences (NARAS), the Grammys, cut the category of Latin Jazz as well as thirty other categories that represent the musical/cultural diversity of American music.

If you were asked where Afro-Cuban/Latin Jazz was born and answered Cuba, you would be wrong. If you answered New York City you would be right. Founded in 1939 by two boyhood friends from Havana, Cuba, vocalist and maraca player, Francisco Raúl Gutierrez Grillo de Ayala, AKA 'Machito' (Feb. 16 or Dec. 4, 1912 – April 15, 1984) and clarinetist, trumpeter, alto saxophonist, Prudencio Mario Bauzá, (April 28, 1911 - July 11, 1993) the Machito Afro-Cubans would be the first group to fuse the rich harmonic palette of jazz arranging techniques with the complex, exciting polyrhythms of West African descent that had evolved on the island of Cuba. They would be the standard bearers for a new, progressive kind of music that would become known as Afro-Cuban Jazz or Latin jazz. Ironically, it was born not in their native Cuba, but in the heart of what was at that time, NYC's center of Puerto Rican and Cuban community, East Harlem, or El Barrio, aka Spanish Harlem. In the 1920s the Jewish hall for hire at 110th St. and 5th Avenue was rented for political and civic activities. Eventually the Park Plaza (formerly The Golden Casino) and the Park Palace above it began featuring Latin music entertainment. It was in this setting that the first rehearsals and eventual first performance of The Afro-Cubans would occur. Although there were many other Latino musical groups performing in NYC at the time, none would have the musical pedigree and hipness exuded by the Machito Afro-Cubans.

Mario's boyhood friend and later brother-in-law, Machito grew up in a district of Havana known as Pogolotti, named after an Italian settler. They grew up listening to the sounds of rumba and son as well the Afro-religious based drumming and chanting of Santeria, a religion that is rooted with the Yoruba people of Nigeria in West Africa. It was in this musically vibrant atmosphere that Machito would learn the skills of a rumbero (drummer, singer, and dancer) and sonero (one who can improvise in the son style). He would also develop a keen sense of clave, the five attack rhythmic foundation of Afro-Cuban music, and his mastery of the maracas. The son of a cigar manufacturer, Machito became a professional musician in Cuba in his teens before he immigrated to America in 1937 as a vocalist with La Estrella Habanera and began working with clarinetist, saxophonist, and violinist Alberto Iznaga's group. Eventually he would work with the famed bandleader Xavier Cugat recording several sides with him.

Mario Bauzá had been a child prodigy on clarinet in Cuba performing with the Havana Philharmonic at the age of 12. He come to the States in 1926 with the charanga (flute and strings) orchestra of pianist Antonio Maria Romeu and became inspired by witnessing a live performance of Paul Whiteman Orchestra playing George Gershwin's Rhapsody in Blue. Eventually he would return to NYC in 1930, making a remarkable switch to trumpet while still maintaining his clarinet and sax chops. In 1933 he became famed Harlem bandleader, drummer Chick Webb's musical director and lead trumpeter. This was no small feat. The fiery drummer's big band was known as the most powerful swing juggernaut of its day. During the period from 1933 to 1939, Bauzá would also perform and record with the bands of Noble Sissle, Don Redmond and Cab Calloway, thus establishing himself as one of jazz's most respected lead trumpeters. It was with Calloway that Bauzá would recommend a young Dizzy Gillespie and expose the young trumpet genius to the world of Afro-Cuban music.

While Mario Bauzá was with Cab Calloway's group he recalled: 'One day somebody in the Cab Calloway band made a remark that our sounds, Cuban music, were like hillbilly music... so I told him: "One day you are going to hear my music sound in a band better than Cab Calloway's!" That's how the Afro-Cubans were born. My brother-in-law Macho would be the front man, singing, etc. I would take care of directing the band, getting and supervising arrangements...'

In 1939 the newly formed Machito & Afro-Cubans hit NYC like a hurricane. Although other Latin groups at the time had some elements of jazz arranging technique, none of them had the jazz pedigree that Mario had attained. By 1943 the Afro-Cubans had established themselves as the founders of the Afro-Cuban jazz movement with a composition entitled 'Tanga', which featured tenor saxophonist Brew Moore, alto saxophonist Gene Johnson, and a trumpet solo by Mario Bauzá that requires virtuosic technique to play. As Dizzy Gillespie stated, "Mario and Machito were the first to do it, not me." The appearances by Machito and the Afro-Cubans under Mario Bauzá' musical direction at the Apollo would become legendary as the multi-racial mix of African Americans, Latinos, and New Yorkers from the Jewish, Italian, and other communities were united under the spell of big band Latin jazz. They also had a secret weapon, Machito's sister, Graciela. An incredible vocalist in her own right, Gracie became a legend when she upstaged Sarah Vaughn at an appearance of the Machito Afro-Cubans at the Apollo. It didn't matter that she sang in Spanish, 'Music...' as her brother-in-law Mario Bauzá once said, 'is an international language.' In 1950 the orchestra was also chosen by legendary Cuban composer, arranger Chico O'Farrill to premiere his monumental Afro-Cuban Jazz Suite, which featured alto sax virtuoso Charlie Parker, tenor sax master Flip Phillips and drum-set phenom Buddy Rich. It was the first extended large-scale work in the genre.

But by the mid 1950s, the supremacy of Machito and Mario's grand experiment was falling by the wayside. Upstart bandleaders like timbale titan, composer, arranger Tito Puente and vocalist Tito Rodriguez, themselves products of East Harlem's El Barrio, were challenging the musical dominance of the Afro-Cubans. In December of 1957 that would all change when the Roulette label, owned by Morris Levy approached Machito and Mario about recording a new album. Since Count Basie was signed to Roulette, it was easy to get Basie trumpet star Joe Newman added to the project as a soloist. Julian "Cannonball" Adderley who was the hot alto player at the time and was playing with Miles Davis would also be added by Levy.

Within the ranks of the band itself, unsung heroes like tenor saxophonists José 'Pin' Madera as well as Ray Santos, and pianist René Hernández, who had contributed some of the most memorable compositions and arrangements in the orchestra's extensive repertoire, would contribute mightily under Bauza's leadership to the masterpiece which would be known as KENYA.

Cándido Camero (b. April 22, 1921) was the third lynchpin to this masterpiece. Arriving in NYC on July 4, 1946 with the Cuban dance team of Carmen and Rolando, he was the first in a wave of virtuoso conga drummers to arrive from Cuba. Known for his incredible co-ordinated independence, multiple drum technique and melodicism, he is considered the father of modern conga drumming.

After a disagreement, Mario and Machito parted ways and Mario went into retirement. Coaxed by Marta Moreno Vega of the Caribbean Cultural Center, a tribute concert was held in his honor at Lincoln Center and Mario came out of retirement. It led to Mario forming his own big band and three Grammy nominated CDs on the Euro based Messidor label, which brought his unique contributions back into the spotlight in the jazz community. Tours of Europe followed to critical acclaim as the jazz intelligentsia wrote about the greatest comeback in jazz history with awe and reverence. Since those early days of the Machito & The Afro-Cubans Latin Jazz has expanded in its scope to include rhythms and styles from all 23 Latin American countries and is performed and recorded worldwide. Today the torch has been passed to those who have dedicated their lives to America's greatest art form, jazz, and the branch of that art form that best represents all of the America's, which started with Mario and Machito in Harlem, Latin jazz.

DOCUMENTARY

MAKING SOME NOISE: THE CIVIL RIGHTS ERA IN QUEENS, NY

Catherine Fletcher

Queens may not be the first borough to spring to mind when you picture New York, but if NYC is a melting pot, then Queens has taken a lot of the heat.

According to the 2000 US Census, Queens is home to 2.2 million people, with 98,000 living in the neighborhood of Corona and 79,000 in nearby East Elmhurst. Corona is located in north-western Queens, near the Triboro Bridge and LaGuardia Airport. To the east is Flushing Meadows-Corona Park, home to the 1964 World's Fair. Traditionally, both are African-American neighborhoods – often referred to jointly as 'Corona-East Elmhurst' – but they lack the romantic, historic imagery of Harlem. This is where the original TV 'King of Queens' and popular (fictional) wife-beater Archie Bunker lived. It also gets a namecheck in Paul Simon's 1972 hit 'Me and Julio down by the Schoolyard' ('*Goodbye to Rosie, the Queen of Corona...*'). These days it is home to growing Mexican and South American immigrant populations.

The importance of Queens to the development of black civil rights in America is often overlooked. During the 1950s and '60s Corona-East Elmhurst was home to legendary African-American civil rights leader Malcolm X and members of the Black Panther Party; also musicians Louis Armstrong, Dizzy Gillespie, Ella Fitzgerald, 'Cannonball' Adderley, and baseball's superstar, Willie Mays.

The Civil Rights Movement in New York was distinctly different from the Southern narrative favored by American textbooks and filmmakers – a narrative which runs from the 1954 Supreme Court decision declaring school segregation unconstitutional

(*Brown v the Board of Education of Topeka, Kansas*) to Martin Luther King Jr.'s assassination in 1968. As Martha Biondi has noted in her excellent work on the subject, the movement in New York took a different form with different goals; rather than start an outright fight against the 'Jim Crow' segregation laws, the New York movement really got underway during World War II, with the agenda of ending employment discrimination and police brutality, creating access to new housing, and achieving representation in government.

You jim crowed me
Before hitler rose to power—
And you're STILL jim crowing me
Right now, this very hour.

Yet you say we're fighting
for democracy
Then why don't democracy
Include me?

Langston Hughes, 'Beaumont to Detroit'

Between 1940 and 1950, during a period known as the Second Great Migration, 1.5 million African-Americans left the rural South and headed for the North and the West. New York's black population rose by 62%. Although segregation was viewed as a Southern phenomenon, many landlords in cities in the North and the Midwest abided by 'whites only' policies. This created a housing shortage and facilitated ghettoization, with many black people unable to obtain mortgages outside recognized black neighborhoods. Migrants moved into Harlem and across the Triboro Bridge to Corona, while the more established black middle class moved into East Elmhurst.

Although the area's industry was thriving, job discrimination was rife. Black employees at nearby aviation plants on Long Island numbered less than 4%. There were community protests and legal fights. At the heart of the community was the Corona Congregational Church, on 34th Ave and 102nd St. Its leader, Reverend George Hinton, pressured city officials at LaGuardia to hire black workers. A prominent realtor organized boycotts of white-owned businesses that would not hire Blacks, in a local version of the 'Don't Buy Where You Can't Work' campaigns that were taking place in a number of cities including Baltimore, Newark, and Chicago. Nationally, union leader A. Philip Randolph proposed a march on Washington to protest against racial discrimination in the war industries, an act that resulted in Franklin D. Roosevelt's issuance of Executive Order 8802, or the Fair Employment Act, in 1941 to prevent the demonstration taking place. In New York, the Ives-Quinn Bill prohibiting discrimination in private employment was signed into law in 1945, the first ever in the United States, despite protests from business leaders including the New York Chamber of Commerce.

> A man's respect for law and order exists in precise relationship to the size of his paycheck.
>
> Adam Clayton Powell Jr., 'Keep the Faith, Baby!'

During the Cold War, the wartime tone of unity gave way to a culture of conformity and patriotism. The FBI created surveillance units like COINTELPRO, and the New York Police Department set up the Bureau of Special Services (BOSS – aka 'The Red Squad'), to keep an eye on domestic political dissidents. 'Red Scare' tensions rose between the Communist Party and the Congress of Industrial Organizations (CIO). The New York-based National Association for the Advancement of Colored People (NAACP) took an anti-communist line and distanced itself from former labour activist allies.

In the 1950s, unemployment in New York's black community was twice that of the white community and the Ives-Quinn Law was not widely enforced. Harlem's first Black Congressman, Adam Clayton Powell, Jr, worked to increase the minimum wage. 70% of Corona's white residents left the neighborhood. Local youth gangs skirmished with rival Italian gangs from South Corona. In 1952, local block associations come together under the banner of the East Elmhurst-Corona Civic Association, to respond to the declining conditions in the neighborhood and the red-lining bank practices that prevented locals being given loans.

The NYPD had a reputation for dubious law-enforcement practices, including a tacit agreement between the police and the Justice Department that all civil rights violations be investigated internally, rather than by the FBI. When African-American truck-driver Jacob Jackson was beaten after an arrest for a traffic violation to the point of needing two metal plates in his skull, NYPD Commissioner Monaghan informed the FBI that civil rights laws only applied down South.

In 1958, Malcolm X moved in to a house on 97th St and established the Queens branch of the New York Nation of Islam's Mosque No. 7 in Corona. Appointed to the prestigious leadership of Harlem's Temple No. 7 just two years after his release from prison, Malcolm X was wildly popular and his years as a prominent member of the Nation of Islam (NOI) saw membership skyrocket from several hundred to around 100,000. Mike Wallace's 1959 TV documentary *The Hate that Hate Produced* introduced mainstream America to the Nation of Islam and catapulted Malcolm X into the nation's consciousness. X had begun to insert the Nation of Islam into the Civil Rights debate.

> I'm not an American. I'm one of the 22 million Black people who are the victims of Americanism. One of the 22 million Black people who are the victims of democracy.
>
> Malcolm X, *The Ballot or the Bullet*

In 1964, three civil rights activists from the Congress for Racial Equality (CORE) on the Queens College campus left New York to register black voters in Mississippi as part of 'Freedom Summer'. They were arrested on trumped-up charges by the Mississippi police then handed over to members of the Ku Klux Klan, who beat them to death — you may have seen the movie, *Mississippi Burning*. Meanwhile, back in Queens, there were ongoing problems with school segregation. As an attempt to remedy the *de facto* segregation that occurred along neighborhood lines, a plan to 'pair' a school in East Elmhurst and one in Jackson Heights was scuttled by a coalition of Jewish parents in Jackson Heights. The boundary between the two neighborhoods became known as 'the Mason-Dixon Line.'

As Stephen Gregory has described, the Corona-East Elmhurst community mobilized on two fronts: residents, local churches and community organizations conceived and founded the Library Action Committee as part of the Anti-Poverty Program, to address their need for a library; voter registration drives were organized by Independent Citizens For Good Government, the NAACP and both the Democratic and Republican Black clubs. In 1965 Kenneth Brown became the first African-American elected to the State Assembly from Queens. He was replaced three years later by Guy Brewer, whose Democratic Club would become as an important center of Black politics for several decades. And, in 1965, Malcolm X's East Elmhurst house was firebombed.

Following the fallout between X and his one-time mentor Elijah Muhammad, the NOI demanded the surrender of X's home, which they owned. The house was firebombed, while X's wife and children were inside. One week later, at the Audubon Ballroom in Manhattan, X dismissed claims he had bombed his own home and publically accused Muhammad.

Malcolm X outside his firebombed home, 1965

> If anybody can find how I bombed my house they can put a rifle bullet through my head.
>
> Malcolm X, speaking at the Audubon Ballroom

Within minutes, he was shot to death.

In 1968, the Oakland-based Black Panther Party for Self-Defense established its New York branch and opened offices in Queens. Its leadership (including Tupac's mother, Afeni Shakur) had a Marxist-Leninist ideology and they established community programs such as Free Breakfast for Children – all part of a larger plan by co-founder Huey P. Newton to create a healthy revolutionary army. Alongside the NOI, local churches and community organizations, the Panthers worked to achieve practical, social needs – medical clinics, help for the homeless, traffic lights at dangerous intersections and, still, a library.

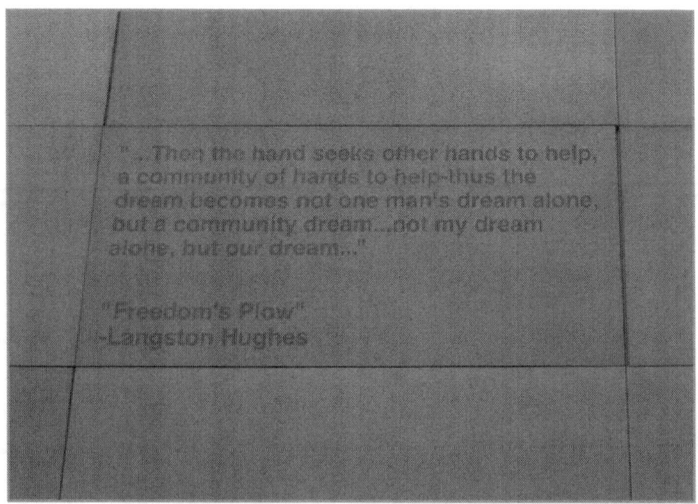

The Langston Hughes Library
© Catherine Fletcher

Finally, in 1969, a former Woolworth's store on Northern Boulevard reopened as the Langston Hughes Library and Cultural Center with a circulating Black Heritage collection and a user-friendly philosophy – both unique at the time – established by directors Tyrone Bryant and Helen Marshall. The same year, twenty-one members of the New York Panthers were rounded up as part of a series of conspiracy arrests.

> We want a black poem. And a
> Black World.
> Let the world be a Black Poem
> And Let All Black People Speak This Poem
> Silently
> or LOUD
>
> Amiri Baraka, 'Black Art'

Though only thirteen defendants were eventually brought to trial, the group was known as the Panther 21. Support for the prosecution's case came from undercover police who claimed the defendants had developed plans for a series of bombings of area department stores and the Botanic Gardens in the Bronx and had conducted classes to instruct those participating in the plot on how to construct explosive devices. The defendants were held for almost two years, each on $100,000 bail, and the case became a cause célèbre, moving Leonard Bernstein to hold a cocktail party for the group's legal defence in his Park Avenue apartment.

The trial began on Sept. 8, 1970, and ran for eight months. In Queens, the Panthers continued their advocacy work, chasing drug dealers away from East Elmhurst's Public School (PS) 127, and establishing the People's Housing Coalition and the Tenant's Grievance Committee to address housing issues. At the same time, their leadership published letters in New York's alternative press calling for more radical action. In response, the revolutionary group the Weather Underground bombed the home of New York

State Supreme Court Justice Murtaugh, who was presiding over the Panther 21 case.

On May 13, 1971, after deliberating for barely three hours, the jury acquitted the defendants on all counts. Eleter Yanes, a jurist on the trial, told the press, 'I used to be a little afraid of the Panthers and not as afraid of the police. Now I'm a little more afraid of the police than the Panthers.'

However, in 1971 there was reason to be afraid. A split within the party led to escalating violence and, in Harlem, Robert Webb – a recently-arrived San Francisco Panther, reportedly loyal to Minister of Information Eldridge Cleaver – was shot when he tried to stop the sale of *The Black Panther* newspaper. The NYPD refused to do anything about Webb's murder so in retaliation Sam Napier, the paper's circulation manager allegedly loyal to Newton, was bound, gagged and shot six times in the Queens Northern Boulevard office, which was then set ablaze. A number of the Panthers left to join the underground Black Liberation Army, who were dedicated to armed struggle. They were involved in several Queens bank robberies and shootouts with the NYPD.

During the 1970s, the insurgent politics of the 1960s, empowered by civil rights activism and reform movement agitation, gave way to the mainstream politics of the Queens County Democratic organisation. Race had served to unify Corona-East Elmhurst but had become less of an issue, as the neighbourhoods' black middle class became more empowered. In 1974, Corona-East Elmhurst elected Helen Marshall to be its first black district leader. Later she was elected to the New York State Assembly and the New York City Council, is currently Borough President of Queens, and still lives in East Elmhurst.

The Langston Hughes Library continues its Black Heritage programming and maintains the largest circulating Black Heritage collection in New York City.

The Justice Department is currently reviewing the murder of

Malcolm X and considering reopening the case.

The Black Panthers' office is now a community centre but the Corona Congregational Church still stands on 34th Ave. They hold services every week. Everyone welcome.

the mural opposite Louis Armstrong's House
© Catherine Fletcher

SHELF LIFE

STRAND BOOKSTORE
NEW YORK

Graham Tomlinson

'Next!'

The sales clerk's voice rang out in the packed but strangely silent shop, and another customer shuffled forwards to the counter with a stack of discounted books. Borders at Pennsylvania Plaza on Seventh Avenue, just around the corner from Madison Square Garden, was a glum place that July evening. This branch, like all the others in North America, was closing down, and the display signs promising 20%-40% off had worked their magic on New Yorkers hunting down one last reduction on the cover price of a bestseller. The chain of booksellers filed for bankruptcy in February this year, and by the time you read this, all of its remaining 399 shops will be gone.

This was my first visit to America and I'd been relishing the opportunity to idle away hours in bookstores. I'd already decided that if there was going to be any excess baggage at the end of the holiday, it would either be in hardback or softcover. With outside temperatures still in the 80s, the combined pleasures of air conditioning and cheap books had been a strong incentive for me to spend time in Borders. I scanned their fiction section, the shelves filled with works by familiar authors in unfamiliar American editions. But I left with nothing. Perhaps it was the atmosphere that put me off, an atmosphere familiar from time spent in other retail outlets at the end of their life: frantic, with an air of quiet desperation generated both by bargain-seeking customers and by staff trying to remain cheerful whilst preparing for a new life without the comforts of a familiar workplace. Or perhaps a new life without a workplace at all.

It was a disappointing start to my quest, and I headed south to my main book-buying destination: Strand, two blocks from Union Square on Broadway. I spotted its red and white awnings from a distance and when I pushed through the shop's swing doors, the sight that greeted me was every bit as frantic as Borders, but its complete opposite in mood. Customers in here were chatting at the checkout line, collaring staff for recommendations, eyeing up each other's purchases. The shopping baskets in the stack by the door were in constant use. Shelves bowed under the weight of ancient leather-bound volumes and single edition hardbacks in slipcases. Tables were laid with face-up modern classics, old favourites and hipster selections, and all at a discount. I was surrounded by books old and new, the justly forgotten and the just-ripe-for-discovery. Slightly dusty and more than a little chaotic, Strand had everything.

It didn't take long for me to realise that this was where my luggage allowance would take a serious hit.

In a city where it can seem that guidebooks list every other bar, restaurant, club or shop as an 'institution', Strand really can lay claim to such a title. It was opened in 1929 at 81 Fourth Avenue by Benjamin Bass, a Lithuanian immigrant who'd first entered the book trade two years earlier, and who probably took his inspiration for the shop's name from the London street famed for its literary associations. Originally it was just one among many such stores on 'Book Row', a concentration of bookshops on Fourth Avenue, mostly between Eighth and Fourteenth Street. The area had developed as the main location for secondhand booksellers through a combination of factors, including the opening in its permanent home in 1854 of the Astor Library, America's first free public library, on Sixth Street and Lafayette, the American Bible Society's large publishing facility at Bible House, also on Fourth Avenue, and the evolution more generally of the area around Union Square as a centre of commerce and culture in the second half of the nineteenth century.

Between 1890 and 1960, there were as many as 40 bookshops in this one small area. By 1971, there were only about half a dozen left and in the early 1990s the last ones had closed. The decline of this stretch of Fourth Avenue as a booklovers' paradise was driven in part by that vital factor in the changing nature of many cityscapes: rent. Small booksellers were inevitably forced out as the ownership of buildings with previously understanding landlords changed hands, and as tenancy agreements were altered, so too was the designation of blocks and neighbourhoods.

Strand moved to its present home on Broadway around 1956, and although the Alabaster Bookshop which opened in 1996 has the distinction of being the only secondhand book store currently on Fourth Avenue, it's Strand which is the only genuine Book Row survivor. And it's also kept its family connections: Fred Bass took over running the shop from his father in the mid-1950s, and today he runs it with his daughter, Nancy Bass Wyden.

After I'd taken in the full spectacle of Strand's bustling ground floor, I walked past the tables and headed for the remaindered volumes on tall shelves towards the back of the shop. As if to mimic the buildings the city was famous for, the shelves rose up high above me, and were separated only by narrow aisles. Stepladders were dotted around the shop but all severely marked as being 'For Employee Use Only'. I ran my eye along shelf after shelf of books, bewildered by choice. But the first book I looked at was not of my own choosing. As I crouched down to look at titles on the lowest shelves, a book struck me squarely on the back of the head. I looked around but there were no other customers nearby and no reason why any book should have left its place on the shelf. I picked up the volume in question: *Chicken Soup for the Soul: Country Music: The Inspirational Story Behind 101 of your Favorite Country Songs*. I thought immediately of poor Leonard Bast in *Howards End*, his ambitions to self-educate cruelly mocked by Forster as the author has him die under the weight of a falling bookcase and its contents. I thought too of the ignominy of being buried alive under a torrent of inspirational stories behind your favourite country songs, shuddered a little, and then moved on, determined to stay alert and alive as I browsed.

Strand famously trades on the promise of '18 Miles of Books'. The slogan is on T-shirts, carrier bags and proudly displayed on the banner of the shop's website. The statistic had played on my mind since I first read it. I couldn't even picture what 18 miles of books might look like. And how on earth would I find anything I wanted? The thought had nagged at me of missing out on something I'd been searching for because I'd never see it, and this was before I'd even gone into the shop.

But as it turned out I needn't have worried. An hour later, and I'd found a selection of titles from the impeccably ordered music and history shelves. I'd read one or two sniffy comments about apparently grumpy staff in the shop and wondered how they'd react when I troubled them for the whereabouts of, say, an academic work I'd spotted on their website about rock music in post-socialist Hungary (*Up from the Underground* by Anna Szemere, if you're interested). In fact, all the staff I spoke to were cheerful and not in the least bit thrown by odd requests. I later learned that customer service wasn't always such a straightforward business on the Book Row of old. Then, some of its quirkier owners might give you only the vaguest clue as to whether or not their shop had a book you were after, and even if you found something you wanted they might still be reluctant to sell it to you. But customers' needs and expectations change, a point I imagined anyone working out their notice at that branch of Borders could have made to me.

I wedged my books under my arm and headed to the basement for half-price new books and review copies. Displayed by the stairs to the lower floor were cuttings and photos celebrating the history of the shop and of Book Row. They confirmed that Strand could boast not just famous fans (everyone from Richard Gere to the late

William Casey, one-time Director of the CIA), but famous employees, many of them musicians. Tom Verlaine of Television worked there for a year in the basement, packing books and making the most of the 50% staff discount. Patti Smith spent a short spell in the basement too but claimed that the place 'wasn't very friendly', preferring her previous job in the retail outlet for publishers Scribner's on Fifth Avenue. Later on I found out that Miriam Linna, the original drummer with The Cramps, built up her collection of pulp fiction titles whilst working at Strand. David Bowie might never have worked there but he told *New York Magazine* that, along with Julian Schnabel's house and Washington Square, he considered Strand one of his favourite places in the city.

Even in the short time I'd spent in the shop, Strand was fast becoming one of my favourite places, too. The basement had yielded yet more treasures and as keen as I was to make my book-buying trip worthwhile, I didn't want 'American debt crisis' to become an alternative description for my bank balance. For perhaps the first time in my life there was actually no need for me to visit every floor of a bookshop; art and children's books on the floor above and the rare book room at the top of the building could wait for next time. I went back upstairs and juggled my finds up to the till where yet another smiling member of staff asked me if I'd found everything I wanted.

'Pretty much,' I said, knowing full well that I could've spent another couple of hours and several hundred dollars. As the assistant scanned in my items, a sign I'd missed on my way in caught my eye. It promised a free gift to every Borders Rewards cardholder.

'Just out of interest,' I said to the clerk, 'what do you get if you show your Borders card?'

The assistant indicated tote bags and notebooks on the shelves behind. We chatted about Borders and I told him that the branches in Britain had closed down the year before last. 'Hmm,' he said, 'I don't know what happened with that store. Maybe they over-reached themselves?'

The clerk rang up the final bill and I fished some dollars out of my wallet. The assistant had been generous about the fate of their one-time competitor, and with a long line of customers queuing behind me it wasn't the moment to have a detailed discussion about the failings of a large multi-national chain. But if I worked at Strand, a one-off shop which had, against the odds, survived more than 80 years of changing tastes, new ways to shop and economic turmoil, I might just have been feeling very slightly pleased with myself. Customers defecting from Borders would get more than just a tote bag if they settled on Strand as their new bookseller of choice.

Strand Bookstore, New York
© Graham Tomlinson

POETRY

THE END OF THE WORLD AS WE KNEW IT

WYOMING ROAD KILL

FISHING IN THE AFTERMATH

Salena Godden

The Puerto Rican coke dealer and I were an unlikely team
we were just like a jail escape movie
hiding out together with our wrists shackled
looking for a hack saw
but not wanting to be separated
after all...

I sat on the window ledge of the cheap hotel room
I was small and damp from the shower
I drank and watched black smoke guff thickly
into Manhattan's postcard sunset skyline.

New York stank of barbecues and worse
nobody ever talks about that
the stench of burning matter.

Nobody talked much about the days after
they talk of grief or recompense
but not the mental frenzied scramble
to claim a piece
and the crazy hoax victims on TV

the shoes in the gutters
the silence
and how suddenly
every bar filled

and spilled with gallows humour
and irony
how we all drank like there was no tomorrow
because for all we knew there was
no tomorrow.

I didn't eat or sleep for days
I hopped bars and pub-crawled
collecting conspiracies
but Cokey looked after me
he bought me a toothbrush and
an omelette I pushed about my plate
devouring vodka and Marlboro
paranoid
scared
wired
word spread there were
concentration camps
at JFK airport...

And this was it
the start of the end
of the world.

The greatest bar on earth was in flame
this was the last party ever
the biggest drink of my life
and I was going out of my mind
holed up in some sleazy Brooklyn motel
with a dark eyed stranger who made sense
he made more sense than the censored TV
and the pool table jokers.

Cokey made love to me
like it was the last fuck on the planet
he told me I was beautiful
of course he did
his brown arms surrounded me
an accent like rum
and sugar cane
and I felt safe there
I thought
this is the way to go then
nice and numb and
easy.

I watched the black sky and told him
there is only one thing we can count on
that the sunset will be there
be here, be unique
each and every day
and we both believed that little.

I knew I'd never see him again.

Weeks later –
when I made it home to London
I was shell shocked and stunned
people
they kept saying
that Americans deserved it.

No.

No life deserves this
our lives, this life
this our beautiful

living breathing life...
no life deserves war and flame
I wish people used indifference
when purchasing cereals
instead of passing blame.

Maybe
there is only one thing
you can truly count on –
that the sun will set
and be there
but be unique
each and every day
even when we are all fried
fried and
done.

We passed river Big Horn
and Custer's last stand,
the sky was on fire ahead of us
behind us we left a trail
kicked up dust and grit
crossed the border
into Montana,
rabbit fur on the fender.

She made me think
Of Mice And Men.
Slow and sloth,
mechanical, medication slurred
her braying laments for Bugs Bunny,
and the bugs smeared.
Splat across the windshield.
Me concentrating on the road
and the wine bottle
between my knees nearly all done.

Montana Mike.
I took off his glasses and baseball cap,
cut his hair and shaved him,
in the shower, he scrubbed-up
good, all firm and wet against
the slippery tiled bathroom wall.

Fucking like mountain rabbits, eyes wide,
strong back legs, freckled forearms,
I remember that much and little.

And the heat and the mountains,
the stars and the air went to her head.
I could say it was in an act of self-defence.
And gutting. Like she took a knife and tore
slashed from throat to belly.
Like *I just wanted to pet him.*
I became an accomplice whilst sleeping
I could say it was drunken misunderstanding.
A bone just needs to be buried.

White morning light sobered,
we drive with the snow capped mountains behind us.
Ahead of us repulsion and hysterical excuses.
Laughing like *I just wanted to pet him.*

At the state line we stop for eggs and biscuits.
She picks up her plate, puckers and sucks up three yolks.
I gag cramped into the stained, chequer restroom.
A condom dislodges, birthed into the toilet bowl.
Rabbit fur on the fender,
should have kept the foot.

Stranded in New York
and all out broke
I go to the 7th Avenue
2nd hand bookstore.

All I have is my books to sell,
Bukowski, John Fante
Seamus Heaney's *Beowulf*
Fitzgerald, Faulkner
and a Richard Brautigan.

He offers $5.50 for the lot,
I say I'm marooned and
I'm from London,
the airports are closed and
the world has gone mad
and so he offers $7.50,
but the *Beowulf* is brand new and
I never even finished *Trout Fishing in America*
I choke, my hot eyes sting
and I leave.

I decide to try Downtown
and take the subway to Broadway.
The train is reassuringly normal
I perk up and decide to visit
a jolly Irish barman
to see if he'll give me a beer
or a job washing glasses,
but he's not there for dust and
the bar is boarded up.

I'm obstructed by
Do Not Cross police tape,
masked TV crews,
emergency sirens like wasps
and the fire station
is flooded with flowers.

Heading back to Brooklyn
the sun is a smoking red coal
in billowing black smog.
A gentle man smiles at me
we get off at the same stop,
I tell him I tried to sell my books,
he says he tried to give blood
but they had enough of his type,
we shake hands and go separate ways,
his calm and his smile remain with me.

I make a pot of tea
curl on my friend's sofa bed
and listen

to the difference
between war planes
and rolling thunder,

then I give up
and go fishing for trout
and finish that Brautigan.

ESSAY

DOROTHY PARKER AND ME: THE ROUND TABLE AND THE NARROW HOUSE

POETRY

PENETRATIVE DISCOURSE
CYNOSURE
ANTITHESIS

Rhian Edwards

I first came across Dorothy Parker in the shape of a birthday card from the only real feminist in my family. She was the aunt who smoked Benson & Hedges fags in a cigarette holder and introduced me to *The Hobbit*. She also posed nude for the front cover of a tax magazine with the strapline 'The New Face of the Inland Revenue', wearing nothing but a man's tie and a pair of tortoise-rimmed specs.

The birthday card, on the other hand, contained a simple photograph of a petite, moon-faced woman with sad eyes, a button nose, bobbed hair, cloche hat and a leopard-lined coat and silk gloves. Under the photograph were the words: 'I REQUIRE only three things of a man. He must be handsome, ruthless and stupid – Dorothy Parker'.

Physically speaking, Dorothy Parker and I were rather similar. At the time I was even sporting the same signature 1920s bob haircut in an attempt to mimic Louise Lombard in the BBC series *The House of Eliott*. For some reason, this is one of the few birthday cards I have ever kept. This may be because Aunty Lynne was something of a heroine of mine, strange, nonsensical and exciting, which meant Dorothy Parker must be too. Thus Parker made an impression by proxy before she made an indelible one in her own right.

Our paths crossed again five years later when I was combing the Notting Hill Buy and Exchange stores. In the bookshop, I happened to find *The Best of Dorothy Parker*, a silver-glittered, creased hardback with the New York skyline as the background and a bottle of champagne on the spine, how could I resist? It even had its own plain grey coffin to slide into. And so I immersed myself in her poems and stories and inevitably the life story of the 'little Jewish girl trying to be cute'.

Dorothy Parker is perhaps best remembered for her razor-sharp one-liners and her chief whip residency at the Algonquin Round Table on West 44th Street, where the crème of New York literati held court and self-aggrandised, (the American equivalent of the Inklings but with a tad more glamour, Prohibition whiskey and competitive pun tennis thrown into the mix). In fact, Parker has often been cited as the greatest wit since Oscar Wilde, a reputation substantiated by such ripostes as 'Brevity is the soul of lingerie', 'Scratch an actor and you'll find an actress' and the most famously misquoted 'Men seldom make passes at girls who wear glasses'. Her mental agility was such that when asked to conjure a pun on the subject of 'horticulture' during an Algonquin parlour game, she replied: 'You can lead a whore to culture but you can't make her think'.

However, Parker was more than a dinner party guest who could dish out a memorable catchphrase. She was also a prolific poet, short story writer, columnist, theatre critic for *Vanity Fair* and book reviewer for *The New Yorker*. She turned her hand to writing plays and screenwriting, particularly with her second husband Alan Campbell with whom she co-wrote the script for the Oscar-nominated *A Star Is Born*, starring Judy Garland and Laurence Olivier. She penned lyrics to a number of songs such as 'I Wished on the Moon', which became a hit for Billie Holiday, Ella Fitzgerald and Frank Sinatra. Less known is the fact she was also a serious political campaigner and lobbyist. She attended political marches and demonstrations and in the thirties even went over to Spain as a war correspondent. Moreover, she bequeathed her entire literary estate to Dr. Martin Luther King.

Everything I read seemed to resonate and heighten my admiration for her. I wanted to be her modern equivalent. However, on re-reading her poems and short stories, I became acutely aware of just how limited her themes and storylines were. They tended to be of the man-done-me-wrong disorder, self-mocking, served with a generous helping of self-loathing; Parker was Sylvia Plath with Groucho Marx delivery. Most of the poems were written in strict quatrains, tight rhymes and a wise-cracking finale. She was a hopeless romantic, an even more hopeless alcoholic and a frequent dabbler in the suicidal arts. I was already in the throes of mirroring many of these traits and in my early twenties began to regard her as something of a kindred spirit.

It was some years later that at the very same Notting Hill Buy and Exchange that I swapped the video of *Grosse Pointe Blank* for *Mrs. Parker and the Vicious Circle* with Jennifer Jason Leigh in the title role and Matthew Broderick in the role of the love rat Charles MacArthur with whom she had an abortion and responded: 'It serves me right for putting all my eggs in one bastard'. Having been a mimic most my life, I discovered I could impersonate Jennifer Jason Leigh's vocal cadences rather well, it was like Katherine Hepburn on Prozac.

It wasn't until my late twenties that I also started writing poems and found I was also a strict rhymer and punster. I discovered that when I read my poems at open mic nights, my Welsh accent had a nasty habit of creeping in or seeping out. This made little sense given the fact I had left Wales at the age of eight and had successfully neutralised my dialect for survival purposes during my England-bound years. I became hopelessly self-conscious of this fact and so relied upon my knack for impersonation as a way of both showing off and avoiding this incongruity. Thus I started writing poems in and for the voice of Dorothy Parker. It was a hit. Audiences seemed to enjoy the seamless transition between Mockney and 1920s New York. And so the poems 'Familiarity Breeds', 'Penetrative Discours' and 'Antithesis' were born.

In the summer of 2005, I supported the award-winning poet Hugo Williams at the Poetry Society. At the end of the reading he congratulated me, particularly on my impression of Dorothy Parker. 'You sounded just like Jennifer Jason Leigh from the film,' he said. I blushed. He was the first person to have ever found me out. And with that I was seduced and embarked upon my first extra-marital affair, which lasted over five years. The very act of being mistress to a literary figure was in itself a Parker-esque copycat crime. And being the 'other' woman meant that the man-done-me-wrong poems were also beginning to flow thick and fast. Though unlike Parker, I became sick of the self-pitying, amorous theme. In fact I was running the risk of becoming a parody of myself. And so I started to broaden my poetical horizons and in the process ceased being a rhymer. I even started allowing my Welsh accent to bleed into my poems, an accent which has returned with a vengeance, even in my everyday speech, since I moved back to Wales two years ago. Although I managed to shed most of my mimicry poems from the set-list, I never quite managed to un-noose myself of the albatross of Dorothy Parker.

In November 2006, I headlined a poetry gig at the Plymouth Arts Centre and the compere Phil Bowen approached me after the reading and mentioned that he had written a play called *Anything But Love* about Dorothy Parker. My heart did a backflip. Surely this conversation was going to conclude with him asking me to play the leading role of the only character with whom I have ever wished to tread the boards. 'Sadly you're too young for the role,' he said. 'You would have been good though.' My heart then did a lousy dismount and scored badly with the European judges. Six months later, I got a call from an unrecognised number. It was Phil Bowen asking me to play the role.

Having played Parker for years in the individual poems I had composed, I unexpectedly found that I was struggling to play her on stage. I found I could play the vulnerability, the poet, the dented romantic, the orphan, the alcoholic, the depressive, the suicide artiste. After all I had been method-acting most of those idiosyncrasies for years. However, it was the tough, caustic and cruel

Dorothy Parker that I couldn't grasp, 'the mistress of the verbal hand grenade' (Tallulah Bankhead), 'the lacy sleeve with a bottle of vitriol concealed in its folds' (Alexander Woolcott), who didn't give a rat's ass what she said or to whom she said it. It was the Dorothy who claimed she married her first husband Edwin Pond Parker II to change her name and distance herself from her Jewish heritage and the Rothschild family name. It was the Dorothy who during her second marriage would introduce her husband as a homosexual: 'Have you met my friend, the wickedest woman in Paris?' and 'What am I doing in Hollywood at my age and married to a fairy?'

Both her husbands succeeded where she had repeatedly failed; both committed suicide. Famously, at Alan's funeral a neighbour asked the widow if there was anything she could do for her, to which Dorothy replied: 'Get me another husband'. The neighbour replied, 'I think that is the most callous and disgusting remark I have ever heard in my life.' 'So sorry,' Parker fired back. 'Then run down to the corner and get me a ham and cheese on rye and tell them to hold the mayo.'

Seemingly, no person was exempt and no event was sacrosanct or immune from her slander. Yet at the same time, she was a woman with grand, political ideals with reams of poems and stories that more often than not were pleas to be loved. It was then that I realised I was far from the reincarnation of Dorothy Parker. My downfall has always stemmed from the desire to be liked and the constant preoccupation with how people regarded me. Her bravery and success stemmed from the fact that she didn't. I simply did not have the capacity to absent myself of kindness or run the risk of being disliked for the sake of a good line.

Even peddling her classic one-liners during the show, I felt like the exhausted performing monkey. This in itself made me acutely aware of the extent to which she simultaneously attacked and pandered to those around her. Despite everything, the play was a success. We even set up a theatre company called Narrow House in reference to my favourite poem 'Symptom Recital', which in itself was a reference to death and the coffin that would eventually house Parker.

We took the play to the Cheltenham Literature Festival, Dylan Thomas Festival, the St Ives Festival, the New End Theatre, Hampstead and the Tobacco Factory, Bristol. We were recently invited to stage the play again in Croydon, but my enthusiasm had waned. After all, we had had a good run. What more was there to be gained from exhuming a role I had played so many times before? In truth I realised I had not been playing her at all. All along, I had simply been playing myself - with a Louise Lombard bob haircut and a voice that sounded vaguely like Katherine Hepburn on Prozac.

PENETRATIVE DISCOURSE

Tonight my rhetoric is running on empty.
Well to be perfectly honest, it ain't
running at all. Instead it's nursing
inertia and candid remarks,
irresponsibly imparted the night before.
Tonight I'm all out of my idiolect
and my signature wit, yet you still hang
on my every like a chimp on a twig.
I mean just look at you!

On the edge of your seat, metaphorical
of course, impatiently awaiting
some sardonic retort. What is this
conversation to you anyway? Repartee
tennis or a derisory blood sport?
Feeling unindulged now are we? Deflated
by a distinct absence of eloquence?
Well I bit you adieu my insignificant other
Because I've done my hard time,
I've completed my sentence.

CYNOSURE

(Cynosure: the dog's tail or Lesser Bear (Ursa Minor),
the constellation containing the North Star itself,
hence anything that strongly attracts attention
or admiration)

Now we have fallen by way
of a window, the motion
picture of a mouth, the faithful
companion of the voice,
staggered by a split
second.

Now we can only see the other
by looking away from the lens,
each the voyeur
conversing with its mark,
tracing over your face
with a cursor.

Now we have come to a blur,
a pixellated mashing of atoms
stock-stilled in vignette,

we re-focus the cynosure
with the fractious waking
of a rheumy eye.

Now we are a screen, a sea
apart. Three thousand miles
as the crow flies, you lean
in for the kiss with only
the blue iris of the camera
to requite it.

ANTITHESIS

Look at her:
all love-lettered
and dinnered free.
Occasionally I wish
that girl was me.

REFLECTION

A COMEDY SEGWAY

Taylor Glenn

I suppose the story of how I became a comedienne in the UK is not that unusual in an age where people hop from country to country and let life happen. In my case, it was falling in love with a Welshman which ultimately made me stay in London. Hey, it sorta worked for Elizabeth Taylor and Richard Burton. Seven years later, I'm still here. Cheerio.

I'd always done improv and sketch comedy in New York as an outlet from my day job as a psychotherapist. Flailing about on stage was a great outlet from staring at depressed and/or anxious people and trying to make them feel better. And I think I knew that's what I really wanted to do some day.

Two years on, I'm a professional comic: an American woman living in London, gigging full time in the UK and Europe. In the past six months I will have gigged in eight countries.

There are bumps, for sure. Performing to a stone-faced audience in Exeter who either didn't like me at all, or all had that disorder where you can't smile. I still hope it was the latter. And getting my head around the cultural differences in such a relatively small space: The Cornish. The Welsh. The Scottish. Northern English. Southern English. East Anglians. Making fun of yourself before you make fun of them is an artform.

Gigging in eastern Europe is a whole other kettle of post-communist fish. I love it. My first run was in Croatia, and in a matter of days I'd learned more about the history and culture than I ever did whilst in America. Because in America, I had simply picked up 'there's some bad shit going down in Yugoslavia.' I also discovered that even with English as their second language they are sharper than many British audiences I've played. And Croats love eating sausage made of up to five different wild animals. My kind of folks. The last run I did there was on the coast, and I performed to 200 English speaking Croats on top of a castle looking down on the Adriatic, and finished at an upscale beach club where the punters sat on marshmallow-looking bean bags next to the beach. Not bad venues, if you like those sorts of things.

Warsaw. Budapest. Papa. Bratislava. Bucharest. Prague. Zagreb. Osijek. Split. Rijeka. 'I've been everywhere, man...' These cities which were lumped into a Cold War pile o' places in my upbringing, such wonderful, quirky, and amazing centres of culture and history. And people who want to laugh. Even at a Yank like me.

There's a hunger for stand-up comedy in these countries. Sitting with punters after shows has revealed two things: one, finding an outlet for laughter is simply part of the human condition. There are few places in the world where the topics of family, love, self-exploration, technology, politics and sex aren't parts of daily life, and worthy of some ridicule. Two, most of the post-communist nations have for years consumed both American and British television and humour, so they welcome it with open arms on the live stage.

In Croatia, even just mentioning the classic British series *Only Fools and Horses* will get you a round of applause. In Warsaw, I got a raucous cheer just for doing a New York accent. And in great contrast to my own nation, nothing is out-of-bounds. Sometimes when I'm abroad I see if I can find something too dark, too offensive for the crowd – it hasn't happened yet. One week after her tragic death, I found a way to mock Amy Winehouse's disastrous run in Serbia as an allegory of the war in Yugoslavia, and got nothing but appreciation. Perhaps they've been through too much to find a joke too hard to handle; maybe some of them have simply been through too much war, strife, and real-life hardship to blink an eye at an American woman saying things which would be deemed 'too soon!' back home.

The glorious part of gigging abroad is being able to see these countries whilst working. In Prague, we decided to explore the city in style, on the two-wheeled mobility triumph that is a Segway scooter. A two-wheeled, upright beauty, controlled simply by the body's leaning. It was like the ultimate symbol of capitalism meets former communism – who needs walking, people? We've got a better way. Step right up. We literally looked like stand up dick-heads.

Prague is beautiful. A colourful, fairytale city. And I must say, the Segway city tour is a hell of a ride. We happily covered a lot of bohemian ground, looking down at the city's spires and quaint orange roofed buildings. Until I got cocky and took a sharp turn by some church steps with an enthusiastic VROOM sound effect. BAM. I fell down like a chopped tree on my American comedy ass. Slapstick has its place.

(If an American falls in Prague and there's no one around, will people still appear and take videos on their phones? Yes. And three weeks later I still have the ass-bruise to prove it all happened. As for the video, good luck finding it amongst all the other Prague Segway crash videos out there.)

As much as I might long to be a European sophisticate, there's always room for being an American dork. That's how I roll. And fall. Comedy's a bit like that. You're sailing, sailing, and then you crash when you least expect it. But even as I sit here, typing with a bruised posterior – I'm eternally grateful I made the segue into European comedy. My next stop is Cyprus. I can only hope their sense of humour is as good as their halloumi. I've every confidence it will be.

ESSAY

SOMETHING REAL: NAN GOLDIN, THE MECHANISM AND THE MOMENT

Jo Mazelis

A woman enters a bookshop on Charing Cross Road. The shop specialises in art books, many of them expensive; even paperback editions and more so imported ones. Outside it's a dry dusty day in London sometime in 1986, double-decker buses trundle up and down the road heading south towards the river or north to Oxford Street and Tottenham Court Road. The pavements carry waves of people; workers, tourists, students, shoppers. The woman moves casually over to a central display table, hovering as if uncertain of what she is looking for, but this is a disguise – the first of many. Despite giving the impression that she is browsing, she has come here for a distinct purpose, which, while it isn't theft might be considered by some shopkeepers as almost the same as theft and certainly not a thing to be encouraged. She selects a recently published American photographer's monograph and, resting it on a pile of books, she first looks at its cover then slowly, savouring each one in turn, she begins to turn the pages. Her eyes travel over every photograph in the book, noticing new details or finding that a previously overlooked image has suddenly increased its impact. Those pictures which are very explicit – a naked man masturbating, a couple making love, for example – she turns the page on quickly. Bad enough to be caught looking with no intention to buy, even worse, if you are apparently mesmerized by the elaborate swirling patterns of black hair on a young man's pale body while he casually, gracefully even, touches himself.

She has done this, looked at this one particular book, at least twice before. She wants to possess this book – to buy it – but it is beyond her means. She wouldn't steal it – too scared to risk that – so she steals it this way instead. By turning its pages, by lingering, staring, memorizing, absorbing with unparalleled awe the audacity, the daring of these images, the way a very intimate world has been recorded and – by means of this book – disseminated. Cock and cunt, tears and laughter, bruises and blackened teeth, Monopoly games and shooting up, babies and beaches and bars.

All of these photos have been taken by an American woman called Nan Goldin and the images are of her circle of friends and family, mostly in and around New York City, but also in places like London and Berlin. No one says 'no' to Nan and her camera it seems; no one raises a protesting arm to block their image, to catch the bleaching glare of the flash in the palm of their hand.

Nan Goldin is not the first photographer to create a body of work that is both autobiography and documentary; Larry Clark did it before with his book, *Tulsa* (1971) and while Clark's friends shoot up, play with guns, 'wait for the man', get naked and encounter death, it's all presented in grainy, gritty black and white – the traditional medium for any serious documentary photography and one which gives a degree of distance between what is seen in the pictures and the here and now. The photos in Goldin's book, *The Ballad of Sexual Dependency* (1986) are all in dazzling colour and might have been taken yesterday. Turning the pages, certain faces and names are repeated; Nan herself, Suzanne, Brian, Cookie. Stories, or at least their traces can be discerned, most particularly Nan's story, which includes friendship, love and sex, and then, starkly, shockingly getting beaten up. Not that the act itself is seen, only its after-effects on her face; the swollen lips and nose, the terrible, hurt eyes flooded with blood and shadowed by discolouring bruises. Her captions are often minimal and blandly factual; this one says, 'Nan after being battered, 1984.'

The woman standing in the Charing Cross Road bookshop in 1986, stealing a look at this work is herself a mainly self-taught photographer. She is around the same age as Goldin and earns her living as a graphic designer on magazines. Sometimes she gets the chance to go on photographic assignments, taking photographs of political demonstrations, of dancers, writers, actors, artists. Her work is predominantly black and white. She gets her film developed and contact sheets made by a photo lab down an alley off Oxford Street. She is always excited to collect her negatives – back then, before digital cameras; there was always a delay between shooting pictures and seeing them that increased the anticipation. In her mind's eye she has a rough memory of the pictures she has taken, but sometimes a particular shot may be marred by something being out of focus, or by camera shake or a faulty exposure – by then of course the moment is passed, you can't reshoot. She collects her negatives early in the morning, on her way across London to work, allowing enough time to go to a café where she opens the envelope with hungry trepidation. She uses a yellow wax pencil to mark up the contact sheet; a large cross through rejected pictures, a happy box around successes and on others lines and cross hatching that indicate how an image might be cropped.

Sometime before, she had attended a week-long workshop in Derbyshire, run by Paul Hill and led by Martin Parr. Brian Griffin, renowned for his surreal editorial portraits in magazines and on record jackets, was also meant to be there, but cancelled due to a family crisis. This was a disappointment, as it was the promise of Griffin that had persuaded her to enrol on the course. At one point Parr had shown the group his recent work – colour slides in gaudy colour – images of brash seaside places, where people wear cheap nylon clothes, surrounded by garish signage, while their children paddle in water bobbing with a tide of washed up plastic and polystyrene packaging. The images are shocking, brazenly banal and unflinching - almost to the point of cruelty.

Later in the week attendees are invited to have one-to-one sessions with Parr during which he reviews the portfolios of work they have brought. When it is her turn he is entirely and obviously uninterested in her black and white efforts whose aim and subject matter are inconsistent and scattered. She feels not only disappointment but a measure of shame – for even daring to show them, or for ever undertaking the workshop.

After this she made an effort to be more consistent; set herself a documentary project, but still resisted the leap to colour, partly because of the cost, partly because she was still enamoured with black and white photography, its simplifying graphic qualities and the control she has when making enlargements in the darkroom.

She stands in the bookshop, turning the pages of Goldin's book with awe, seeing the future, but still not able to change her own practice.

Time passes. Now she is working for another magazine, and happens to notice on the book editor's desk a shining new copy of *The Ballad of Sexual Dependency*. It has arrived with an invitation to interview the photographer, Nan Goldin, who is in London because the slideshow of her work is due to be shown at the ICA. No one from the magazine is planning to take up the invitation to meet Goldin, so she asks if she might. The response is a shrug of the shoulders – sure, why not? Though they won't publish the interview and offer her instead a 200 word blurb to go along with one of the pictures from the book. She contacts another magazine and asks them if she can do the interview for them – she feels she must have the legitimacy of a definite feature before she contacts the press office at the ICA – they agree.

She's conducted interviews before and taken photographs to accompany articles, she's travelled to different parts of London, gone to publishers' offices, hotels, theatres, studios and found herself face to face with famous and not-so-famous strangers, most of whom are kind and obliging, submitting themselves to her camera lens and carrying out her instructions to sit there, look here, turn towards the light. They trust her. She acts with confidence in these situations. Another of these disguises, this confidence – inside she's a bag of jittery nerves, fearful of messing up, of being unmasked as an impersonator – not the genuine article at all. But of course, unlike the person who pretends to be a brain surgeon or a pilot, the impersonation of a photographer (as long as there is film in the camera) transforms the actor into the real thing.

She goes to the ICA at the appointed time, taking with her a portable cassette, a list of questions and her camera loaded with black and white film.

The woman she meets at the gallery is glowing with life and health and positive spirit, and welcomes her warmly. Goldin had recently turned her life around, going into rehab, where one of the first things they did was deny her use of her camera. In New York she had lived for years either a nocturnal existence or one conducted in rooms and apartments with boarded up windows and thus many of her images were taken with flash. She explained how during recovery she had rediscovered light and thus, in recent self-portraits, she had shown herself with daylight streaming into the hospital room, almost, but not quite, receiving the light like a contemporary Danaë seduced in a shower of gold.

Goldin talked about her slide show; the way her work had developed, the way it was meant to be seen, of how she was strongly influenced by the 1962 Chris Marker film, *La jetée* – a narrative film (that prefigured and influenced *Twelve Monkeys*) which is entirely made up of still images. Goldin's slide show had a musical soundtrack, 'I'll be your Mirror', 'Downtown', 'This is a Man's World', 'All Tomorrow's Parties' – the choice of song adding to and indicating the subject matter on the screen.

Nan talks about her older sister's suicide over twenty years before, an event that was and is an abiding influence in her life. The two women are alone in a dimly lit auditorium, the interviewer (in her disguise) whose tape machine is still purring along, suddenly has the impression that their conversation has strayed into confidences which Goldin might not want made public. Is it some strange inbred British reserve of hers which makes her think this?

Or politeness? Or inexperience – her confident disguise of worldly reporter slipping slightly?

She has forgotten perhaps that in Nan's introduction to *The Ballad* she had not only written about her sister's death, but reproduced a snapshot of her standing outside the family home. The revelation, or what had sounded like a revelation, was already out there. It was no secret to be jealously guarded. Where is the borderline between the public and the private? How is it utterly stripped away for some individuals and kept intact for others? Does it depend on the life-changing trauma of a family member's suicide, after which secrecy and silence and control are abandoned? The place of suburban conformity blown apart.

Or is it something to do with the American psyche, which is not constrained by politeness, or class, or tradition. Or just the difference between these two women, one of them in the disguise of someone more legitimately there (because otherwise she will fall apart), the other who has no disguise whatsoever, but whose 'no disguise' might be like an inverted version of the emperor's new clothes?

Nan had written about wanting her eye to be her camera, for there to be 'no mechanism between me and the moment of photographing'. The other woman had wanted this too, but more perhaps because of a wish to be invisible, or at least invisible in terms of taking photographs, because unlike Nan's lovers and friends, she is certain those close to her would not wish to be recorded at all and every moment, caught forever, irrevocably, a butterfly skewered on a pin.

'How do your friends feel about the pictures you take of them?' the interviewer says, reading from her list of scribbled questions.

'Nothing is taken without their complete collaboration. There has to be trust. They always know and often initiate it. The problem is, sometimes people go through periods of personal revision where they don't want aspects of their lives to be shown, so I try to respect that. One of my big motivations is to leave a record that nobody can revise, because both personally and socially I come from a revisionist culture where history is constantly rewritten.'

The interview comes to its close; the interviewer asks if she can take her subject's photograph. Nan agrees and says she'd like a cigarette, maybe they could go outside? In the afternoon light they sit together smoking, chatting now about alternative communities in the US and the UK, about Tepee Valley in Wales and the convoy and Thatcher and Reagan and AIDs. Broken dreams and broken promises.

Then the time comes to take the photograph. In their respective practice, one of them photographs what is there, is real, is a moment out of time. The other creates it, art directs it, choosing a location, relying on natural light, asking her subject to sit in such a way, to direct his or her gaze in a particular direction. One of these women is already a success, is on her way to world renown, the other is a shadow. Now on the broad flight of steps next to the ICA, the shadow is lifting her camera and photographing the photographer. There's a roll of black and white film in her SLR and a wide-angle lens fitted. The steps provide an interesting graphic effect, receding into the background like an exercise in perspective. The American woman sits on the steps. She is very relaxed and comfortable, easy in her own body. Two, three, possibly four shots are taken, and they're done.

They part company, each thanking the other. One promising to send the published article to the other when it comes out.

But it never does – the magazine that in a sense sponsored the whole affair decides that it can't be of any interest to its readers as no one knows who this American woman, Nan Goldin, is.

Time passes. Shadows shrink and grow, the sun rises and falls many times over. Nan's fame and influence grows. She is celebrated for her honesty, her single-minded vision, originality and consistency – then damned by some for the same.

The other woman takes a different path, moves home several

times, loses the original cassette on which she recorded the interview, misplaces the written transcript and the negatives for the portrait, mysteriously has only one half of the written up article and can only lay her hands on one print from the photos she took. It's in a frame, she has to remove the tape and pull out the framer's points to open it up. She places it on the glass surface of the scanner. It's over twenty years since she took it. But here it is – something real.

over: Nan Goldin

REFLECTION

THE EYE OF AN OUTSIDER

Tamar Yoseloff

Recently a ten-foot-high statue of Ronald Reagan, whose presidency has been reassessed positively since his death, was erected in Grosvenor Square, outside the American Embassy. When I left the United States in 1987, Reagan was President. I was 21 and had just graduated; it was impossible to find work in New York with a BA in English. It seemed like a good time to make an escape, at least temporarily. I remember thinking as I boarded the flight to London, clutching my one-way ticket and my copy of *The New York Times* (the Iran-Contra affair still very much in the news) that things would improve by the time I returned. I didn't know then there would be worse to come – the Gulf War, the long years of the Bush presidencies, 9/11, the war in Afghanistan – and that I wouldn't return, apart from a week or two a year for parental visits. I doubt now, twenty-four years later, that I ever will. I have lived more than half my life here in Britain. People ask me if I ever get homesick; how can I be homesick when I am already home?

Nathaniel Hawthorne said, 'the years have a kind of emptiness when we spend too many of them on a foreign shore. We defer the reality of life, in such cases, until a future moment when we shall again breathe our native air'. I used to believe that; I don't any more. What living 'on a foreign shore' has given me is a shift in perspective. My childhood understanding of the world from a fixed point in New Jersey comes into everything I see and say, but so do the attitudes of my adopted country. Being both American and British is what I am. The two cannot be separated. I can't say what my life would have been like had I stayed – quite simply, I would have been another person.

I can't say what my poetry would have been like either. I am often described as an 'American poet living in London', but that's not how I would describe myself. I'm a Londoner first, and the particular experience of living in this city as opposed to anywhere else in the world is what informs my work most. But I arrived here with the eye of an outsider, and I will never cease to be amazed by the city's archaeological layers, the ancient and the contemporary cheek-by-jowl (coming as I do from what is, by European standards, still a new country). Not being born here has its advantages; everything was new to me when I arrived, which meant I took nothing for granted.

I think of poets like Eliot or Plath or Michael Donaghy, whose work appears in both British and American anthologies; not because, to quote Hawthorne again, 'between two countries [they] have none at all', but because they inhabit both the Britain they made their home and the America of their imagination. I say 'imagination' because it's true that what you've given up you can never regain, not in the same way. My vision of America is New Jersey in the 1970s. That place does not exist any more so it is necessary to keep inventing it, or different versions of it, to keep it alive, at least in the mind. In a way we all have to do that, no matter where we are from or where we end up. But somehow my childhood in New Jersey seems further away, in years and in miles. Nevertheless, I have never lost it, just like I have never lost my accent.

THE WIRE

ESSAY

RE-GENERATION, RE-UPS AND RE-TELLINGS

Tom Anderson

Go when the wind is up. You'll get the smell of the muddy Bristol Channel, pollinating the pools and mossy patches that grow in the sunless lee of swanky yuppie pads. On the oily surface at the quay-sides, among clusters of floating debris, birds swoop in search of food. The place may seem asleep, or off guard. But it isn't.

Listen hard. This is when just the slightest hints of the past, its old identity, hang faintly in the Cardiff Bay air. Strain your ears further, and see if you don't pick up, on the wind, the haunting voice of a lost soul: Old Tiger trying to remember who she once was. And this is also the time when you're most likely to be strolling with the place's people – the ones with a real story to tell, those who are still here despite the fact the redevelopment, or *regeneration* as official parlance puts it, was an effort in displacement. Sometimes of people, certainly of values.

Walking recently through the beautiful gloom of the face-lifted docklands of Wales' capital, I have several times felt as if I'm in an episode of *The Wire*, HBO's critically acclaimed mega-series. Hardly surprising when you consider that Cardiff's Inner Harbour, the man-made freshwater lake created by the barrage that eliminates the effect of the tide over the mudflats, took its inspiration from Baltimore, the setting for the series. In particular, I think of the montage and the end of the much-debated Season Two – when Nico Sobotka peers through a fence at the changing faces of Baltimore harbour, at its docks and declining stevedore community, overrun firstly by crime and then commercial and industrial progress. It would be too simple here to say that Nico, about to go into witness protection with a partner and young child, is lamenting the passage of time, or even taking a last moment of nostalgia, before walking away – uphill. No, that would negate the peculiar, complex beauty of this television moment. Hardcore *Wire* fans either love Season Two – the show's one solid break from the 'projects', the mostly black public housing estates of the city dubbed by its inhabitants as 'Bodymore, Murderland' – or are deeply critical of its inclusion. Personally, I think the second season appeals to my having felt that same moment of melancholy as Nico, albeit on a smaller scale, in Cardiff Bay.

Season Two's inclusion, I'd argue, was one of the several strokes of genius that elevated *The Wire* to absolute greatness. Like Shakespeare, *The Wire*'s richness is partly due to its meticulous yet fluid blurring of the boundaries between good and evil, to the extent that those terms themselves become near redundant. To become elevated onto the level of universal human drama, the show had to go beyond the basic 'cops and robbers' concept upon which it is essentially founded. Season Two's exploration of Baltimore's Polish and Greek communities, its unions, and their infighting with corruption and crime both petty and organised, added the first of the many dimensions that, three more seasons later has produced that has produced what I see to be a complete understanding of human nature in all its guises.

Of Shakespeare, Sir Ian McKellen once said 'The range of characters is enormous. He could write about the employers and the employee, about the king and the subject, about men and women, about young people and old people, people in love, people who are ready to kill. There is no area of human life [he] didn't seem to be in total contact with.' But it's not mere range that makes Shakespeare – and David Simon, creator of *The Wire* – integral to my own humble understanding of the human condition; it is the layers within the characters.

And it's precisely this recognition of these layers that exist within *people* that is missing from most commercial developments.

The lack of these blurred lines is what flaws the theory of regeneration from the start. The process doesn't take in the idea that life is not black and white, good and evil, ying and yang. Beauty should be a challenging idea, and any viewer of *The Wire*'s second season will attest to the unspecified but inescapable beauty of Baltimore's docks in decline. A land and seascape that was the primary inspiration and case study for Wales's own major cosmetic upgrade, itself the progenitor of films like John Mills' *Tiger Bay* and fiction like Sean Burke's *Deadwater* or John Williams's *Cardiff Dead*.

These links between Cardiff Bay and Baltimore aren't something that anybody has tried to hide. Or not very hard, at least. In the mid-eighties, a Welsh Office team visited several North American cities for ideas (a level of research one supposes the public purses may not be as eager to accommodate these days). Their conclusions were, to use a phrase I'm guilty of over-using lately, like something straight out of *The Wire*: 'In Boston, Baltimore, New Orleans and Dallas we saw remarkable examples of what can be achieved in the restoration of run down urban areas... we must build the barrage to achieve the full potential of Cardiff Bay. We say this having seen how Baltimore have played on their superb waterfront as a means of changing their image and in so doing have attracted investment all over the city.'

I look at these words now more than twenty years on, myself accustomed to Cardiff Bay as a leisure village of hotels, restaurants and an opera house and wonder if something is missing. Tiger Bay, pre-regeneration, say the people behind the desks, 'suffered from serious dereliction as a result of the long-term decline of its port and associated industries'. Adopting the 'Baltimore model', the developers resolved to 'adhere to a highly researched, long-term and visionary strategy,' one which 'sought to create a new social and economic centre of gravity for Cardiff'. This exercise in displacement was summarised using the stripped-down language of the press release, as 'a programme of renewal, driven by a group of business people and a cross-sectoral partnership,' which became the 'springboard for renaissance'.

One could argue about the 'social and economic centre of gravity' in a port city cut off from the very sea that was its reason for existence. Cardiff was built on coal from the South Wales valleys, just as Baltimore was built first on tobacco and then on sugarcane from the Caribbean. Now both cities have embraced the service industries to counter their industrial decline. In doing so, they have created inner harbours that amount to leisure villages, physically and psychologically divorcing the docklands from the oceans that created their famously diverse and open-spirited communities in the first place.

For, if *The Wire* is to be believed, it is characters – people – who really define a place, and this is something a bit of architecture and a bottomless, relentless bombardment by cash may not control as easily. Two of the show's drug dealers, Bodie and Poot, seem to have recognised this before anyone: 'The city is about to destroy the Franklin Towers: I'm not just talking about missing a building, I'm talking about people, memories and shit,' says Poot – before his supervisor notes, 'That ain't the same! Look, they gonna tear this building down, they gonna build up some new shit. But people? They don't give a fuck about people.' Universal sentiments; universal observation. On the other side of the ocean, *The Western Mail* stated that the attitude of the Bay's local community, pre-development, ranged from 'scepticism over the benefits... to outright hostility.'

Oh, hindsight... Had *The Wire* existed then, those responsible for social policy could have just couched themselves in for a quick sixty hours of TV to learn how a community really is an autonomous, organic, constantly changing and utterly complex being.

Of course, money will talk, and it did in Baltimore – but with a language of its own. Where the show is concerned, I am drawn to the so called 'civilisation' of Marlo, the ruthless drugs baron born in the violence, fear and hatred of Baltimore's poor, ignored underworld – maybe one of the few characters in *The Wire* who does appear to exhibit elements of pure evil, or 'callous unemotional traits' as psychology now dubs it. 'It's hard work civilising this motherfucker,' says the infinitely more humane Proposition Joe (despite being responsible for human trafficking and drug purveying on a mammoth scale).

Money reacts to its recipients, who in turn behave in a manner that the banking system and establishment can predict about as well as basic oceanography can assess the prospects of a British summer. Money has a mind of its own – like Marlo, whose background has forever forged a concentration of all that is ill with this shunned society.

The people of Baltimore, as represented through the extensive range of characters present in *The Wire*, never resemble symmetrical, poster-perfect samples of human life (although Dominic West and Idris Elba have both garnered quite a following). They have acquired depth that even soap personalities forged by teams of writers over decades cannot enjoy. David Simon speaks of *The Wire* as being essentially a 'television novel': '[For] people watching a show like this in real time, it's like reading a book. And I'm not picking a book and saying it's as good as this book, it's just a book that we all know – *Moby Dick*. The main character goes to the inn, there's no room, they give him a room with Queequeg, a guy with all these weird tattoos. He has to share a bed, he goes to church, the homily is given with all these maritime metaphors, and that's the first couple of chapters. You don't meet the whale, you don't meet Ahab. You're basically getting to know Ishmael, and people are comfortable with that because books have always been a patient narrative... TV has been ridiculously impatient.' A shake-up of this convention is what Simon sought to bring to the moving screen – and he and writing partner Ed Burns, a former homicide detective, have done just that. Over five seasons, the power of the perpetually battling, possessed but endearing Bubbles, as he fights the addiction that has brought him to the edge of reason, is a plight we feel with such intensity it lingers long after the fact. The demons circling police, perpetrators and victims are convincing and compelling. I can still sense the palpable fear we have for the possibly redeemed Cutty, released from a lengthy jail term into a world where going straight and doing the right thing are, well, *wrong*. The schoolchildren of Season Four have scarred my psyche, permanently informed the way I see childhood, education, adolescence, cause and effect.

And then there's Omar – for many the show's greatest entertainer. When asked by a lawyer in court what he does for a living, one of the funniest lines follows, in a sentence that makes perfect grammatical sense in Cardiff's own dialect: 'I robs drug dealers.' This is moments after, getting sent to buy clothes for his court appearance, he returns in a wholly inappropriate, but perfectly in-character get-up of party-sized tie and loudest possible shirt. But this is a man who has suffered, and does suffer, pain and anguish of immense proportions. A Robin Hood maybe, Omar is also openly gay, vulnerable and compassionate; a new kind of Macduff for twenty-first century America.

Omar, like many of the show's characters, is played by a person who has had first-hand life experience of the world he portrays. The actor Michael K Williams's facial scars are the remnants of a fight before his screen and stage career. But the most famous of these 'real-life' actors is arguably the teenage girl assassin, Snoop, played by Felicia Pearson. Pearson has herself become a prominent apologist for forgiveness and new beginnings, after serving time for second-degree murder before The Wire's producers noticed her power as a method actor and rescued her from what may well have been more of the same.

If it is to be judged as a 'television novel', then the show's use of language, both colloquial and standard, is what again sends me reaching for the 'S' word ('Shakespeare', that is – not the lovingly imitated 'sheeeee-it' of the wicked but charismatic Senator Clay Davies). Those born and raised in the underbellies of society can be just as articulate as Henry Blofeld or Stephen Fry. Language is language; even if it hasn't been formally taught and grammar dogmatically applied, the song will still be sung. We need only look at a snapshot of street corner dialogue to see the razor wit and its ability to allude to the deep and meaningful. Take the tormented 'soldier', D'Angelo Barksdale's chess lesson to his young recruits: 'Now look, check it, it's simple, it's simple. See this? This the king-pin, a'ight? And he the man. You get the other dude's king, you got the game. But he trying to get your king too, so you gotta protect it. Now, the king, he move one space any direction he damn choose, 'cause he the king. Like this, this, this, a'ight? But he ain't got no hustle. But the rest of these motherfuckers on the team, they got his back. And they run so deep, he really ain't gotta do shit.'

And if we're claiming greatness for the language of *The Wire*, one can't avoid the legendary 'fuck' scene too – where detectives Bunk and McNulty carry out an entire murder scene reinvestigation using only various nuances of cussing's most versatile word.

Finally, for giant, rolling, grand plotlines of character development played out on the widest scale, *The Wire* is unrivalled too. The show's social commentary rises through ranks over the five seasons from corner and copshop (Season One) via importers and puppet-masters in the docks and local politics, right through the inner-city schooling system (Season Four) and ultimately a race for high office and the newsroom of the *Baltimore Sun* (Season Five). David Simon and Ed Burns appear, through this structure, to see the press as top of the pile in terms of power. This summer the UK has witnessed media mogul Rupert Murdoch and police chief Sir Paul Stephenson hauled before Parliament in a manner that might seem far-fetched in a comic book, let alone a crime novel or TV series. As the triangulation of corruption between politicians, police and press unravels, time will likely judge Season Five's assessment of the food chain to be an astute call.

Among these plots, the rise to office and erosion of values courted and suffered by Mayor Tommy Carcetti is the storyline that best captures the Faustian pact humankind makes with power.

In one of his first days in the job, Carcetti, already facing up to the naivety of his earlier idealism, is given profound advice from an experienced politician. Here is where we get the horrid analogy of daily 'bowls of shit' that the new mayor will be asked to eat by every faction of the community he represents – a metaphor for the impossible juggling act ahead. From Baltimore-Maryland to Body-more–Murderland, and Tiger Bay to Mermaid Quay, it's relevant not just to regenerated docklands but to all human societies.

One afternoon this year, under April gloom, with a feisty sea breeze in the air, I arrived early for an engagement in the Bay. Killing time, I strolled towards the Pierhead building, its redbrick clock tower seemingly out of place amid all the chrome and glass. It was open, but a security guard at the doors put me off wandering in. Here, it felt, was a relic. Defiant, the building has anchored itself in, an irremovable hark-back to something that has been glossed over, but isn't quite lost.

I thought of its now redundant role, the heyday it once had. And I thought of Baltimore, a place never quite put on the map by a regeneration project, but now embedded in the cultural psyche of many for an iconic series that will stand forever in the canon of television drama. Baltimore's battle with split personalities has formed the basis for television's richest experience. And we just happen to have its equally schizophrenic twin in our Bay.

Sea winds pulling at my coat, I looked across at the barrage. Would that someone can one day tease out the real story of this place, I thought. If it is ever to be done, they'll probably have to start on one of those dark, windy, run down but authentic, gloomy days when the Bay still sings to those willing to listen.

REFLECTION

COMING TO AMERICA

Yahia Lababidi

I thought I had it, ages ago. Attending American schools, K-12 (albeit in Kuwait and Egypt) meant I was familiar with the lingo. Even though I spoke some Arabic at home, I never formally studied it at school, which translated into reading, writing, and dreaming, in *English*. What's more, I had gone to college in the States, so there really shouldn't have been any sort of culture shock for me when, around five years ago, I made the US my home.

But, my college years (in Washington, DC) were a kind of reactionary blur where I'd spent most of the time with my nose buried in a book, experimenting with things like philosophy and silent fasts instead of taking in the New World around me. Seasons came and passed without my noticing, and I would go back home anyway at the end of each semester. So, when I decided to move to the US I was, for all practical purposes, living in America for the first time - the same way they say that you never know someone till you *live* with them.

Thus, in spite of my early Americanisation, landing in the States in early 2006 I felt like an untitled, and near penniless, version of Eddie Murphy's African prince character in his 1988 hit comedy, *Coming to America*. A series of cultural confusions during my first year of orientation, featuring my then-college-sweetheart and soon-to-become wife, convinced me that I was 'off the boat' and that Project Integration was still underway.

Sure, America had changed, and I had too, since those college years (this was the tail end of the Bush Years, and pre-financial crisis) but somehow I had not wrapped my mind around the basics last time I was here: like the credit system. So, when my partner disclosed to me the amount of her mortgage ($115K) I was genuinely scandalised. After I candidly told her I thought such debt was criminal and she should do time for it, I gave her another piece of my overwhelmed mind. 'In Egypt, we have a saying,' I volunteered, '"extend your legs to the extent of your blanket."' Meaning if your blanket/means are limited, no need to stretch/splurge.' She heard me out patiently, and brushed the whole thing off, assuring me I was over-reacting.

I'm a poet, which means that I send out countless packets of my work to magazines across the country, like quivering arrows, in hopes a lucky few might hit their target. One day, my wife brought back an envelope to me. 'You need to include the state and zipcode,' she said. 'I did,' I replied. 'No, you *didn't*' she continued matter-of-factly, 'you just wrote Portland.' 'Oh no,' I shot back rather smugly. 'I read that one very closely, dear. It said either Portland or the zipcode; and the 'or' was written in caps.' Very slowly, as though speaking to a small child, she let me know that OR stood for Oregon.

Meantime, I was looking for work and without much success, when I came across what seemed like a plum position. I could not contain my excitement. 'Diana,' I nearly hyperventilated into the phone 'come over this instant and check this job out!' She tumbled into the room, also breathless, like a happy puppy. 'Where, where, let me see...' 'You're going to need to sit down for this,' I cautioned, presenting her with the job description. As she scanned the form, I volunteered: 'I know, I know, it's a military job... but I'm willing to swallow my principles (I'm a die-hard pacifist) for a salary like that... and sell my soul to the devil to buy my freedom.'

'What are you talking about,' she ventured cautiously. 'Keep reading, *please*.' I bounded across the room and pounced on the page, forefinger landing on the key paragraph: 'There!' I exclaimed. '401K,' I mouthed it like a miracle. 'Can you imagine, for an editorial job? I'll do it for a couple years, then quit! Plus they can keep that extra one thousand...' She gave me a look – half incredulous, half pitying – and burst out in a fit of uncontrollable laughter. A 401(k) is a standard type of retirement savings account in the United States, and has absolutely nothing to do with my fantasies of fortune and early retirement.

INTERVIEW

GODFREY HODGSON

TALKS TO GARY RAYMOND

Journalist and political historian Godfrey Hodgson has been 'in the wings' during some of the most significant events of the twentieth century. As Washington correspondent for The Observer *during the Kennedy and Johnson administrations, he also befriended a young Martin Luther King Jr when a postgraduate student at the University of Pennsylvania in 1956. As well as his biography of King, Godfrey has written many books on some of the more interesting figures of American history, including Henry Stimson (US Secretary of War during World War II) and Edward M. House (Woodrow Wilson's indispensable advisor). He was in the room when Robert Kennedy was assassinated, and he was working in the offices of the* Washington Post *when Woodward and Bernstein broke the Watergate story. As well as* The Observer*, and a colossal canon of books about American political history, Godfrey also worked at* The Sunday Times *(where he headed a team of staff-writers who went to the US in '68, resulting in the bestseller* An American Melodrama: The Presidential Campaign of 1968*), and as Foreign Editor for* The Independent*. In more recent times he spent many years as Director of the Reuters Institute at Oxford University. Gary Raymond visited Godfrey at his Oxfordshire home on a day filled with that particular English greyness, just as he was putting the finishing touches to a new biography of President Lyndon B. Johnson.*

To reach Godfrey's study is to descend a small staircase at the end of a book-lined hall – many of which are American paperbacks; Hammett, Chandler, etc – and to enter a vault. The room, light and airy, is one half library and one half workshop. A large table in the centre is piled with hardback tomes by the likes of Schlesinger, a volume of biography of one US president is propped up by the collected letters of another. Godfrey, in his late 70s now, is still a big man, not without hints of former athleticism and a certain suavity one would easily associate with Washington of the Fifties and Sixties.

'I was in Washington for the first time as a journalist in '62,' he says, 'which was an interesting time; it was still the sort of Camelot time – everybody in Washington was still very thrilled with Jack Kennedy. He was still being portrayed as young, vigorous and as a family man whereas the truth was he had several very serious medical conditions – life-threatening – and he was not a particularly staunch family man and his wife, I know, was particularly upset by his philanderous nature.'

Godfrey talks candidly, often, about his experiences and his interpretation of his experiences. He talks very much in the style of the man who ruffled more than a few feathers with his *The Myth of American Exceptionalism* in 2009.

'I remember getting rather annoyed by everybody always going on about how young they (the Kennedys) were as I was only 28 and they were all about 45.'

Godfrey shows me a sequence of photographs on his computer screen from the *New York Times* archive; Lyndon Johnson morphing from a genial pose into a towering, scowling bully. Godfrey suggests, with a smile, that this is the perfect representation of the man as he remembered him.

'I was one of the very few journalists who expressed an interest in Johnson, so when Jack Kennedy was assassinated I was one of the very few people who had contacts in the Johnson world. And furthermore I was aware that the general stereotype of Johnson and his people at the time by Washington journalists was that they were complete louts. In fact they were extremely capable people.

'I was quite aware of the intense ambition that Johnson and his people had for a really major programme of domestic policies that he had termed 'the Great Society'. Now the thing about Kennedy was that he undoubtedly had ambitions to do something significant in the same vein – Kennedy and a lot of his people had been reading this book *The Other America* by the Irish Catholic intellectual Michael Harrington. Harrington pointed out that contrary to the 1950s orthodoxy there was in fact a great deal of poverty in the cities; black poverty in the cities, sure, but also real poverty in the South and the Appalachians etc and Kennedy wanted to make that the central theme of his second term.

'I went to see Kennedy's man on domestic policy Kenny O'Donnell and I asked him about civil rights. Now, at this stage there was no Civil Rights bill, they hadn't yet got near to committing themselves to that, but having been put on the spot – this was '62 – it was '63 we had the Birmingham riots – and it wasn't until then that they were rather reluctantly persuaded that they had to do something; that was when they drafted but never got around to passing the Civil Rights Act. They [his people] absolutely worshipped Kennedy and they greatly exaggerated just how liberal he was, really.

'I was a sceptic about the Kennedy people. I wouldn't say from the right because I wasn't really on the right, but I was sceptical of the certain facile liberalism which sort of – you know (adopts a snappy East Coast accent), "you find out what the problem is and you sort out a programme and put in some guys from Harvard and the problem will go," you know? I was very sceptical of *that*.'

'When Johnson came along it seemed to me that his limitations and weaknesses were obvious – he could be incredibly crude he was a bully.' Godfrey nods toward the sequence of photographs on his computer screen. 'But he was really serious about these things and he had a commitment to equality and in particular racial equality that went way back. And I spent a lot of time in the South covering the civil rights movement and I did manage to understand a sense of the complexities of the South. There was both the kind of quasi-fascist system and at the same time there was an enormous amount of good will and desire for change. The South was much more complex and divided than it was seen from the editorial corridors of the *New York Times*. These people were very snobbish. And there was a degree of snobbery about the whole Kennedy crowd, too. These were people who had been well treated by life. And, quite an interesting ambiguity actually, one of Kennedy's sayings, actually, was 'life is unfair'. What he meant was that his brother had been killed, his family had been dogged by ill health and bad luck. But what other people interpreted that to mean was that, okay he and his brothers and sisters each had a 10 million dollar trust fund, *so what!* and there was a kind of insensitivity about the man. But at the same time he had immense charm and he could be very agreeable.'

Godfrey leans back in his chair and a mischievous half-smile emerges on his face.

'Twice I had a one-on-one with Kennedy, but the time I thought was very revealing was the time I was in the West Wing – this was before there was a press room and we just used to hang around in this sort of lobby and there was this big round table that we'd all throw our coats on when the weather was bad, and there were various doors – one went down to the press office and there was another door that went to what was then called the 'fish room' because there was a huge stuffed fish on the wall that had been caught by FDR – it's now called the Roosevelt Room. That was the way through to the Oval Office. Anyway, so I was leaning in a somewhat loutish manor on this door and the door was suddenly opened and as one does when ones weight is on a door that is suddenly opened the result is to go arse over tip. Well, I went arse over tip on top of a small man who turned out to be the King of Morocco. And Jack Kennedy was just showing him out; doing him the courtesy, this ruling monarch, of showing him out. Kennedy obviously intensely disliked the king of Morocco and he just thought this was the funniest thing he'd ever seen. So I was told I must go with him, the President of the United States, along Pennsylvania Avenue to the Blair House. Of course I'm tongue-tied, extremely embarrassed and can't think of much to say. I wasn't really in the business of saying, 'So what do you really think about General de Gaulle?' but I marched along with this rather debonair 40-something man and this small ruffled angry monarch whose torturers were noted for their ingenuity and ruthlessness. I was just blessed and thanked my lucky stars that this incident had not happened in Rabat.'

Godfrey laughs at the memory, but then, another thought comes to him, putting the incident into the context of an historian's evaluation.

'Kennedy did have his great charm. He had lines like this – which was his, I don't think for a moment he had it written for him – he gave a dinner to the 40-odd American Nobel Prize winners, mostly in medicine and science and he stood up and said, 'Gentlemen, I don't suppose there's been as much talent assembled under one roof since Thomas Jefferson last breakfasted here alone.' He was very fertile in these kind of attractive one liners. Of course, he had at least two life-threatening diseases and he was always portrayed as being young and vigorous in comparison to Richard Nixon who lived to be 95.'

The laughter that follows this observation is coarser than the one that came after the anecdote about the King of Morocco, suggesting a darker vein of humour that must have been (and perhaps still is) needed to work in a place like Washington.

'I went to the *Sunday Times* and I went back [to Washington] to cover the 1968 election with two co-authors. It was in a way an anti-Teddy White book, because Teddy White had written this rather fawning series of books on the Kennedys that started with the 1960 election. I'd only met him once and he said to me – literally the first thing he said to me was, "O, I hear you're one of these three young men – the three wise monkeys – you think if you type long enough you'll write Shakespeare." For no reason at all. I hadn't met him before. He was obviously just nervous about the fact we might damage the sales of his book. Which we did. The book was a great success. The last and only time I've written a best-seller. Much to my disappointment as I didn't have the rights to it. I was paid a wage by the *Sunday Times*. So there we are. It bought a cottage. As one could do for £500 in those days.'

But the 1960s saw the beginnings of something much darker than back-biting emerge in Washington.

'I think I was aware of, but greatly underestimated, the rise of the right. In 1964 I covered Johnson's triumphant campaign against Goldwater. And although I did interview Goldwater and I got to know some of his people, '64 was a bad time to assess the nature of the new right; because although in fact the new right was springing up at the time it was absolutely hammered by Johnson in the '64 election. It would have been hard to appreciate how strong it was. Nixon won in '68 by the narrowest of margins over Hubert Humphrey, and Humphrey was catching up in the last few days.

'Well I was away from all that for some time – although I obviously retained an interest in American politics. The first thing I did after that was to get involved with Robert Maxwell and those lawsuits and a lot of unpleasantness. By the time I sort of got back into American politics, Watergate had happened.

'But it wasn't really until Philip Whitehead and I did some programmes about Reagan that I really took on board just how big a shift there had been to the right. What happened was that the swing to the right in America, of which there were different components, a brake was put on it by Watergate. I was told by a very leading right-wing operator that something like 40 Democrats were getting ready to become Republicans by the beginning of '73. Then suddenly in January/February professional politicians began to say "whoops, this is not the moment to become a Republican" because that was then the Irving hearings were taking place – one of those moments when the whole of the US was glued to the television screen. That went on for several months and by the end of it the Republican/conservative surge was on hold – it was postponed.

'Philip Whitehead and I interviewed over 100 people who were associated with Reagan – enemies, friends family etc and we came to have a sort of grudging respect for Reagan and even a certain affection for the man – he was a very pleasant man. The idea that he was a sort of stupid cowboy was completely wrong. What he was was very right wing. And what happened it seems to me was because of this delay in the right's ascendancy, American society adopted a lot of conservative ideas that I happen to think is damaging, destructive and wrong – which is basically the idea that government should stay out of people's business. One of these ideas is this idea about taxation; the idea that taxation is immoral, it is the stealing of people's money. That has reached a real kind of wild view under the Tea Party people: they literally take the view that all taxation is immoral. Not just that it's a waste or ineffective or is badly used but actually that it is wrong to take money away from people.'

When talking about current trends, even just touching on the Tea Party movement, Godfrey's tone takes a noticeable turn of disappointment, disenchantment, even.

'In terms of my own personal development,' he goes on, gathering himself from the edges of a rant, 'I was so shocked at the Bush administration – not just by Afghanistan and Iraq. Afghanistan, it seemed to me, was inevitable. I remember sitting in this room here and my daughter came in and said you'd better go and watch the television. And I caught the second of the two planes going into the Towers and it seemed to me absolutely inevitable that a president of the United States would have had to lash out on behalf of a country that was angry and frightened. What was completely crazy was Iraq. And it seemed to me that Iraq had to do with, "they're the guys who tried to kill my dad." Plus a lot of Neocon support for Israel; plus an arrogant fantasy that the US would be able to turn the Middle East into a sort of replication of Iowa or Nebraska. That's when I started writing the last book I wrote – I wrote two books; one was called *More Equal than Others*, and the other was *The*

Myth of American Exceptionalism. I think there's actually a lot of logical flaws in the idea behind that book. What was I saying? Well I was saying that America was less exceptional than America had been led to believe. And it was most exceptional in the early nineteenth century before the civil war, before the mass invasion of immigrants, and urbanisation. The US has become rather like a European state only richer. But actually, over time, not much bigger or richer than Western Europe. Americans have developed this idea of their effortless superiority as in the time when that phrase was invented in Britain, and it was connected with imperial ambitions.'

From here there is no avoiding the murky waters of the current state that America finds itself in.

'Now I think the United States, at the moment, is in quite a lot of trouble. Maybe we all are. But it seems to me at the foot of all this is that the American economy is in spectacularly bad shape considering the position it seemed to be in. On the other side the American political system seems to me in a jam at the moment, also. Both sides seem to be completely unable to solve their major problems. I was quite early in being sceptical about Barack Obama. Just as in '97 I was one of those who thought how wonderful it was that Tony Blair had become Prime Minister, in 2008 I was one of those who thought Obama was a great hope. We were staying, my wife and I, in America at the time with some very dear friends. We all thought it was wonderful, a blissful moment and then really quite quickly after that he began halving the distance between himself and the right and I began to contrast him with Johnson and with FDR and the sort of orthodox view among liberals was that it was just too bad that he couldn't get his healthcare bills through, and I was thinking how Lyndon John got two massive healthcare reform bills through in the same year. And then, of course, I began to meet people who knew him and began to find out that he is rather shallow – that, in short, he is neither Kennedy nor Johnson.'

'I have been both disillusioned and alarmed at the way matters have been going particularly with the banking crisis. It seems the bankers have lectured the rest of us about their own superiority. I'm very depressed about this and I also think there are some very profound things wrong with it. The initial question has been kicked down the road. There is a sense that, yes, the grosser forms of discrimination have disappeared but after 25 or 30 years African-Americans are still absolutely at the bottom of the pile. The other thing is that the country seems to think that the point of the civil rights movement was in order to give African-Americans the chance to become rich. A sort of Oprah Winfrey effect – not that I have anything against her, you understand.'

'The Kennedy brothers had this idea, that was carried out by Johnson, that it was outrageous and indefensible that there should be a system which discriminated against people coming in from Northern Europe; of course, they weren't really thinking about that. What they were thinking about was making it easier for Irish girls and boys to come over and get jobs. What they and what Johnson did in their name – Ted Kennedy was very, very devoted to this – was to open the doors to immigration on a massive scale. The only problem was that half the people that came in were from Mexico, and another quarter were from other Central and South American countries. This was really not what was intended. If the law of unintended consequences is not a law then it is certainly a fact of life.'

'At the moment there's still a slightly goofy thought that we're all so multicultural but I do think in actual fact that the whole nature of American society, if you like, is in the nature of being changed. I mean, both East Asian and Hispanics have very different cultural values. Some of them are very admirable – for example, a stronger sense of family. But they also have very little real cultural commitment to democracy. Neither Mexico nor China are strong examples of a working democracy. What I do think is that there is an optimism about America that has proved immensely attractive. I suppose speaking as a man in my late 70s, instead of disappointment there is a rather disagreeable element of, "I told you so". What is much more profound and meaningful to me is this sense of disappointment. Many Americans that I like and admire most seem to share this concern.'

'One thing you have to understand is the very real significance of the IT revolution. It is true that those technologies with their immense impact on the way we do everything from medicine to culture actually came from the US, but came from a rather particular thing; it came from the culture of the great Graduate School. Now, it's also true that these things whilst immensely liberating are also in some ways destructive. I mean it's clear that a world where children sit in front of a computer all day is inferior to a world in which children run around in the open air and throw balls around. I do also think there is a kind of privatisation of life which is reflected in American politics and in America society.'

The morbid curiosity surrounding the Tea Party movement from this side of the Atlantic draws us, inevitably, back to that subject.

'The Tea Party is a rather strange phenomenon as they are bringing to their aid a mainly fictional historical narrative. I mean at the most serious level there are two areas where the Tea Party movement has roots going down into serious intellectual movements. One is Law where there has been a school of interpretation of the constitution which is basically that the law should be based on the original intentions of the Framers. That seems to me to be outrageously foolish. The Framers lived, for a start, in a completely different emotional world. They did anticipate the problems of a democracy. The crucial difference seems to me – it was not the first democracy but it was the first democracy on a continental scale – there are all kinds of structural constitutional problems. And then of course the Tea Party roots go down into very simplistic economic doctrines that have been disproven over and over again.'

'So where do we go from here? J.P. Morgan once said, "Only a fool would bet against the United States." Well, in recent years many people have done very well betting against the United States. The Communist Party of China, for one. On the whole, betting against the United States of America in many, many ways has been the right thing to do in a way that was absolutely not true between 1865 and 1945. The US has been through crises and problems and has shown considerable pragmatic institutional savvy in how to deal with these things.'

And this is no longer the case?

'For example, there are many things that Americans believe about the world that are not quite true. It's not so much that they have a strange relationship with the truth as it's a consequence of having a powerful political ideology which is rooted in semi-religious beliefs about being onward and upward and doing well by doing good. What is true, I think is that protestant religion, even in that particular guise of Irish Catholicism, which is kind of Protestantism for obvious historical reasons, is fundamental to American political ideology. Richard Hoffstdeter once famously said that, "Our misfortune is not to have an ideology: we are an ideology." A very clever remark. There are obvious religious aspects to the American story – the members of the constitution are the apostles; you have the holy trinity of George Washington, Thomas Jefferson and Abraham Lincoln – you could go on forever with this. The sacred texts of American political system. I don't think the realm of politics has that religious component anywhere else.'

'People in America are actually brought up to believe in American exceptionalism. A British journalist asked Obama at a press conference did he believe in American exceptionalism and he said, "Yeah, just like the British believe in British exceptionalism and the Greeks believe in Greek exceptionalism..." Well, that's not what exceptionalism is about.'

'The Democratic party has a really deep existential problem which goes back to the fact that it was always an alliance between the moneyed south and the northern working class. The dramatic thing about the Democratic party is this contradiction of the south, which stood for some great ideas, but ideas that were also rooted in institutional racism and for 100 years after the end of slavery continued to defend what they called "our way of life" which was, of course, to hang on to as much of slavery as possible. I'm as blunt as that about that. In the 1950s and 60s most black people in America lived in their own separate parallel world; separate hiring ladders in jobs, in neighbourhoods there were subtle structures of red-lining which meant segregation and it was deep in the fabric of society. And that was the Democrat's problem. Lyndon Johnson's greatest achievement was that he managed to keep it in balance long enough until he smashed it. And, of course, in the process of smashing the system he smashed the Democratic party. My interpretation is that if you take the voting rights act of 1965 and use that as shorthand for the whole process whereby gradually more and more black people were registered to vote. All of this was changing and then rather suddenly in the late 60s and 70s conservative white people in the south who would profess to vote for a Democrat if he were a yellow dog, they suddenly became Republicans. It was quite something. Trent Blott is a very good example. He was an ambitious young Democrat politician and two years later he was an ambitious young Republican politician. And then House Majority Leader. Black people were coming into the Democratic party and it was moving to the left. And the Republican party was moving to the right by squeezing out liberal Republicans like Ed Brooks is Massachusetts. I remember having a conversation – excuse the name dropping – with Bob Kennedy about something or other and we got into a bit of an argument when I said, "What I don't understand is why you don't have a party which represents the 'have nots' being as the country is so divided geographically and ethnically and so on." To my amazement he'd thought a lot about this and he fished out a shoebox of research on the subject. The orthodoxy then was that "you in Europe have class parties, haves and have nots, left against right. We lucky Americans don't go in for that kind of thing; we don't have class divisions." But of course, suddenly, by the '80s, they did. The Democratic party had become the party of the have nots. And the Republican party now do unimaginable things like saying there should be tax cuts for those who earn over $250,000 a year. That would have been inconceivable that anybody could have proposed that in the 1930s or '40s.

'So, I'm quite pessimistic about these things. Whenever I go to a conference of academics we all seem to have the same furrowed brows, but the great American majority still remains convinced they're above it all. It's difficult to see where an economic recovery comes from for them. There are certain enormous strengths they have. One is they have a large population who are, on the whole, rather well educated – actually I should put that differently. It's such a large country a rather small proportion of them are well-educated but in absolute terms they are a large number of people. Interestingly the United States is now by no means the place where everybody has success at tertiary education. The drop-out rate is really spectacular. Something like 70%. Due in large to cost. Which, of course, means that the UK is doing a very odd thing in trying to follow the model.'

Godfrey Hodgson is one of those great conversationalists from a certain generation of battle-hardened thinkers and commentators.

Over lunch of beer and devilled-kidneys in the local pub he tells me of his time as anchor for Channel Four News: 'It's interesting to work in a profession where you are seconds from going live on air to look down and see you have a script in front of you made up of two page twos, and no page ones, and to know that the person who has given them to you has done so because they want your job.'

I leave him in late afternoon to return to his biography of Lyndon Johnson, the president he knew best.

THE RACONTEUR

POETRY

THE UNITED STATES OF PORN

Heathcote Williams

Amerigo Vespucci, of Florence,
A peddler of pornography,
Gave his name to America.

The name Vespucci didn't sound right
Otherwise the world would be living with
'The United States of Vespuccia'

But when Martin Waldseemuller,
A sixteenth-century map-maker,
Was looking for a suitable name

For a particular landmass to the West
Which Waldseemuller thought held a short-cut –
The fabled North West Passage to India –

Long sought after by navigators who hoped
That it might spare them circumventing the Cape
On that continent's treacherous, southernmost tip.

Waldseemuller thought at first of calling it the North Indies
(In line with the West Indies and the East Indies),
Until the name of Amerigo Vespucci entered his mind.

Amerigo, a senior steward of Lorenzo de Medici,
Had travelled both to Guinea and to Brazil
And then had written accounts of his adventures

In which he'd reveal that he'd lived with Amazon Indians
For all of two weeks, during which he'd made a discovery
That his hosts in the Amazon rain-forest were naked.

This of course was appropriate on their part –
Their being nearer the equator than Florence –
However their beady-eyed guest foresaw a market

In the drawing-rooms of Italy for some spiced-up tales
In which he'd detail their customs then invent some more.
With a tabloid glee he'd make out the Indians to be outlandish –

Frolicking in the sun, having carefree orgies; then fecklessly killing
Unwanted children, on whom Amerigo insisted they snacked.
In his view the indigenous people were erotomaniac cannibals.

His readers lapped up his exploitational gallimaufry
Set in a paradise untrammelled by Church or State
And his salacious tales became an Italian best-seller.

Even though Amerigo was never in fact to set foot upon it,
Waldseemuller would give the US's future territory his name.
It was business: Waldseemuller sought to give his maps kudos

By capitalizing on the notoriety of Amerigo's accounts.
Thus America, along with its dream, was named after a porn writer
Who worked for the Medici, the mafia of the Middle Ages.

'In my beginning is my end.' wrote Eliot in the Waste Land
And Amerigo's now bankrupt landmass survives on pornography
And on the profits from the sale of its instruments of killing.

Chatsworth, California is the HQ of America's Pornocracy
Where the vulnerable are herded by the voracious
Into the maws of a multi-trillion dollar industry.

An industry strewn with suicides who've lost their identity
To repetitive grinding in exchange for money and drugs
In a forlornly unfulfilled wasteland frantic for a hole to fill.

A new porn video is produced in the US every thirty minutes,
Where ninety-seven percent of all pornographic web pages
Are generated for a global food chain of interlinked PCs.

. . .

When Adolf Hitler was preparing to invade Poland
The lecherous, lip-smacking troll Dr. Goebbels
Hobbled beside him, straight out of a Wagner opera.

Goebbels was an expert on how to debilitate opponents
And, in the case of Poland, he'd make pornography a weapon
Targeting Polish officers in an erotic PsyWar.

They were infiltrated with pornography by the Nazis
As a matter of state policy, for Goebbels thought
That if they possessed it they'd put up less of a fight.

Goebbels believed pornography worked as an anaesthetic –
His enemies ironically being softened by being stiffened –
And his opponents could be maddened by graphic portrayals

Of their wives, at home, in the Polish officers' absence –
Dr. Goebbels knew his Freud and his Bernays and his Adler
And how psychosexual mechanisms worked.

Still more is known now through hooking up lab rats
To electrodes that stimulate the pleasure centre of the brain
When they're placed in a cage with two buttons to press,

One is dispensing food and the other dispenses orgasms.
Typically the rats will soon starve themselves to death
If they haven't already died from exhaustion.

Goebbels knew sexual stimulation to be a powerful method
Of social control and that's why it's now permitted –
For its soporific effect on consumerism's lab rats.

Particularly handy in a pre-revolutionary situation
With levels of inequality such as never seen before:
Pornography is capitalism rewarding political apathy.

Pornography is the sensual soma of 'Brave New World'
The un-admitted tranquillizer that neuters collective action
So that in the U.S. few are angered by just 50 people

Having as much wealth as 150 million other Americans,
And few are provoked by another 150 new billionaires
Joining the American billionaire club every year,

While 20 million people die from hunger and disease
And while the average billionaire annually spends $25 million
On food; entertainment, then more food and entertainment,

Which is enough to feed 70,000 hungry people for a year.
Imperial Rome spent fifteen percent of its tax revenue on its war
machine,
The imperial US spends 54% of its tax revenue on its war machine.

Or rather on Defense Contractors – the body guards of an elite –
Because the more money that corporate America hoards,
Then the more weapons it needs to protect itself.

To protect itself from the consequences of its own actions
Amerigo's country is founded on the genocide of its first Nations
And sustained by genocide in countries all over the world.

Amerigo's country has sponsored serial holocausts
In Central and South East Asia, and the Middle East,
All with the same motive: capturing others' resources.

46% of children who lose an arm and leg in the world,
Lose it to a weapon manufactured by a U.S. company.
The U.S. government receives $2,650 billion in taxes each year,

Of which 54% goes towards war and destruction.
'We are bankers. You are nothing, and when our greed
Gets the better of us, you must help us out.'

The sex toy industry is valued at $15 billion this year.
It's enough to provide for the healthcare needs of all women
In impoverished countries. But 'We are American bankers,

We invest in sex toys. They have a high yield. You are nothing.
We are money's oligarchs. We are happiest when making money;
Making money by people pleasuring themselves with machines.'

As befits a country named after the murderous Medici's gopher,
America spends more money on weapons each year
Than the whole world spends on food and drinks.

In 1998, Lockheed Martin refused to give free prosthetic limbs
To children maimed by its weapons.
'We are American bankers. We invest in weapons. You are nothing.

We are citizens of the United States of Porn.
We are kleptomaniac oligarchs, you are nothing.'
We live in an armed Imperialist pornocracy.

'A few thousand miles of cannibal land' was how Robert Korner,
CIA Adviser
To John F Kennedy, described resource-rich West Papua before both
Backed an invasion to the benefit of the US Mining company
Freeport.

Similar allegations of cannibalism to those Vespucci once made
Allowed the Papuans to be slaughtered by the American Empire –
To be treated as unpeople and therefore ripe for exploitation,

Whilst back in the USA, in the cradle of another civilization,
Porn barons bewitch their tame tribes to act out primitive rituals.
Smeared with oil, and sporting latex sheathes, they eat each other.

There are 22 million women in the world who spend five hours a day
Collecting water for their children and families.
During the financial crisis there were American bankers

In Wall Street who watched porn for up to five hours a day.
But a marriage between such unfeeling profiteers from poverty
And porn addicts is an ideal marriage since both bankers

And porn addicts distort the way you love your fellow man.
'We are financiers, we crunch numbers. You are nothing,
We're the money oligarchs, you are nothing. Pass the Kleenex.'

Bigger than Hollywood, porn pump-starts the US economy –
The cream-filling in its military-industrial sandwich
Upon which the rest of the world is now force-fed.

Every second in Amerigo-Vespucci-land thousands of dollars
Are spent on porn by 250 million citizens
Who look away from their porn screens

To wave wet Kleenexes at their Statue of Liberty
Then smile, slack-jawed, 'Look Mom, look at what we can do'.
Then back to the infantilizing screen in every terminal.

Porn screens in the Pentagon; porn screens in the White House;
Porn screens in the Senate offices; porn screens in Congress.
Two hundred and fifty million militarized masturbators

Are enslaved by billionaire pornocrats relentlessly promoting
Cybernetic snakepits of squirming bodies, all gasping, 'Ah!'
'Ah!' 'Ah!' 'Ah!' 'Ah!' 'Ah!' 'Ah!' 'Ah!' 'Ah!' 'Ah!' 'Ah!' 'Ah!' 'Ah!'

Porn stars can be paid by porn barons to eat excrement
To self-harm, to use babies and animals as sex objects,
Always with a brutal triumphalism: 'Take this. Take that.'

While all are in denial: 'I don't like cocaine, I just like the smell of it'.
'It's got nothing to do with sexual belligerence, it's harmless.
If people want to see people holding women down. So what?'

Yet romantic arousal is now mediated by favorite porn clips;
One addict confessed to logging on to three hundred vaginas
Before getting out of bed – it's causing synaptic change.[1]

'What pornography is really about, ultimately, isn't sex but death.'
Said Susan Sontag, and she was echoed by J G Ballard:
'A widespread taste for pornography means that nature

'Is alerting us to some threat of extinction.'
'When liberty comes,' said Wilde, 'with hands dabbled in blood
It is hard to shake hands with her.' Equally hard to shake hands

With those sweating and throbbing due to a repetitious distraction
Induced by Miss Porn USA and her all-enveloping porn cloud that governs
The global weather, despite pornography being as dull as golf.

In the caves of Lascaux, prehistoric man drew virile penises on stick figures
But which may not have rooted him to the spot while he pleasured himself
For instead he'd leave the darkness of the cave and pursue his own history –

Being sensible enough to know that compulsively playing with himself –
Preying on his own energy and milking himself for hours on end
While watching flickering images might make him prone to predators.

Amerigo Vespucci, of Florence, a peddler of pornography,
Set his seal on America: trillions in debt; its economy sexualized;
Stealing others' resources at gun-point, and unable to feed itself.

'They are living like parasites off the global economy'[2]
Vladimir Putin said of America, now lacking only William Burroughs,
A former pest control expert, to describe its final death-orgasm.

America's stripped of its Triple A gold-plated credit rating,
Its life-blood's drained by a population of digital sex zombies
Then topped up by killing third world children with drones.

If Amerigo's land were personified it'd be as a sex criminal
Bringing irate women with rolling pins out onto the streets
Demanding protection from a slathering, dead-eyed pariah.

To fake an emotion can damage your immune system,
Inviting opportunistic diseases;
'Got wood?' porn producers bawl to start their wooden shows

In a nowhereland that Amerigo never visited[3]
Where plotless stories are crammed with climaxes to sell in billions
Via porn barons' multi-platform production outlets;

Whose actors may be trafficked, or be willing slaves – few can tell,
Only that America constitutionally defiles love.
For its pornographic power has blended sexuality with death:

Letting it kill for pleasure whomever it chooses;
Its Statue of Liberty is mounted upon piles of imperial corpses
And now it holds a torch that's ignited by porn.

The American dream becomes a meretricious nightmare:
A fake country living on fake orgasms;
Porn's a ploy to smother you as America devours the world

'We are Americans. You are nothing.'

Notes:

1 Davy Rothbart, 'He's Just Not That Into Anyone Even, and perhaps especially, when his girlfriend is acting like the women he can't stop watching online.' New York: *New York Magazine*, Jan 30, 2011.

2 Putin addressing students in Lake Seliger, Russia, Aug. 1, 2011, Reuters.

In this passage I have drawn freely from uncredited online postings on 'Injustice Facts' and the 'Overt Dictionary', notably for the statistics relating to the US Empire and economy.

3 I owe this comparison to Malcolm Ritchie, following comments he made on seeing an earlier draft.

REFLECTION

I AM NOT & ALWAYS WILL BE AN AMERICAN

David E. Oprava

I am not & always will be an American. My twang doesn't bend or blend in well with my surroundings: I stand on buildings rather than in them. But America is an anomaly to me, something unhealthy & unnatural that has consumed a continent aiming for a world. I chose to ride away from the sunset to wallow on an island with no dawn. Things I miss: decent kosher hot dogs, truly open space, candour, waitresses who touch your shoulder every time they pass, the anonymity of being a thing with room to breathe. Things I hate: narrow-minded bigotry, self-fulfilling prophecies, Pax Americana & Twinkies. That's a lie, I love Twinkies.

I wrote a book once that ten people read called *American Means* and it meant that my country is mean, uses means to get what it demands, and is demeaning. It was 96 pages long and was one poem. It had all I had to say about America in it and then I was tired, I looked like a drying rack naked after that so I shut up my shop and called it a mouth and kept a small acetylene flame alight somewhere in my underwear drawer for the day I might return. I call it memory.

Don't get me wrong. I still believe. I believe in the idea of America more than ever, it's just the reality that gets me. Don't think anywhere is any better – I've been. It's not. It's not the country that's wrong or the history or the language or Wal-Mart or tourists or guns or white socks with sandals – it's humans. We have issues. Like weeds we pop up all over the place in different shapes and sizes and a Welsh weed is still a weed as an Arkansan weed is still a weed and lots of people smoke 'em & drink stuff made from them and we are all as peculiar as a drunk porcupine on mescaline & that is kind of beautiful. Hell, it doesn't matter. I mean nationality is a lost cause, because when the aliens land we all get to be human again. Again. As if we ever all were.

When people ask me where I'm from I state the obvious, unless you think I'm Canadian & then we have problems, I just am as is & gave up on pride a long time ago when there was more to be ashamed of than gloat over so call me HUMAN & forget we won a few wars.

Our beer has gotten better & we still make the best hot dogs. It's not a pissing contest. Go to Disneyland & tell me all about how great Florida & New York are. I'll smile as I point out that everything in Florida is trying to kill you from the fire ants to the mosquitoes, the category 5 hurricanes to the razor grass to the alligators to the goddamned heat. Hell, I should know; I lived there. But I'll tell you all these things in my mind & keep smiling, because you had a good time. By the way, I like your sunburn.

See, it doesn't matter.

And as to matter, let's look at our molecules. Are mine red, white, and blue? Perhaps yours are too. In a parallel universe we are all gods, maybe just not the same one.

See, now you can avoid me on the street & that is fine with me. I won't open my mouth & you will never know I am American. I often forget I am. My kids can't tell the difference, I'm just dad: the only thing that matters. Thank god. Or whomever.

ESSAY

AN AMERICAN SAGA

Gary Raymond

George Orwell once described England as like a family but with the wrong members in control. There is a truth to this nowadays should one apply it to any nation. Orwell was not talking about the Prime Minister *per se*, or the person of the King at the time; he was alluding to the nature of ruling classes. The ruling classes, after all, do not always hold public office.

Whereas the United Kingdom has seen itself travel an interesting road in the story of its elected leaders since Orwell's time, a journey that has gone from the gates of Eton all the way to the gates of Eton, the United States has been a muddled 'family' of a different hue. America has had leaders who have embodied the American Dream – farm boy presidents, four star general presidents, movie star presidents, Catholic ones, a black one. America, a country that wowed intellectuals such as Alexis de Tocqueville for its equality in its early years, seems to have had a better go at choosing which family member will sit at the head of the table than we have. Or has it?

What is a country if not only a faction imposed by geography? And what is a family if not a faction imposed by birth? The truth is that the idea of 'family' to the American myth *is* merely one of faction; it is the natural result of the ghettoised visions of an immigrant nation. The idea of political parties, for instance (an idea that the Founding Fathers explicitly opposed), is merely a concentration of unstable power. And America has shown time after time that as the interests of one family can splay out into the community, and that community splays forth once more across a county, a state, a nation of states, it is naturally to the family that America eventually ends up looking. Take the post-war period, for example, to see a nationwide infatuation with the Kennedys, as well as the dynasty of the Bush family, not to mention the successes of such microcosms of the American ethos, such as the Ewings, the Galts, or even the ludicrous middle-class dysfunctions of *Desperate Housewives*.

It is a full circle, as from Eton to Eton. And family, whether at the top of the pile or the bottom, is just a band of ill-matched people, bound together by the tensions that push them away from solitude.

As Francis Bacon pointed out, 'those that are seconds in factions do many times, when the faction subdivideth, prove principals,' and thus when parties, or factions, boil down to dynasties, it is just as likely that a creature of such undistinguished achievement as George W. Bush will rise to the top.

In January 1998, somewhat bewildered after four months spent studying Classics in the small Welsh university town of Lampeter, I slung a guitar over my shoulder and set off for America. I was eighteen.

Of course, I was by this point steeped in the folklore of the Beats, and Kerouac was my guiding light, as he had been for so many before. Nobody had captured the sense of adventure, the deliciousness of freedom, like Kerouac seemed to – not since Jack London had the world seemed so winnable. This was the high-point of my love affair with the place; everything that's come after it has been just as trying as a settled relationship, specked with glimmers of glory and intense passion, but mainly a narrative of subdued companionship, compromise, and long thoughtful silences.

America – often referred to as the land of our cousins across the pond. It is no cousin to me. But it is certainly family. I have just as little in common with it as I do other family members. And just as much. America and I have that colourful mix of the alien and the bonded. We have our lives. But we are linked.

Most likely millions upon millions of people across the globe will have the same experience, most likely without really noticing. America, since the war, has become the master-hegemony, infiltrating all aspects of life from diet to fanaticism, from language to posture. The American myth has grown, often using little more than the vulgarities of glamour to trap its prey. Oh, and heavy artillery.

But America is the home of 'homely', is the hub of bubblegum simplicity and rosy cheeks; the apple pie, sweet and indulgent cooling on the window sill, is its national dish. In casting off the shackles of European imperialism, it also slowly walked from out of the shadow of that Georgian silence, almost sidestepped the Victorian muteness. America was to be a utopia-of-sorts when it was conceived as a nation apart from Europe. It was to be the land of equality. De Tocqueville was so blown away by it he left New York and went home to start the French Revolution.

But building a country is hard work, and it claims lives, and it claims sanity. The European tribes that reached America ghettoised the land, tightened into factions bound by tongue and tradition, but over time they formed into something greater, something nobler. Family is important all over the world, obviously, and it is important to more than one species, but it grows in weight when it can mean more than a bloodline. The archetypal American family believes itself to be a microcosm of the nation at large – or at least the *idea* of the nation – and that nation is the *greatest on earth*. Opposing beliefs, therefore, are non-American; not a part of the family.

Of course this is all very middle class – the most significant class in the classless society. There was a time when America was a middle-class country. It was Eisenhower time. The richest of the rich paid 90% income tax. America was the most powerful nation on earth. It glowed. But the right of the Republican Party could smell the fruits of exploitation by the '70s and despite the seven year sojourn after Nixon's resignation, Ronald Reagan, a TV soap salesman from California brought the Dream to an end. Between Reagan's election as president and the end of the century the average wage of the American rose 10%, whilst during the same period the rise for chief executives was 157%. The land of the equal no more. And that disparity has continued at the expense of the very existence of the middle class.

The American middle-class family is the bearer of those very aspirations that fill the American Dream with its impetus. What the family units of the ruling classes have done so well, in the name of the American myth, is to convince the middle classes – and even some of the working classes – that they all exist on a sliding scale. The reality is that, just as in the UK, transgression of class is very rare, and is not entirely associated with wealth. But as Gore Vidal pointed out in the mid-80s, social mobility in America has never been more available, it's just that 100 years ago no member of a wealthy family, no matter how reckless and penniless, would have been allowed to slide downwards.

America the family has always had its archetypes, its favoured, romanticised dynasties. While the best of the nation's novelists and poets have told of a country with solid middle-class ideals, ones of freedom, liberty and justice, but a country of fragile humanity, its politicians have created a country that survives only in the mind. Perhaps that is why, nowadays, it would be a shock to hear a politician talking about the alcoholics of Eugene O'Neil, or the dispossessed youths of Flannery O'Connor, or the guilty fakes of John O'Hara, all of them struggling within and without of their own family units. But rather one can often be treated to essays on the value of Ayn Rand and her one-dimensional *ubermensch*.

Rand, although never a truly popular novelist this side of the Atlantic, has a peculiar hold over certain right wing politicos in the US (notably Paul Ryan and Rand Paul, with their suspiciously anagrammatical names).

For those unfamiliar with her work, she was the great progenitor of the idea of the 'undeserving poor' in the minds of post-war, post-Depression America. Her works have titles such as *The Virtue of Selfishness*; she regarded homosexuality as 'disgusting', advocated the terms and conditions of European colonialism, and termed the working classes 'parasites', 'moochers' and 'looters'. Of course, Republicans cite her Objectivism as the core of the American Dream – where anyone can become a millionaire if they are willing to put in the hard graft. But the truth is that there is something deeper in the figure of Rand that Republicans can allude to, like a secret handshake. Ayn Rand was a racist, a snob, a homophobe and a hypocrite. Wink wink.

It is interesting that Rand has undergone almost nothing in the way of a revisionist makeover, such as, say, Ronald Reagan has in recent years. Reagan, of course, has been reinvented as the right search for an icon in the toxic shadow of Bushism. The exploitative nature of Reagan's 'greed-is-good' economic policy has been rebranded as a call-to-arms for dynamic entrepreneurialism. Forgotten are the Iran-Contra criminalities, the Central American genocides, the back-slapping economic policies that (just as Thatcherism did in the UK) has filtered down a generation and left us in this god-awful mess. But, it seems, Republicans are not yet done with the myth-making of Hollywood. Reagan, no fool but neither was he in any way remarkable (apart from his ability to sell) is currently an Augustinian figurehead for the thinly-veiled cruelties of American Republican politics. So good is the right at creating father-figure myths that even many Democrats find themselves nodding in agreement when Reagan is lauded.

Earlier this year Donald Trump (of the Trumps – it's okay to laugh at a man filled with such wind who walks about in a skyscraper he has named The Trump Tower), the epitome of the smoke-and-mirrors billionaire, announced his candidacy for the Republican nomination for president. Trump is and always has been a rather unpalatable joke to anyone who doesn't see their own ambitions embodied in his lack of talent. Born into enormous wealth he has sunk project after project with family money. He has filed for bankruptcy more times than would rightly be deemed possible by a moral society. And yet Trump would have met with Rand's approval according to her advocacy of a society where the rich pay no taxes, where government's only role is to use force to perpetuate hegemony and ensure civil obedience.

What the GOP almost had in Trump was a true face of their Objectivism, for where Trump is a billionaire with no money, an entrepreneur with no obvious skills in business, the Kitsch ideal, lacking in all modesty, irony, and wit, the American Dream in all its garish absurdity; so Rand made her name as a figurehead of individualism, a guru of the triumph of the will, an anti-statist standard, whilst at the same time she claimed social welfare under her married name of Ann O'Connor.

This is where the basic hypocrisies and deceptions of the right become complex contradictions forced upon them by reality. The (almost) great hope Trump is the broke billionaire, while the matriarch Rand is the State sponger.

Is America more susceptible to neediness than other nations? One problem is that when thinking yourself the greatest nation on earth, you sometimes need to look to someone to provide evidence.

The initial supposition – assertion – is the creation of (or for) a very simple mind. And so the American right have almost always seen the evidence for this lying in the most simple of paradigms. God. Killing. Wrath. Defeat the enemy with lightning bolts.

The American right, loud as it is, is not the entire country. And yet here we encounter the continued adoration of the family as nation, and as quasi-regal-dynasty as family. The differences in the nature of these two factions inevitably brings them closer to one another than pushes them away.

Perhaps the signs for this were there from the beginning, with the paragon of libertarian values in the guise of John and Abigail Adams. John Adams was one of the guiding forces behind the American cessation from Europe in 1776, and was the second president of the United States. The marriage began America's first great dynasty, one that included the sixth president, John Quincey Adams, and numerous other extremely distinguished figures. But it was the written correspondence between John and Abigail during the turbulent building of the nation – John Adams spent many years in Europe during this time as consul to Paris and London, and secured important bank loans from the Dutch – that captured the minds of the American public.

Published decades after they had both died, the letters established a focus for the ideal of Americanism, as just, as hard-working, and as family-bound. To create a just land where equality meant more than anything else would be the greatest gift to one's children, and to one's children's children. Generations that came after, as energising stories of the fight for the liberty of their new land were told, became aware of the love and stability of the Adamses during harsh, epochal times. As family after family fled unfurling social disasters across Europe, the Adamses seemed, not only like a good example to follow, but almost like the flesh and blood of the archaic, classical, iron, untouchable virtues of the statue on Liberty Island.

The left have their love affairs with those they perceive as thoughtful leaders, and the Adamses certainly fitted that bill. The New Deal was a thinker's response to economic devastation. JFK *thought* his way out of the Cuban Missile Crisis. Johnson's Civil Rights Bill was pragmatic if nothing else. The right prefer to see sabres rattle.

The diplomatic skills, not the martial roaring, of John Adams ensured American cessation. The new right in America, along with the tumultuous Tea Party (a collection of disaffected middle-class white-folk whack-jobs), ignore the truths of the Founding Fathers

– no, wait – they rewrite the history of their own country to fit their prejudices. And what is a family without prejudices?

Centuries after the Adams' epistles, as the class systems of the old lands inevitably began to reform in the light of the breed, dynasties rose out of the blood, sweat and tears of the aftermath of nation-building. As commerce was joined by industry, and political ideals were joined by exploitation, wealth, once again, began to dictate who ruled and who served. Was European gentility returning? As the frontier became tamed America saw politicians begin to reach for crude symbols of its own brief past – and Theodore Roosevelt decided to go out hunting.

In the nineteenth century the Roosevelts, over three generations, had gone from importing hardware to sitting in the Oval Office. The American public looked up to Teddy Roosevelt as a man of the people, a hunter, a frontiersman, a man immortalised in a studio portrait in 1885, six years before he became president, that depicted him as a vibrant young man, rifle in hand, dressed in the tassels and bear-skin hat of a Badlands hunter. He was not necessarily perceived anywhere near his truth, a chronic asthmatic who, in his last two years at Harvard spent $2,400 on clothes and club bills – six times the annual income of the average American family of the age.

TR spent a 'lost weekend' – more of a publicity drive, if the truth be told – in the Badlands of the Dakotas hunting and butchering wild animals on a scale that would impress even the most bloodthirsty of voters in late nineteenth-century America. And he carried out these massacres of elks, bears and bucks with such child-like relish ('By Godfrey, this is fun,' he is recorded as cheering during one early expedition) that it is no great leap to move forward a century or so and see the columns of journalists lining up to watch another frat-boy inheritor, George W. Bush, shoot geese or, even, drive a golf ball. The urge, a convincing one, to portray the privileged, to believe in them, as common-folk, who hunt and golf and work for a living, has never changed. There needs to be, at the desk in the Oval Office, a man taking his rightful position at the head of the family table.

In the case of both Theodore and George Junior (and other examples between) an obsession with physical prowess, with physical courage, comes from a psychological drive to compensate for the lack of moral courage in their political and 'real' lives. The most potent symbol of this would surely be George Junior's display of martial vulgarity when he donned flight gear and stood before a 'mission-accomplished' banner on the USS Abraham Lincoln after the fall of Baghdad in May, 2003. But the obvious hypocrisy, the simian comedy of the pose, the lack of irony, did not fill the American public with revulsion, but rather helped get him re-elected in 2004.

The American people voted for a man who they perceived as the great protector, a man who could shoot a rifle, share a beer (although he is a recovering alcoholic), win a war, sit at the head of the table. Just as Teddy Roosevelt had flip-flopped his way through the ranks of the Republican party, backing whichever drive, no matter how abhorrent, suited his ambitions best, so George Junior, one year into a war now in its tenth year, declared mission accomplished, cocked that lop-sided southern grin, and moved on to the dessert course.

All that the Republicans understand is the loudest shout of the American Dream: that anyone can become successful. What they cannot hear is the whisper that underlies it: that not everyone *is* successful. Individualism depends upon the failure of others, and in society failure rarely comes without a domino effect. Gore Vidal may have been right in the '80s, but is the family unit of the upper classes just as watertight as it was in Theodore Roosevelt's time?

Ayn Rand said in an interview with *Playboy* in 1964 that the role of government had only one real function: 'the protection of individual rights'. This is the essence of the modern Republican

Party, and the eternal essence of capitalism; to protect the individual's rights to live, to make money, the right to exploit and the right to be exploited. Perhaps Rand is a peculiar role-model to the Republican family, maybe a less peculiar choice for the members of the Tea Party movement. Or perhaps Rand's hypocrisies and contradictions suit the moral confusions and blanks of the American right.

Opera is at its best when it is tragedy. The American saga, on the whole, is just that. *The Godfather Trilogy* is perhaps American cinema's greatest moment. And why is that? Mainly because of how it takes the story of an American family and uses it as a metaphor for history, for ethics, for ideals and for the politics of a nation built by immigrants, soon to be destroyed by Americans.

Talking of metaphors, one lurches forward when you start to look at the health issues of America's great dynasties. The Kennedy's ill-fortune is a byword for tragedy now in the same way that Oedipus is a byword for close family-ties. In the modern era (by which I mean post-Industrial Revolution, not post-World War II), extreme privilege paired with pervasive ill-health and early death seems to be an overriding theme of such American families.

Theodore with his asthma and his 'feebleness' (as a Harvard's President Charles William Eliot once remembered him); his brother Elliott Roosevelt, an epileptic who died from alcoholism at the age of 36; Anna, the elder sister, suffered from a disfiguring curvature of the spine. His father, Theodore Senior, had died from cancer at the age 44. FDR's polio, although now well-known, was never spoken of whilst he was running for president, and when he took office, he gave every televised address from behind a desk, concealing his braces and wheelchair from the cameras and America's burgeoning love affair with full celebrity disclosure.

Jack Kennedy himself, portrayed always as the dashing man-of-the-house, young, athletic, devoted, was, of course, a serial philanderer who suffered from potentially crippling Addison's disease. The left may have worried had it been common knowledge that their man, adored by heavyweight east-coast intellectuals such as Ken O'Donnell and Arthur Schlesinger Jnr was not a Mallorian Arthur at the head of the round table. The right, however, were happy with lazy, drunken frat boy George Junior, as long as he fired a rifle and tipped that folksy grin. Keeping it in the family.

The American right is now, once again, rather than learning from its unflattering mistakes of personality that have dominated its past, lurching even further into the mire. Look at the figures waving from lecterns in hope of the Republican presidential nomination. Each of them – to a man and woman – plastic, homophobic, delusional, hypocritical, gun-toting, Christian-fantasist, historical-revisionist, family-heads.

The obvious name to evoke here is Sarah Palin. Not just the head of the family, but the head of the family that all other alpha-females look up to. She is strong, a hunter, a governor of not only her family but her State. The fact that she has been proven time and time again to be a shallow, publicity-seeking overseer of a family of quasi-comical dysfunction does not seem to spoil the image that her supporters crave.

Michelle Bachmann, another potential nominee, is a devout Christian who believes the Pope (literally!) is the Antichrist. She has attested (it is a matter of public record) that God himself came to her in a vision and told her to become a tax attorney. She runs, along with her husband, a clinic whose sole purpose is to cure people of their homosexuality. She is a climate-change denier. She has received an income of over $260,000 in government subsidies for her farm in northern Minnesota whilst at the same time standing in the US senate and denouncing the farmer's union, and calling farmers scroungers because of their 'dependence' on such subsidies.

But to a growing number of Republican voters she is not just one trust-fund away from an insane asylum, but is a symbol for the successes of the working mother, the ambitions of the matriarch. Bachmann is a woman who professes to put family first, as does Palin, and her family, by implication, stands for America.

John O'Hara spent much of his career prodding at the cracks in the family ideal. Julian English, the tragic hero of his 1934 novel *Appointment in Samarra*, is the symbol of deep dissatisfaction beneath the façade. English has everything – his family is the fake statute by which he becomes an American of worth. He has the perfect soap-advert family. He has the car and the country club memberships. The novel is a masterpiece of fragmented worth. It should be taught in primary schools across all the red states.

Vladimir Nabokov said that when he bestowed an item from his past onto a character in one of his novels, that memory would 'pine away in the artificial world' until it became 'more closely identified with my novel than with my former self. In the intellectual chaos of American public life the opposite is true. Old fictions are teased from aspects of the country's brief history and embraced into a strange meta-reality, one passionately believed, but largely fake. America is an idea that swirls with misinformation and lies, a country of honourable conception that strives, for the time being, on misconceptions.

Hunter S. Thompson

REFLECTION

A HISTORY OF GONZO JOURNALISM FROM ACID TO ZZZZZZZZZ

Dan Tyte

Okay so let's rewind a few decades to how it (*it* being gonzo) began. It's best to have solid foundations to these things, set some boundaries, some house rules. Just so as we all know where we stand. We wouldn't want this to be a magazine equivalent of the parable of the man who built his house on the sand. Well, I wouldn't. Fuck knows what you would want. Or who you even are. I mean, who are you? Wait a second. I'm sorry. I got sidetracked there. Regardless of who the heck you are, let's find out who gonzo is. And to know who he, or it is, we need to see where he, or it, came from.

It started with a journal no better or no worse than the one you're holding in your hands or pinning down with your skinny chai latte or whatever overpriced gunk it is you put into your body under the auspice of a healthy lifestyle. It was called *Scanlan's Magazine*, the year was 1970, the piece was 'The Kentucky Derby is Decadent and Depraved' and the writer was Hunter S. Thompson. And while we're at it, bears shit in the woods and the Pope is Catholic. But either way smartarse, you've got to know where you came from to know where you're going. Anyway, back to the gonzo part. Why the Mary Magdalene did they call it that? A hepped up hack by the name of Bill Cardoso (working on the *Boston Globe*) read Hunter's ride and said it was, 'totally gonzo.' Eh? Cardoso thought the name came from the French Canadian *gonzeaux* (n) meaning a shining path. Although he took so much medication he could have got the wrong end of the stick. Or the right end of the stick. Hunter S.

himself thought the name came from a 1960 song by Big Easy rhythm and blues man James Booker. And others reckon the song title came from a movie called *The Pusher*. Which in itself was from a 1956 novel by Evan Hunter called, well, *Gonzo*, obviously.

Reader: Fucking/bloody (side of Atlantic dependent) get on with it all will you. What does the name matter?
Me: It TOTALLY fucking bloody matters.

Gonzo was the presentation of fiction as fact and facts sprinkled with fictions. The Who; What; When; Why; Where; How, as the Who the fuck is asking; What the fuck does it matter; Why do you care; Where's my drink; How do you drive this thing and How the hell do we get out of here. What started with the myth on the verisimilitude of the name gonzo was propagated by its prime pen-pusher. Namely, the aforementioned Mr Thompson. Although he was 15,000 days old (give or take) before Cardoso christened his canon, Hunter had been heading towards that light since he first touched a typewriter. From his early sports journalism through to the reputation-making Hells Angels reportage, he made the fingernails of his subjects bleed and smeared himself in the story with the blood.

If the *Scanlan*'s article was the entree, then the main course was *Fear and Loathing in Las Vegas*. Manic, mescaline-addled, meddled with by the narrator and a mainstream success, what started out as a real-life *Sports Illustrated* assignment ended up as an altered reality Johnny Depp film. The catalyst was a trip Thompson took to Las Vegas to cover the Mint 400 motorcycle race, with a source for another article he was researching in tow to interview on the way from L.A. (N)ever the multitasker. Prominent Mexican-American activist and attorney Oscar Zeta Acosta rode shotgun and morphed into 'Dr Gonzo', a '300-pound Samoan attorney' in the retelling. The 2,500 word manuscript was 'aggressively rejected' by the jock mag, at which point, Hunter thought what the fuck and turned the tale into a first-person account from the autobiographical/made-up (delete as applicable) journalist Raoul Duke. Some fact, more fiction, 'five sheets of high-powered blotter acid' and a facing up to the failures of the 1960s counterculture movement later, gonzo journalism had gone global.

The following year, the fear and loathing left Las Vegas and hit the hustings. Reporting for *Rolling Stone* – who kept him in clean pants until his death in 2005 – Thompson turned his attention to the 1972 Presidential campaign between his lifelong nemesis Richard Nixon and defeated Democrat George McGovern. The manifesto read, 'Objective journalism is one of the main reasons American politics has been allowed to be so corrupt for so long. You can't be objective about Nixon.' From highway to hotel room, the near 500 pages of amyl-analysis brought politics to the potheads. Only trouble was, not even Hunter was gonzo enough to blur the truth of the result and kick Nixon out of The White House. Not that the truth tampering was strictly a new wave, gonzo's chief exponent died and lived by William Faulkner's idea that 'the best fiction is far more true than any kind of journalism – and the best journalists have always known this'. Some hack called Hari at *The Independent* and *Huffington Post* just caught hell for exactly this.

★★★★★★★★★★★★★★★★★★ HOLD THE PRESS ★★★★★★★★★★★★★★★★★

I forget myself there. We really should have done this at the start. How remiss of me. There are rules and regulations to follow. We must have rules and regulations to follow. The *Instructions for Reading Gonzo Journalism* of November 1971 detail that the reader should inject 'half a pint of rum, tequila or Wild Turkey... straight into the stomach' to 'experience the saga under the "proper conditions"'[1] and that the 'mind and body must be subjected to extreme stimulus, by means of drugs and music.' Choose your own adventure people. Those of you with work in the morning may just want to turn the page and read about *Uncle Tom's Cabin* instead.

****

Suitably refreshed? Then I'll resume.

Legacy time – Gonzo begat/was part of a wider New Journalism movement. In his introduction to an anthology in 1975, Tom Wolfe howled it 'might be possible to write journalism that would read... like a novel'. Or vice versa. But from Wigan Pier to American wanderlust (Kerouac's *On The Road* was 'a long rambling piece of personal journalism' according to Thompson, and anyone else with half a brain), this was old hat. While Wolfe played with punctuation and typography, and Capote, Mailer and James Baldwin blurred boundaries between journalism and fiction, Hunter wasn't convinced. They were more resolute reporters, sure, but innocent bystanders, the storyteller never the story. Gonzo was about going for it, getting involved, making the act of observing evident on the narrative, causing stunts, taking drugs, pushing your persona into the spaces between sentences and shaking things up. Less man bites dog, more reporter bites reader. Or as someone else put it, Wolfe 'mastered the technique of being a fly on the wall, Thompson mastered the art of being a fly in the ointment'. Hunter believed that by interacting in the story, by getting between the lines, you could change things... upset the status quo. From pissing off Presidents, documenting the sacking of Saigon and taking the temperature post-9/11, Gonzo fought the power. Hunter was a misshape, gonzo incarnate, a pain in the arse, but unfortunately not a paradigm shifter. The great and the greedy remain. Best to get shot to the stars in a sky rocket.

'Objectivity is a myth.'

So that was gonzo journalism. Make up your own mind.

Le Chapeau Noir

ESSAY

BRIGHT LIGHTS, DARK CITY: HOW NOIR EXPLODED THE AMERICAN DREAM

Robert Lewis

Land of the free, home of the brave, cradle of its own mystical, national, eponymous dream: the United States is famously a country of vision and of visions, and has been right from its very inception. The Declaration of Independence neatly and poetically embodied a set of principles so noble and humane that simply to read them, even now, is to share the yearnings of its signatories, whatever your nationality might be. That these principles were based on ideals far removed from the true, slave-owning, Indian-massacring American nature of things goes without saying. It is the purpose of a vision to defy reality.

Born out of visions, America quickly became a nation of believers. The country has been sustained and shaped by its powerful dream of itself ever since, however far-fetched and impossible that dream may be. It isn't just crass and anti-American to portray the States as a mindless and consumerist culture – as so many European writers have done – it's false. Because power and abundance are on their own not enough for America, as they might be for some other countries. America also craves righteousness, or at least the future promise of it. Its supremacy must be the symptom of virtue.

At times this can lead to attitudes that to non-Americans appear ridiculous or arrogant, but this need is deep-seated and enduring and pretty much universal. Truth, justice, the American Way: Superman's inseparable triptych resonates in far loftier places than comic books. Hollywood, Wall Street, Washington, all sing from the same star-spangled hymn sheet. Sure, there are flavours and tones, there is a left and a right, there is argument and division within the national dialogue, but America must see itself as an inherent force for good. This positive self-image, this national belief, underpins every aspect of its shifting, evolving identity. Despite how the States sometimes appears, despite its fundamentalist Christians and rabid neoconservatives, it truly is a free country, and as a whole it will tolerate just about anything, *unless you question that belief.*

Woe betide those Americans who truly call the country's moral integrity into question. Communists, socialists, liberals, Muslims: all these groups and more have felt the brunt of a burning hatred because they were seen as disbelievers of the American project. Just as those who set fire to the flag can be arrested, those who tear apart America's shining idea of itself are classified as enemies of the people. And yet oddly, one of the country's most popular art forms – and I would submit its greatest literary style – did exactly that. True, its heyday ended decades ago, but its influence was felt around the capitalist world: noir fiction has always been about the dark reality which defies the American dream.

The People's Pulp

Noir was never a self-conscious literary movement. It started in the twenties, when there was a hungry market for quick, action-filled, pared-down stories in throwaway periodicals, and it was crafted by down-at-heel writers who were trying to turn a quick buck. Pulp magazines like *Black Mask*, *Dime Detective* and *Detective Fiction Monthly* provided cheap entertainment to the reading public. And what a public that was. It was an age when people still read for kicks, not because they considered the written word to be culturally superior but because it was cheap and diverting. There was no glamour or status in writing for these magazines, no promise of book contracts or full-on publication. In fact it was years before the publishing houses, being the august literary institutions that they were, realised there was anything in them that might prove worthy of an actual novel.

The prose in these stories grew to match their tone, and the world in which they were produced. Noir prose was blunt, brutal and cynical; in fact it became so cynical it practically elevated itself into a literary trope. The word people used to describe it at the time was 'hardboiled'. It was without equal in the world of letters, except perhaps for Hemingway, who spent his writing life establishing a voice that was equally minimalist, but without the wisecracks.

The noir outlook was bleak. Money corrupted, completely, and money was everywhere. The wealthy in noir fiction are either immoral or ineffectual or both. The police and the politicians are their tools. The rest of the population is divided into two groups: criminals who want that wealth and dupes who are too stupid to realise they're being played by everybody else. Love, whether familial or romantic, evaporated in the face of this rampant avarice. Father always turns against son, mother turned against father, lover against lover.

Into this social collapse the noir writers weaved their hero, the private eye. He was both an everyman and a white knight, lied to and exploited by everyone, yet somehow able to survive without compromising his sense of self. And that was often his only victory. Noir detectives are not the sharp, observational computers you find in British crime novels. Sherlock Holmes and Hercule Poirot solved crime like it was an intellectual puzzle; noir heroes like Sam Spade or Philip Marlowe lived through it. Though they did solve mysteries, the hardboiled gumshoe's biggest prize (apart from his daily wage) was the ability to go home alone, always inevitably alone, and think himself unsoiled.

As exciting as noir is, with its girls and guns and liquor and slang, its attraction is incredibly modest. It is, in essence, that there is such a thing as an honest wage, that putting food on the table didn't mean you had to be a schmuck or a plaything of the wealthy.

The girls and guns and liquor were always prominently featured, I grant you, but I'm not aware of a single classic noir novel that doesn't have a scene where a lowly-paid detective tells a millionaire to go to hell. The wealthy in noir are in no way to be emulated or aspired to, which in itself is something that stands the American dream on its head.

The Price Paid

Though it stood at odds with much of the cultural mainstream, and the capitalist status quo, noir wasn't a pose. Although never overtly political, its disaffection and muted anger was sincere, as becomes evident when you look at the lives of the men who wrote it. Hard-boiled fiction threw up a couple of truly masterful writers, authors whose books have never gone out of print, and their biographies remind us that however stylized their genre seems, it comes from a real and very dark place.

Dashiell Hammett, the first noir great, came from modest farming stock, although his family moved to Philly when he was small. Growing up he became a ferocious reader, the kind of kid who read Kant's *Critique of Pure Reason* aged thirteen, and academia beckoned. But his father couldn't hold down a job and money was tight so by the time he was fourteen he left school to find work. And so, in a roundabout way, the smart young Hammett ended up becoming a private detective himself, working for the infamous Pinkerton agency. What he saw and heard of while with the Pinkertons shaped him for life: district attorneys framing suspects, masked vigilantes assaulting unionists, detectives sweeping away incriminating evidence. Frank Little, a strike leader in a mining town in Montana, was lynched and hung by Hammett's Pinkerton colleagues for a $5000 bonus. The America that noir writers grew up in was as corrupt and fearsome as their books. As the years went by prohibition, gangsterism, the Wall Street Crash and the Great

Depression did nothing to make it any safer or fairer.

Raymond Chandler, noir's other colossus, had a slightly better start. Exotically, he spent most of his childhood in the UK, and attended Dulwich College in London (which means, extraordinarily enough, that somewhere in the mists of English literature there is a still-unnamed Dulwich English teacher who in the space of a few years educated three pupils who would go on to be fantastically successful authors: Chandler, P. G. Wodehouse, and C. S. Lewis). He later returned to the States, settled in California, and eventually found work as a bookkeeper for an oil company. Only after he lost his job in the Depression did he turn to writing, where he started off writing for *Black Mask*. From there he took Hammett's harsh, punchy style and developed it into a jaundiced poetry, into what Jonathan Lethem referred to as a 'ruined romanticism'.

The key word in Lethem's quote is ruined, not romantic. However striking the idea of the lone, hatted man in the streetlight, or the blonde femme fatale at the bar, the noir world was one of complete alienation. And it was an alienation that was felt and lived by its creators. Despite their successes, Hammett and Chandler, as well as writers like Cornell Woolrich, all lived lonely lives full of broken relationships, alcoholism, depression, disease, seclusion and the occasional suicide attempt. All of them made it to Hollywood, all of them made a small fortune: it didn't save them. I doubt any of them ever expected it to. The great noir writers were true outsiders (unlike the plethora of fake poseurs who came along in the sixties), sufferers of a tremendous anomie.

Cornell Woolrich lived with his mother most of his life, and after her death, a series of tawdry hotel rooms. When he died they discovered his estate was worth almost a million dollars. He just didn't see anything worth spending it on. Nowadays we'd probably consider him psychologically ill, but Woolrich spent his life casting the same judging eye back at us, and his diagnosis was equally damning.

Noir never really survived the Second World War, and was pretty much extinguished in its original form by the Cold War. Soviet Russia gave America a Great Satan to fix its patriotic glare on, instead of having to look into itself. Chandler, Hammett and Woolrich all died drunk and alone, although they locked Hammett up for a spell first, because they thought he might be a communist. None of them were anything really, apart from tired, talented men without solutions.

Noir became a joke, and then it became unfashionable and almost obscure. It's white and it's masculine and it's violent, which makes it largely unacceptable to today's literary hipsters, but never in either fiction or film has America ever been so honest with itself. Now the War on Terror is drawing to an end, and America is left without enemies (one hopes), and the country can refocus itself on the banking bail-outs which have brought money madness to new heights, I hope the States will produce such writers again. Hard-working, unprivileged authors who can write in a simple and popular and beautiful way about commonplace injustice, instead of Columbia graduates farting off twee forty-thousand word novellas about how their girlfriend can talk to dogs. Well here's hoping.

Here's looking at you, kids.

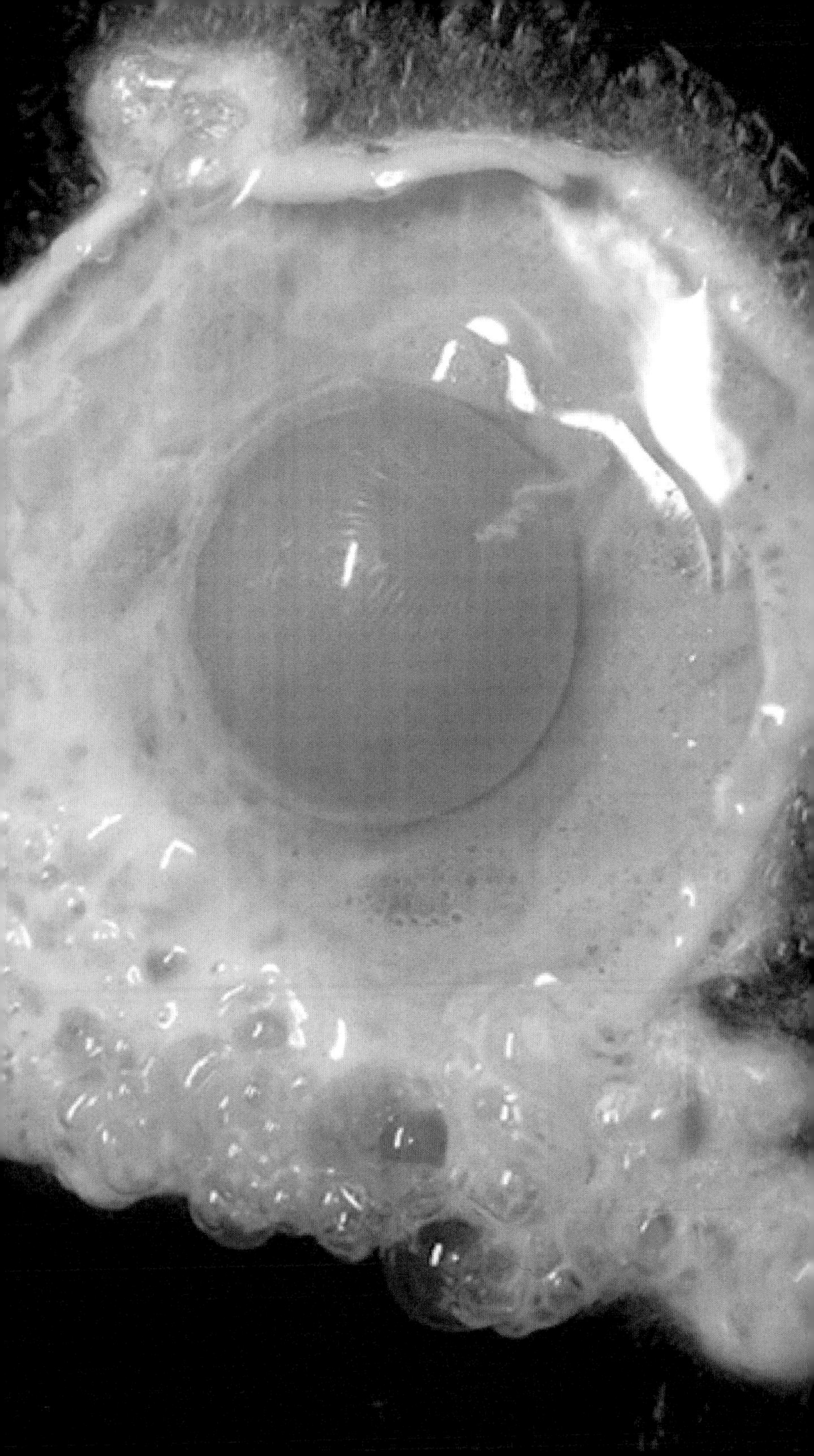

FICTION

SUNNY SIDE UP IN EASTERN KENTUCKY

Tom Abbott

In Magoffin County, Eastern Kentucky, a small wooden house sat on its own, and two boys were in the shade of its front porch where the older of the two was sitting and the younger of the two stood in the doorway.

You ain't supposed to be out here, kid.

Ernie moved his gaze over his overall clad brother Stan, who stood in the doorway itching his stomach.

Who says I ain't.

Pa.

Well Pa ain't here.

Ernie picked a pebble from his pocket and threw it towards the door. Stan stepped back inside as the screen door shut in front of him. The stone rolled abandoned on the floor. Ernie thought hard and then muttered:

Okay you can come on out.

There was a pause.

Get out already, he shouted.

The screen door crept open and Stan stepped out hesitantly.

You ain't staying for long though.

Ernie picked up another stone and threw it over the railing and watched it bounce across the dust until it came to a standstill in a rut. Stan went over to the other chair and sat down.

Where is Pa anyways, Stan finally said, his voice like that of a girl's.

Ernie shrugged his shoulders and then reached for his knee to scratch it.

Just left this morning, just up and left, ain't said no kinda nothing about where he be headed.

Stan looked thoughtful as he sent his pinky to work in his nostril. He said as he picked:

Pa ain't gonna come back is he?

Both the boys shrugged and didn't talk because both of them knew the truth. They had heard the endless sobs from the kitchen all morning.

Their mother had laboured over their breakfasts in tears. Little Sally had pulled at her apron strings all the long morning and the boys, Ernie and Stan, who now sat surveying the land from the porch, had sat quietly at the table, nibbling on biscuits and pouring strong black coffee into their throats, speaking only with the occasional knowing look at one another. They had heard their mother's long sad moans as the stove groaned with heat and the egg and sausage fried in the pan filling the air with the merest suggestion of comfort.

You reckon Ma could do with some company, Stan said across the porch from his brother who was now thoughtfully inhaling on a cigarette.

Ma don't need no kind of male company right now, the boy replied in an adult way, smoke gesturing around his teenage face which wore a rough line of sparse brown hair above the upper lip. Besides, Little Sally is in there with her. They cleaning things up now and from what I knows about women, that's probably the best thing for them right about now, he said.

Then there was a long silence and after another deep pull on his cigarette he uttered:

Pa has up and left for good this time I reckon.

He then looked over at his little brother, Stan. Stan sniffed and pinched his eyes to stop the tears he knew were on their way. Pinched at his eyes as his head bowed and around his little pale fingers tears crept their way out.

Ain't no good you rollin out them tears, Ernie said to Stan.

Stan let his tears go though and thought to himself, Ma ain't the only one gonna have to cry from time to time. That's my Pa done up and left.

A few hours later the boys were in a playground. Breakfast had long since been finished and the events of the morning seemed like a long time ago. The sun now past being modest and cool on the low horizon presently hung high in the blue and its heat raged down on the boys below. They hung tired on the swing set in the playground. The two of them sat in silence and watched a dog resting in the shade of a stripped and rusty car, its tongue lying out of the side of its mouth on the worn earth. The dog watched them back without interest. Stan imagined the smell of its warm breath as he swung back and forth lethargically on the swing. He remembered how the dog had circled them excitedly as they rode the see-saw up and down before it became too hot to move and they went over to the swings. After sitting on the porch and hearing their mother cry through the walls of the house they had come right to the playground. Anything to rid them of having to think about their father walking out of the door and out of their lives as they were just waking up.

Stan watched his big brother peel himself from the swing and walk over to the dog. The dog didn't move, except for its eyes, which rolled lazily to the side at the approach of Ernie.

Why you going near it, you know that thing might could have rabies, Stan called from his swing, as he too climbed out of his no longer swinging seat.

His brother turned and gave him the finger.

You don't never tell me what to do, y'hear.

Stan shrugged.

That's right.

Stan stepped up behind Ernie as Ernie squatted beside the dog and ran his hand across the dog's side.

He ain't no harm, he said. Reckon Ma would be right pleased if we brought this dog back.

Stan listened to his brother then cocked his head and thought for a second.

I reckon Ma don't want nobody or nothing coming back home right about now with Pa just leaving.

You're wrong, Ernie said, looking for a collar in the dog's long and unkempt fur but finding nothing but dust and heat. Then he said:

I reckon Ma might appreciate it. Appreciate that we was thinking about her anyway.

Ernie got up from his squatting position and left his little brother with the dog and wandered over to the heap of trash in the far corner of the play area. Old discarded metal shone in the sun. He kicked at the trash, levered plastic up with his foot to take a look underneath. He sought rope. He reckoned that if he could find some rope he'd be able to tie one end around the dog's neck, and then him and Stan could get the dog back home and hopefully Ma would have stopped her crying and she'd be happy to see them come home with a dog. He found no rope and so he wandered back over to where Stan was sitting with the dog beside the wrecked car. Stan looked up.

Ain't found none?

No. Reckon we might have to get you to take the laces out your sneakers, Ernie said.

That ain't fair, Stan responded as he looked up at his brother who stood there cracking the knuckle in his right thumb.

Neither was Pa leaving us to look after Ma, said Ernie, and Stan then nodded slowly in agreement with his brother as he begun to untie his laces.

Nothing ain't fair, he said as he got his laces mixed up and had to start all over again.

In neighbouring Breathitt County, a decade or so later, a truck sat with its engine running as the two brothers unloaded it.

It ain't exactly my idea of a dream home, Stan said as him and

Ernie finished taking Stan's belongings from the truck.

Between two lines of pine trees they stood in a worn out clearing where there were ten or so trailers set up at random before them, in all types of angles, as if the trailers were at odds with each other, contending for whatever small amount of space with which their occupants could forge a life for themselves, to raise families.

Ernie shrugged:

Well I ain't far away so if you need anything, just holler.

They shook hands. Stan looked at his brother but his brother didn't look back. Ernie instead just climbed back into the truck, and in a yellow cloud of dust was gone. Stan spat onto the ground and then walked up to the trailer that was now his own, unlocked the door, and over the course of a long afternoon scattered his few belongings throughout the trailer in no certain order before sitting down on the porch steps and cracking open a Budweiser.

Over the course of an evening Stan got drunk sitting on the steps. He couldn't understand why no-one had come to talk to him. They hadn't even acknowledged him. Once or twice people had passed and he had nodded at them but their eyes were on everything but him he reckoned. There was more beer though. That's one thing his brother had made sure of, that his first night would at least be a drunken first night. As it got darker outside he muttered to himself:

It ain't fair that Ernie found himself a lady, it just ain't fair.

He banged on doors later. He was told at one door to:

Go to bed. My family are trying to sleep.

And so he moved onto the next. There were similar reactions there and so he moved onto the next trailer.

If you knock on my door again I'll come out of here shooting, was the next response and this time Stan laughed and in his high voice replied:

I'd like to see you try.

Then there was silence and Stan giggled to himself, returning to his trailer with a smile on his face and sitting back down on the steps proud of himself and hungry. Early the next morning Ernie arrived in his truck and his hungover brother slung himself sulkily into the passenger seat and they drove off in silence to the mine.

Years passed and a shadow moved on a black wall and there was just one light and it moved above Ernie's face. He used his pick to dig into the coalface and to lever the coal back into a cart that he'd then send back down the track, and then it would return minutes later to be filled again. He was cold and the only way he could combat the near freezing temperatures was to keep working away at the coalface. All he heard was the sound of his pick and then the echoes that carried throughout the tunnel. He was hungry and soon he would stop for lunch. In a tin attached to his belt was a pastrami sandwich and an apple. Before he could start his lunch though there was what sounded like a massive yawning beyond the wall and then an even louder crack. Ernie thought about how he could get away from such a loud sound but within seconds the tunnel was reduced to rubble. Ernie was instantly killed by the sheer weight of the mountain on top of him.

Stan laughed into his beer. He sat apart from the others in a bar. He kept looking over at them, thinking to himself how pitiful they were that they'd spend their time actually caring about what their wives and girlfriends might be up to when they were out drinking, or when they were out mining. Stan didn't care about what Sandra was doing. The only things he wanted from her was three meals a day, done in the way that he preferred, and possibly a violent fucking every now and again when he wasn't too drunk to get a hard-on. Not that he blamed the lack of a hard-on on the amount of Budweiser and whiskey he consumed every day. No sir. The lack of a hard-on he blamed on Sandra's incompetence and inability to pleasure him properly, so he'd just let loose on her with his fists and his feet instead before storming out of the trailer. He laughed again and drank his beer. He finished his beer just as there was a commotion at the door and he looked over to hear what was going on. There had been an accident in the mine. Stan got up from his stall. People had died. Stan launched himself at the man that spoke the news.

A number of years later, a woman stood at a stove within a trailer making breakfast, and a little girl sat at the small table beside the window.

How you want your eggs this morning, Teresa said to her daughter, Ellie.

Just the way you reckon is right best, Ma.

Ellie got up from the fold-out table and wandered over to where her mother stood at the stove.

Smells good, Ma.

Smells just like normal, Ellie. Ain't nothing special about it.

Teresa gave her little girl a quick smile as she briefly took her attention from the eggs.

Gonna scramble them up for you, she said as she took a wooden spoon from the brown ceramic vase beneath the window.

She looked back at the stove, raised the heat a little, then worked the spoon into the eggs, smoke dancing above them before Ellie's eager eyes.

You gonna put some pepper in those eggs, Ma?

Now Ellie, you know I only put pepper in the eggs on a Saturday. I understand that it's still your vacation but the Lord ain't gonna think it proper to fancy up the eggs on a Sunday.

Ma, come on, just this once.

Ellie, all the while, danced impatiently on her tiptoes, her little hands on the plastic-wood sideboard. The sink beside them was half filled with murky and soap-sudded water. The smell of the eggs made her eyes get all big and excited. Teresa looked down at her little girl, a movement in her heart as she stirred in the egg and felt herself giving in. She winked at Ellie as she reached for the pepper, picked it up and handed it to her daughter.

You have a go at it this time, she said.

Ellie's mouth raised up on both sides into a smile, the likes of which cure whole towns of badnesses Teresa had always reckoned.

Oh Ma, thank you so much.

Teresa turned and put her hands into the pits of Ellie's arms and lifted her up. Ellie turned the top of the pepper over the eggs and she watched as brownish and purplish spots appeared on the eggs. Then Teresa gave her a peck on her forehead and then put her down and folded the eggs over the pepper. She worked the wooden spoon through the eggs and scrambled them up until she felt they were just right. Ellie hummed a tune from a children's cartoon on Nickelodeon she had been watching that morning as she returned to the table to wait in anticipation.

Ellie stepped out of the trailer still wearing a look of great satisfaction. The scrambled eggs had been even more delicious than she expected and her mother had been in a good mood the whole time, telling her stories about her forefathers. Ellie jumped off the final step. She kicked at the tufts of weeds that bordered the asphalt path before setting out around the side of the trailer to look for whatever fun was going to happen on what would hopefully be a long and sun filled Sunday.

But I thought I only had one father, she muttered to herself. Not four.

Maybe Ma was making some kinda joke, she thought to herself. Teresa had let Ellie go after a quick reminder to not go down by the river again. After two days ago when a great storm had passed through, the water was said to be mighty high and moving at such a rate that any child beneath five foot tall was being swept away in it before they even touched it with a toe. Ellie was sensible though. She only wanted to see if Billy was going to be allowed out so they could go and climb trees. The trees overlooked the whole trailer park and you could see just about anything that went on below. Ellie navigated her way around trash and bicycles. A cat pranced from behind some steps and bounded across the worn out grass, diving into a hedgerow before creeping out of the bottom, watching Ellie as she hummed her way through the mess of the park. Ellie wiped her forehead. The sun was sitting in the sky now at such a height that its brightness covered all. There was no escaping it. Ellie shaded her eyes as she glanced up at the sky. Not a single cloud. Just a long dark blue. Like a blanket laid across the sky. Ellie reached Billy's trailer and whistled for him but just as she did she heard a screen door swing open and quick steps coming from behind her.

Ellie span around. A woman rushed towards her, her hair flying out on both sides like a cartoon. Her face was red like a tomato and her eyes mad as anything Ellie had ever seen.

Get your mother now, she screamed at Ellie. You go get her right now.

Just as Ellie started to move she saw a man stumble from the same trailer. Ellie knew him right off as a man that didn't mean any good to anyone. Her mother had always said to steer clear of him. A man who is only seen in a wife-beater and boxers at all times should not be trusted. But apart from his usual clothes he'd got a shotgun in his hands this time, the butt of which rested in the crook of his sun-red arm. Ellie began to step away as the woman turned to face her husband. The woman crept back away from him until she stepped behind the Jeep that stood parked sideways to the neighbours' trailer. She wore little jean shorts and a white tank top and her hair was tangled, sweat clinging like Saran Wrap to her forehead. He stumbled drunkenly towards her and raised the gun up.

You get away from me with that, Stan.

Ain't no bitch wife gonna tell Stan what to do, he said and Ellie thought for a second that he sounded almost like a girl as he swung the shotgun around and took out the wing mirror with a careless shot.

That's the last damn time you serve me the wrong kind of eggs, he screamed at her.

Glass shattered to the floor and Ellie felt and heard herself jump and scream as she turned to run. Bang. She didn't see that shot.

She ran as fast as she could back from where she'd come from. Another scream and a bang. Ellie had seen Stan with that shotgun before. She and Billy had once spied on him down by the river taking shots at cans he'd lined up on the hood of an old car. Then one time they watched him as he'd brought a bottle up to his lips and necked the liquor before loading up the shotgun and sending bullets through half the cans and putting the rest into the river and all the while saying in his high voice: Folks ain't right about nothing. He had a bad aim. But this time he wasn't down by the river taking potshots at cans. He was now taking shots at his wife and his aim had got better. Ellie arrived breathlessly at the door of her trailer. Her mother awaited her.

Honey, get inside. Get inside now.

She pulled Ellie up the steps and threw her back into the trailer.

Get under the table, she shouted.

Ellie crawled back across the floor and looked up at her mother standing in the doorway, leaning out to look to where the sound was coming from. Then there was another bang.

Stan stood in the doorway, shotgun held in his hands and pointing at the ground. Teresa lay at his feet, her head leaking red onto the 'Welcome' mat inside the trailer. Ellie stared at him as her heart pounded and she felt the wall of the trailer hard up against her back as she pushed her small sneakered feet into the floor.

I don't want nobody knowing I would kill someone over some eggs, he said to Ellie.

But it wasn't like he really said it to her, he said it more to the inside of the trailer, as if for some reason he said it simply to hear his own voice, like to see if he even still had a voice. But then he looked at Ellie.

Gonna work my way around this damn place until I got anyone who was in earshot of all that.

He pointed outside where the sun burnt the browning and worn out earth of the trailer park.

Okay, said Ellie between sobs.

He raised his gun and Ellie quickly looked up at him and said:

Please don't.

He looked at her as Ellie heard a screen door open from somewhere behind him. He turned around, raised the gun and let fire. Bang. He then said out into the open air:

Alright, you can leave.

Ellie got herself up from the floor and ran out, not daring to look down at her mother who lay half in the trailer, and half out, her legs out in the sun between the legs of Stan who now aimed his shotgun at every trailer in sight. Ellie saw a body lying in the centre of the clearing.

Get out of here, he cried. Damn wife and her damn mistakes. All I wanted was scrambled eggs and not the fucking sunny side up she brung me this time.

Now a haggard and defeated middle-aged man, Stan sat on the steps of his trailer. He eyed the way the distant trailer shape became the hedge shape became the tree shape. He watched the road as the last person fled. He rubbed his hands over his knees and then he licked his upper lip with a swish of his tongue and then he rubbed his knees again.

Folk says that's it for us kinda folk, he said out of the loose side of his mouth. The other side was stolen shut by a cigarette dangling like a mouse-tail from a rafter.

Folk sometimes is right, he heard his brother's distant voice say.

And the sun came in flat as an egg that was cooked just right on the horizon.

It ain't the first time they been wrong though, he said and then he heard his brother's now more distant voice say:

And ain't the first time they been right.

The back and forth-ness of this went on until he heard sirens and when he heard sirens he looked at the barrels that looked like the shape of a number eight that swayed before him before steadying his hands and moving the cold metal into his mouth and then with a bang that to Stan lasted no more than a split-second, a round of shots took the back of his head off and covered the trailer door in blood and bone. Later that day the Sheriff, who was lucky enough to be blessed with a higher intelligence than most of the men he worked with, wisely decided to keep to himself that he believed the chunks of bone found ingrained in the screen door somewhat resembled, from a distance, broken eggshells.

REFLECTION

ON GOING NATIVE

Mimi Thebo

My first novel for Random House, *Welcome to Eudora*, is a light-hearted look at love, witchcraft and corporate abandonment, set in the American Midwest. I was delighted, then, to go 'home' to the Midwest for the reading tour. Delighted, that is, until my home town newspaper, the *Lawrence Journal World*, ran a half page profile about my visit. The headline was, 'British Author Recalls Mid-Western Roots.'

British Author?

'Bloody hell!' I gasped and waved the offending page at my mother. 'The cheek!' I cried. My mother knows what I need in times of crisis. Very quickly, but first warming the pot, she made me a cup of tea.

How had this happened?

It started with trying to make myself understood. I learned to go up on a lift, pull on a jumper and wear court shoes to work. I learned to shop for loo roll, ask for a plaster if I cut my finger and that my favourite food was evidently chocolate gateaux.

But I am, by nature, exceedingly nosy, and so it went further. I investigated Britishness, especially Englishness. I learned *The Two Ronnies* routines and the offside rule. I went to the cinema and drank pints of bitter in public houses. I read the Saturday *Guardian* obsessively, and carefully noted what was 'Going Up' in style and what was 'Going Down' in the magazine.

And later, when I did the MA, all this paid off. I could write in two languages and because I am so interested in narrative voice, this additional lexis became a whole new playground. I published my first novel about an American in London, playing with words and phrases. I then published three children's books in the voices of young English boys. I could never actually write just as me, because the only people who would enjoy it lived on a raft in the middle of the Atlantic. But I had doubled my market and extended my readership, and I felt very, very clever.

Then I began my PhD and began teaching. And this, this is where I went too far. First of all, I wrote a completely unpublishable in thirteen voices novel for my PhD dissertation.

But even that's not the worst of it.

I began listening to my colleagues about literature. Worse still, I listened to my literature colleagues about literature. They liked American literature. They liked James, Woolf, Carver, Franzen and Atwood. One of them also liked Joyce Carol Oates.

When the one who liked James began talking to me about James, I wanted to quote Mark Twain, that James was our greatest lady novelist... but I didn't, because everyone else was nodding sagely, so I nodded sagely, too. I didn't particularly like James, but he was clearly Going Up. Like skinny jeans, James would have to be on my shopping list.

My favourite authors would clearly be on the Going Down list, if anybody ever thought of them at all. So I, in public, anyway, abandoned them. I sold Twain down the river, I blew off Steinbeck and I shot down Hemingway. I abandoned my favourite stylists – Runyon shot craps, Lardner struck out and I slipped Chandler a Mickey Finn. I certainly didn't champion anyone more marginal; I left Erdich, Kinsella and Alexie on a reservation. I ploughed under Wendell Berry. I left Gary Snyder out of my meditations. I buried William Least Heat-Moon under the *PrairyErth* and paved over him with a *Blue Highway*.

And I went from feeling very, very clever to feeling very, very stupid.

Especially in the classroom. Because although I also love British literature, the prose I know best, the prose I naturally reach for as an example of, say, economic characterisation or revealing dialogue or elegant sentence construction is... well... not to put too fine a point on it... American. VERY American.

Trying to fit in had meant whittling off bits of my intellectual heritage in order to fit. And all that did was make me look stupid, as well as foreign. And at last, I saw this, and realised that I had been trying just a little too hard.

2010/2011 was my third postdoc year. This year, I brought William Least Heat-Moon into my MA class. I brought Thoreau (Henry David not Paul). I brought Erdrich and Steinbeck. My students loved them and could easily see how what they read was useful to their own work.

And this year, I wrote one book two ways; in both my native tongue and my second language.

I have recovered. I am happy that I am not a British author, or a British academic. But I also know I am not unBritish, either, and that I am no longer, after 27 years abroad, wholly American.

'Going Native' is a term from the time of the Raj, the British rule in India. British men and women who 'Went Native' were considered irreclaimable. They were pointed out as examples to others of what could happen if one didn't keep to one's own culture.

This is what has happened to me. And I wouldn't change it for the world.

REFLECTION

DRIVING AROUND COLORADO

Joao Morais

The Air Force Base

In Vietnam, Gene Hartmann was awarded a Purple Heart. At nineteen, he was shot in the arm while defending a bunker.

However, I wasn't told any of this. Not at this point, anyway.

We've driven across the Front Range to the Base Exchange. Cheapest beer in the state. You fight for your country, your reward is subsidised alcohol. They don't do that for our guys in the NAAFI.

We approach the checkpoint. It's the same guard as yesterday. The one with the pistons for forearms. His head is bigger than a bull's balls. His buzzcut hairstyle looks like it was cut with a lawn-mower.

He checks Gene's military ID again. He asks for my passport, again. He hands the passport back through the window, leaning over Gene's body. It feels like the SUV comes up on two wheels.

Top of the morning to ye, he is saying to me. The same thing he'd said yesterday. After we'd talked about those really famous Welsh people, Diana and Charles. He could be taking the piss. He could be attempting jocular familiarity.

We don't say that in Wales, I find myself saying.

He tenses the lids around his left eye. I swallow all the saliva in my mouth. In that instant, I know why he wasn't sent to Afghanistan.

We drive about three miles through the residential block. The tract housing on base is perfect. White fences, two cars to a driveway, lots of flags. The BX is a giant, beige strip mall in the centre. Where most comparable-sized places would put the cathedral.

It's important to Gene that we buy Budweiser. Not the American version, full of gas and preservatives. The Czech one, that's made according to the *Reinheitsgebot*. This is what he imagines his ancestors got *besoffen* on in Bohemia.

The old man at the liquor store checks Gene's ID. We ask for the Budvar. The carved ridges on the old man's forehead look impressed. He gets out of his stool, and clumps to a shelf. The crate looks too heavy for his daisy-stem arms. When he drops it on the counter, I hear all the bottles knock together. The old man clumps around the other side of the counter. He looks at me, waiting for a payment. I turn around and can't see Gene. When I look down, he's crouched behind my legs.

I jump back a bit. My lower back scrapes the counter. I'm about to say something when the old man's hand touches my shoulder. Stay still, he is whispering. Your buddy there is back in the jungle.

I can see the thinning blotch on Gene's crown. He's on his hands and knees.

Lots of guys are coming back from Iraq now, the old man is saying. We get this kind of thing a lot.

The Mountain

You can see the Pike's Peak Massif from across the Front Range. Downtown Colorado Springs is at the bottom. Behind Pike's Peak, its skyscrapers look like a twee model village.

Gene tells me we'll have a beer at the top today.

But it's three times higher than Ben Nevis, I am saying. It took me two days to climb Mont Blanc.

He gives me the steely stare he must have given to the Contras. Before he taught them how to throttle a Sandinista or two. I go out to the garage. I put eight bottles in the SUV's boot. Before we leave, I put on my most comfortable black trainers.

We drive past the USAF Base where we got the Budvar from. After four miles of scrub and bush, we hit the famous pink scree of the mountain. There's a toll booth for the car park at the mountain's foot. Gene pays the attendant. She wears her shorts high, in the middle of her waist. She must have been a looker, 40 years ago. Same as Gene. Before Vietnam, Honduras and Panama.

I take my seatbelt off as we drive away. You'd better put that back on, Gene is saying. The road gets hella bumpy when the tarmac stops.

Aren't we parking up now, I am saying. To climb the mountain.

He smiles as he keeps his eyes on the road. Despite the conflicts, he has those perfect, white American teeth.

We ain't walking up. Hell no, he is saying. We'll park when we get to the top.

I attempt some form of cognition. This mountain wouldn't be out of place in the Western Alps. We are driving to the summit. It is at this moment I realize what's going on in Iraq.

Gene drops the SUV into its 4x4 mode. The ascent comes quick. After an hour, at the half-way point, the road starts to zigzag. We go round a W bend. We climb. We go up another. There is no barrier, just more of that pink talus. All the signs tell us we're probably going to die.

As we near the summit, the air quality decreases. Make a fist. Put the nearside, where your thumb meets your index finger, to your pursed lips. When you breathe, this is what the air is like. I feel like lighting a cigarette, just to fill my lungs with something.

Pike's Peak is actually a plateau. It's about half the size of a ball field. There's pinkish boulders guarding the cars from its steep sides. Gene passes me an opened bottle. He points out the red sand of New Mexico. We can work out the yellow of Oklahoma, and the green of Kansas.

The cold kicks in on the second bottle. The thin air makes every swig feel like ten. I tell Gene that I live at sea level in Wales.

We'll take a picture and then leave, he is saying.

Another tourist holds the camera while we pose. He's about Gene's age, but with twice the neck fat. The summit totem is peaked with ice. It is July. Gene and I hold our elbows, like in the comic books.

Oh. I see what you're doing, neck fat says. You're pretending to be cold, huh.

I smile without showing my teeth or changing my eyes. As the camera goes off, I don't know what's faster. The flash of the camera or Gene's dive behind my legs.

We descend the mountain in second gear. At my insistence.

Downtown

It's the third and last day. Gene doesn't want to leave the house. I was warned this might happen. He's watching a re-run of *Boston Legal*, waiting for 12pm. Then, he'll let himself open the last of the bottles.

I'm going into town, I tell him. Go see a museum or something.

He doesn't take his eyes off the telly. Downtown, huh? He is saying. How you gonna get there?

I show him the printout of the bus times. Where I'm from, I am saying, you can get around OK on the bus, like.

Only freaks take the bus. Get a cab.

I'll be alright then, I am saying. The bus will be just like the 61 Pentrebane.

It takes twenty minutes to walk to the community gate. The sand-shaded prefabs wouldn't look out of place in the Cotswolds. When the bus comes, I pay my fare and take a seat near the front. There's only one other person on the bus. He is sat opposite, to the right of me.

After the eighth Baskin Robbins, I look to the ceiling. The other passenger is looking at me. He's about my age, maybe younger. His red, stretch-fit visor is worn to the side.

I nod my head. You're not from around here, huh, he is saying.

No, I'm from Wales.

Wales, huh? I've never been to England, he is saying. He tilts his cap backwards.

I turn to look at the Taco Bell going past. The other passenger coughs.

Brandon Murphy Berwin, he is saying, as he offers his hand. His palms are smooth, warm and dry.

Call me Joe, I am saying. Most people do.

When he smiles, his teeth make me feel homesick.

Is everyone dark-skinned like you in Wales? He is saying. I thought you were a Moslem.

I think of all the different ethnic groups I'm supposed to be. I add another tick.

No, I am saying. My dad is black. That side of my family are from a small African island. Near Senegal.

Wow, he is saying. I've never met a British African-American before.

He turns his cap back to the side. I let the journey continue in silence.

I alight from the bus when I see the first skyscraper. Brandon Murphy Berwin gets off at the same stop.

Hey. I'm sorry, he is saying. I just wanted someone to talk to.

I turn to face him. It is cold in the shadow of the buildings.

Oh. you just wanted someone to talk to.

Look around, he is saying. There's no one else here. It's just you and me for eight blocks.

I look down both ends of the street. I follow the traffic up to their vanishing points. Not even a pigeon.

He carries on. Everyone's in their cars, he is saying. You have to drive everywhere here. If you ain't got a car, you ain't got anything.

When I breathe out, it is with a large sigh. Fine, I am saying. Just take me to a bar. I could really do with a bottle of Budvar.

FICTION

HANDBALL

Todd Zuniga

What I'm good at is soccer, so when my hand's lopped off in a car accident, a clean cut sutured bloodlessly shut, it's not the biggest deal. I trade insurance cards with the other driver, draw my autograph on his forearm, then head right home. In my bedroom, I juggle my hand like a soccer ball to relax. My housekeeper walks in, sees my hand flopping in mid-air, hitting my knee, flopping in mid-air, off the instep of my shoe, flopping in mid-air, off my head, and faints. She's like that, the big baby.

After a shower, I duct tape my hand to my wrist, drive over to the house of the girl I've been fucking, and we go at each other like horned-up llamas.

To play a joke, I put our interlocked hands above her head, and wriggle my wrist free from the duct tape. Then I start touching one of her boobs with my nub. She moans with her eyes closed. Then I put my working hand on her other boob. When she realizes she's holding my detached hand, she freaks, bucks me off and yells, 'Porter''

Which is my name. She flings my hand away with an expletive, and when it hits the wall I say, 'Hey, careful,' like it hurts. But I don't feel a thing. The hand's dead, and I'm a soccer player who doesn't need it, so whatever.

But she's coloured ghost white, presses into the wall's corner to get away from me, so I play along and apologise. To calm her, I reach over to touch her hair, but accidentally lead with my nub. She screams like it's my fault – but this one-handedness is so new!

'Just go for now, okay?' she says.

I scoop my hand up with my toe and start juggling it.

'God!' she hollers. 'Grow the fuck up.'

'Up fuck the grow,' I say, to make her laugh.

'Off *fuck*,' she says.

I juggle my way out the door.

My cell phone rings and it's my dad saying my mom's dead from cancer.

Just kidding.

He really says, 'I saw the game last night, you played great!'

'I played okay,' I say because my mom, who doesn't have cancer – at least not yet – always told me to be humble.

'You had two goals!' my dad says. He talks in exclamation points, since his hearing is busted from Vietnam. I buy him all of these high-powered hearing aids, but they all go missing.

'My hand fell off.'

'Your man sell cough?!' When my dad mishears, he repeats what he's misheard, without even trying.

'My hand fell off!'

'Like you need it! You scored two goals last night!'

After practice Coach tells me that I made the All-Star team, along with my teammates Devenpeck and Ruiz. 'But yer a fockin' starter, Porter,' he says, and tells me ESPN will announce it later on. Coach is from Switzerland, so he cusses like it's punctuation. 'Now let's go celebrate by eatin' a fat fockin' stack of pancakes.'

I untape my hand and hold it in my other hand, like my right hand is shaking my left only upside-down. Just to show him. 'Well,' he says, scratching his grey beard, gauging it's effect on my future. So, I start to juggle it: knee, foot, knee, chest. He says, 'Haha! Brilliant! Now let's fockin' eat!'

At the restaurant, Coach orders pancakes for every table in the restaurant, even the empty ones. He shouts, like he's drunk, 'We got a goddamn All-Star soccer player in our midst, and I fockin' bet he's willing to sign anyone's fockin' flapjacks with maple syrup!'

I sign eight stacks of pancakes. One kid puts a syrupy pancake in his pocket, and his mom looks at me like I'm to blame.

A day after the All-Star Game announcement, I'm asked by a man named Sandy to be the featured cover athlete for *FIFA Soccer 2013*, a video game made by Electronic Arts. They fly me to Vancouver to get my face scanned so my doppelgänger in the game looks as real as possible. While there, I see Luke Skywalker, which is so unbelievable, I can't help but go over to him.

'Luke Skywalker!' I say.

He laughs, shakes my good hand, and says, 'Hey, Porter, nice to see you,' like he's known me his entire life, even though, of course, we've never met before.

'Quite a grip,' I say,''I guess that's the benefit of getting a mechanical hand after your father cut off your real hand with a light-sabre.'

He laughs again, his head wrinkly and old, and asks why I'm in Vancouver.

'I'm on the cover of their next soccer game, and they're pretty much scanning everything but my cock. You here doing Jedi shit?'

'I'm here to record a voiceover for *Medal of Honor: Stop the Genocide*. I'm playing the part...'

'Luke fucking Skywalker,' I interrupt. 'I mean, I can't believe it.' Which is true; he's like royalty!

'Call me Mark, please,' he says, kind of serious.

'Right, code names. Then call me "Bag of Dicks."'

He excuses himself and walks off. I look at his hand while he walks away, imagine the metal inside, moving when he uses it.

The media build up to the All-Star Game means I get lots of attention. People are freaking out about my hand. The newspaper headlines make me into a virtual hero:

STAR PLAYER FACES TOUGHEST CHALLENGE HEAD-ON WITH HAND OFF

COURAGEOUS ATHLETE HAS 'HAND' DO ATTITUDE

SOCCER PLAYER 'HAND'LING OF ADVERSITY MAKES HIM ROLE MODEL

I like the idea of being a role model, so on my day off during the three-day All-Star break, I agree to give a talk to a group of one- or no-handed kids.

At the event, I tell a group of children, 'I used to avoid handless or one-handed people. But now here I am, standing in front of an entire room full of you!' I wave my non-hand in the air. 'What I'm here today to tell you is that you can live a full life! I mean, don't try to be a mechanic, or a jewellery maker, or a secretary. Try to be a professional soccer player, an Olympic runner, or a Jedi. What I'm saying is you might not have hands, but it's not like you're retarded!'

I'm disappointed when there's no applause, but, duh, none of them have two hands. I walk out feeling pretty good.

That night my publicist calls and says, 'Wow, *thanks*.'

'What?' I ask.

She reads me two headlines:

SOCCER PLAYER TAKES LOTS OF CREDIT FOR OVERCOMING A MALADY HE DOESN'T SEEM TO BE HAVING A PROBLEM WITH

GIVE HIM A HAND: SOCCER STAR MAKES ROOMFUL OF KIDS CRY

I tell her, 'Some people just don't get it.'

She tells me, 'That's exactly right.'

My only brother, Alvin, calls me. Alvin uses Jell-O in the place of hair gel, paints his fingernails with deer blood and eats his own shit. So, yeah, he's pretty awesome, but in some ways he's a total downer. Maybe I'd be a downer too if I wasn't a celebrated athlete who almost everyone loves, who gets to autograph pancakes with maple syrup, and has a hot girlfriend who loves to bone.

On the phone he says, 'Are you coming to my new exhibition?'

'Is it in LA or New York?'

'No! It's here, in Kansas City –'

'Oh, then yes.'

'I'm a failure,' he says.

He takes a bite of something, and I wonder if it's shit.

'Are you still eating your own shit?'

'Dude, I was two years old! Like I knew what the fuck I was doing! Are you *telling* people that?'

'Of course not,' I say.

Tragedy has a sort of way of striking when you don't expect it. My girlfriend breaks up with me on the phone, and says she's sorry she's not doing it in person. I thank her for not doing it in person.

'Why?' she asks. 'Why do you say that type of shit? That's so you, encapsulated in that sentence. You're such a coward. And how could you say those terrible things to those children? My brother has Down's Syndrome! Like *you* care. I just...'

I hang up on her because, whatever, right? We're broken up. Life is for the living!

A week later, we're playing in snowy Chicago against our most hated rival. Whenever I touch the ball the crowd claps for me.

'Man, all this attention is great!' I say to Chicago's center back, Ben Jenks, and pat his shoulder.

'You dumb turd,' he says. 'They're clapping because you only have one hand.'

'Oh!' I say, glad that the mystery is unravelled.

Later in the game I'm slide-tackled, and take awhile to get up. While I'm down a bunch of people in the crowd roar with applause, throw fake hands onto the pitch. The hands are flexible and rubbery, but they still hurt.

EA cancels my appearance on the cover of their game because of 'budgetary problems'.

'They're the richest company on the planet,' I say. 'But problem solved – I'll do it for free.'

'I'm sorry,' my agent says. 'Their decision is final.'

'There has to be a way.'

She tells me the truth: the Canadian government thinks I've faked the loss of my hand, and because of this, they've banned me, or any images of me (posters, digital photography, etc) from entering the Vancouver city limits.

'Whoa, really?'

'No, Porter,' she says before she hangs up. 'Not really.'

Back home in Kansas City, I see a girl in a bar. She makes my heart hurt she's so pretty. When I sit on the stool next to her, she says, 'No thanks.'

'I'm not selling anything.'

She asks me to please go away.

I tell her, 'But I'm Porter.'

She calls for the bartender and asks him to make me go away. The bartender asks me to go away.

'I'm single,' I say to her.

'No kidding,' she says.

One night my ex-girlfriend calls and says, 'I didn't like the way we got off the phone the last time we spoke.'

'Okay,' I say.

'I hate you,' she says, and hangs up.

I call her back.

‘What?’ she snaps.

‘You don’t deserve the last word,’ I tell her.

She sighs like she’s given up.

‘Look,’ I say, “ am light. I am invincible. I move through the world with a lovable stupidity.’

“ou move through the world stupid,’ she says.

I call her back.

‘Hello?’ she says.

‘It’s me,’ I say.

‘Me who?’ she says.

‘Porter!’

‘Why are you calling me?’

‘Because I don’t want you to have the last word.’

‘But I’m on the other line with you.’

‘Oh,’ I say.

‘I’m hanging up on both lines, now.’

I call her back.

She picks up and hangs up without saying a word.

I call her back.

She picks up and hangs up.

I call her back.

Her answering machine comes on. ‘If this is Porter, please stop calling.’ There is the sound of a phone hanging up, then a beep.

I call her back.

I call her back.

I call her back.

POETRY

A BRIEF RESPONSE ON THE TOPIC OF NATIONAL DREAMS

Graham Isaac

'Tell me of your life
and sell me the American dream.' – *John Polsom Jenkins*

John,

Anyone can be a pimp in Vegas. *P-I-M-P.*
I rode the bus today behind Earl The Pearl,
who taught *all* the South Seattle Motherfuckers how
to get shit done, still basically *runs* Skyway,
grew up in Vegas and there it is easy.

I am late for work.

That's the short answer; everything you need to know
about entrepreneurship, opportunity
and frustrations of geography, but
when have I ever given a short answer?

blinking constantly and coughing hard, I have plenty of time
to contemplate the common narrative: boy gets job at local
store selling shoes and with hard work, pluck and a gleaming
smile becomes head salesman. By the end of the story he's
got a wide office in a big city, has forgotten and been reminded
of *where he's from*. Probably by a child. In *America*, we may not
believe in class but we do believe in roots, mobility upward and

lately,
downward; by the time you get to the job interview

your face hangs off your skull and you've forgotten
the answers to all questions; silences as the
interviewer takes notes have you
itching for quick flight. This is that space between
boot and strap and silver spoon that most
find ourselves in;

there is no '*the*', there are many –
the salesman, my arts-commune friends in coastal towns
too schooled in collegiate Marxism to accept their dreams
as *American* but

this casual dissidence
with little to fear besides
strange looks from farmers is just
as American an ideal as anyone
on Wall or Main or Washington –

As for me, still bottom-runging it, shaking down couches,
stitching half-paychecks into a living, but that life isn't for long;
a year from now I suspect I'll
write a very different reply,
but that, as they say, is a very American way to think,

even in my corner of the country, where our ancestors
ran because it was the last place to go before Canada,
where we've taken the density of our isolationism to
the awkward extremes of paying money
to read silently in public rooms. Where you are headed is
friendly and welcoming but there is less to do
and the food, I hear, will kill you.

If you're still hesitant after all this, forgive my meanderings;
the only job I've ever been fired from was Sales.

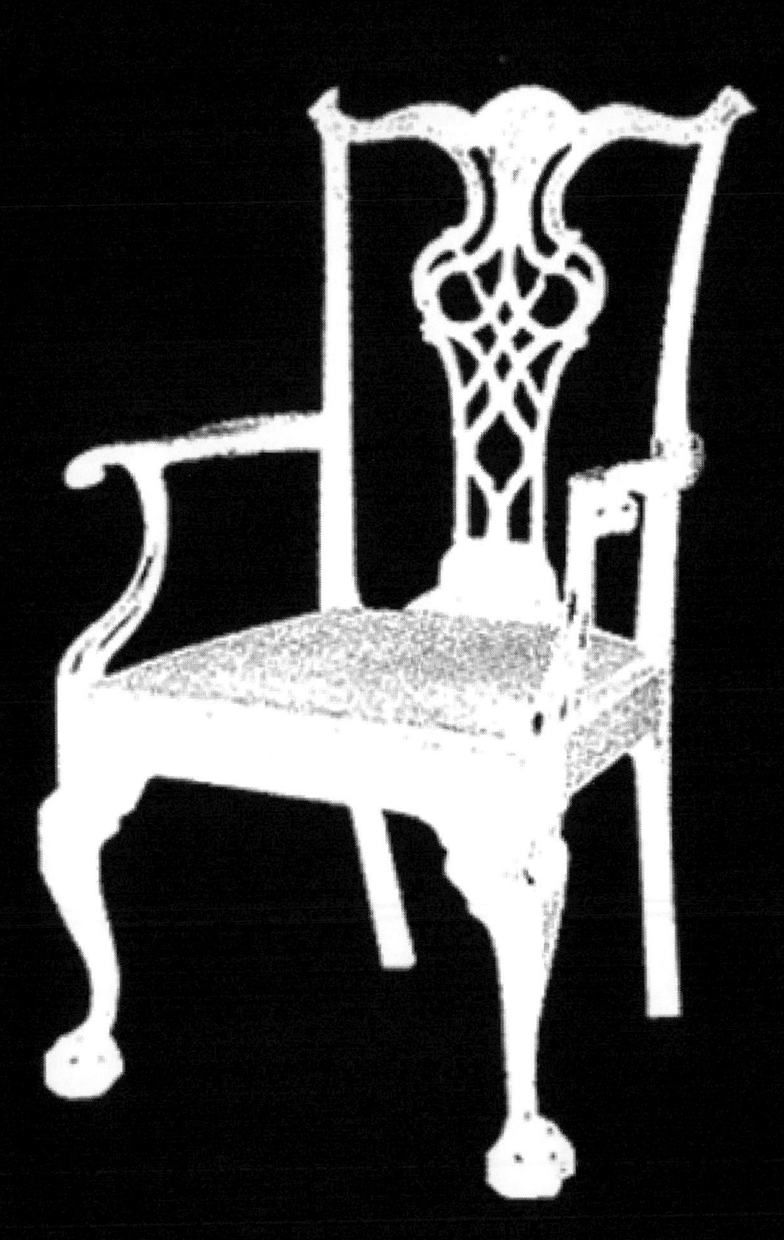

THE RACONTEUR

HAPPINESS IN MAGAZINES

MCSWEENEY'S

Susie Wild

You can't really call *McSweeney's* a magazine. For one thing, over the years it has tried very hard to look like many other things: a box-shaped head, a broadsheet newspaper, a bundle of mail, a cigar box, playing cards, and a hardback book. For another *McSweeney's* also, really, includes the award-winning publishing house McSweeney's Books, the website, McSweeney's Internet Tendency and a family of well-adjusted siblings that takes in McSweeney's Grew Up aka monthly cultural magazine *The Believer*, the scrumptious foodie journal Lucky Peach, and the technologically aware younger sibling *Wholpin*, a quarterly DVD magazine featuring short films, documentaries, and animation. Not forgetting the charitable educational outreach programmes (826 Writing and Tutoring Centers) that began with 826 Valencia's pirate supply store and later inspired Nick Hornby's UK equivalent Ministry of Stories. Magazine, meta magazine or cardboard box, *Timothy McSweeney's Quarterly Concern* is one of America's best-read and widely-circulated literary journals, with another festival of followers across the pond.

I became a fan of Dave Eggers before I became a follower of *McSweeney's*. I realise in terms of literary crushes I am 100% predictable, but I have no regrets. If the loves and lusts of your impressionable youth are meant to inspire and educate, then the oddball sweet nothings that Eggers, and in turn *McSweeney's*, shaped me with don't appear to have done me any great harm. I certainly wouldn't burn the letters, anyway. The magazine-rack dreamy reams of them. Purchasing *McSweeney's* you can never be entirely sure what the new issue will bring, or where the unshelvable issues have actually been shelved, and therein lies their fortune-cookie pleasures.

The literary journal *Timothy McSweeney's Quarterly Concern* started life, edited by former graphic designer Eggers, in 1998, but it was 2001, after devouring *A Heartbreaking Work of Staggering Genius* in my new home of London, that I discovered there were more words of wonder ready to break my heart. I swooned for *McSweeney's*. I liked the gift that kept giving aspect of it. The unpredictable offbeat design. The playfulness. The way they set out to only publish work that had been rejected from elsewhere, but had already caved on their best laid plans by Issue 2. This probably had something to do with the people who have wanted to write something specifically with *McSweeney's* in mind: Denis Johnson, William T. Vollmann, Rick Moody, Joyce Carol Oates, David Foster Wallace, Heidi Julavits, Jonathan Lethem, Michael Chabon, Ben Marcus, Susan Straight, Roddy Doyle, T.C. Boyle, Steven Millhauser, Robert Coover, Ann Beattie, and many others. Or perhaps it was down to the specifics of their new submissions guidelines, which in Issue 2 read: 'There are no restrictions on the size or content of submissions, other than that they should all be 2,300 words and about relationships. Any submissions that are not 2,300 words long and about relationships will not be considered, unless they are 2,300 words long and about talking animals. If they are not 2,300 words long and about relationships or talking animals, they should be 670 words and concern problems of race...'

Timothy McSweeney is a word wizard, and the master of reinvention. He is a well-oiled literary machine, elaborate, smart and shiny. With a real, big, pumping heart. With feelings, too. That he is loved by the big names and the small, and stocked by independent booksellers worldwide is down to one thing. *McSweeney's* is equal to great writing, writing that is often but not always funny. They have reinvigorated the life and readership of the short story, something that shall always win me over (see Issue 12, which also features Jennifer Egan). They unearth new voices including Gabe Hudson, Paul Collins, Neal Pollack, J.T. Leroy, John Hodgman, Amy Fusselman, Salvador Plascencia and Sean Wilsey. They also support the under-appreciated talents, especially another of my favourite American writers, Lydia Davies.

There are detractors, sure. People who think it isn't highbrow enough, or hate the big in-jokeness of it all, the irrelevance, the heavy-weight avoidance. People who I have little time for. People who miss the point. 2011 marks one whole decade of my relationship with *McSweeney's* and I am not bored yet. They have not stopped being irreverent and inventive, they may have occasionally missed the high bar they set themselves but they have not screwed it up.

McSweeney's is a fan of lists. Most decades get at least one Best Of list. So, it follows, here are my Best of *McSweeney's* lists:

List 1: The Best of *McSweeney's* Literary Experiments

1. No.33: The 2009 San Francisco Panorama, in which *McSweeney's* becomes a 320-page old-fashioned broadsheet newspaper complete with a comic and an understandably outstanding book section that reminds you of what newspapers are supposed to be. Featuring articles by Stephen King and Michael Chabon, the paper's entire print run sold out in less than 90 minutes.
2. No.36: The issue that was a more-or-less life-sized head-crate of a pink sweating balding man containing a 100-page annotated fragment of Michael Chabon's lost novel, ace new stories from John Brandon and Colm Tóibín, Jack Pendarvis's 'Jungle Geronimo in Gay Paree,' and a play by Wajahat Ali. Not at all impractical, it can also double as a handy shelf-based hat stand.
3. No.4: A cardboard box containing 14 separately bound booklets, each containing one short story, including my

favourite, Lydia Davies' paragraph-short 'A Mown Lawn' and new work from Haruki Murakami.

4. No.17: The most difficult to shelve, this infamous issue looked like a bundle of direct mail, and was made up mainly of humorous nonsense including a sausage-basket catalogue; a flyer for slashed prices on garments that are worn by more than one person at a time; and a new magazine of experimental fiction called *Unfamiliar*.
5. No.13: The Comic Issue, this clothbound hardback edited by Chris Ware contained the work of comic-book artists R. Crumb, Art Spiegelman, Daniel Clowes, Lynda Barry, and Julie Doucet, as well as essays from Michael Chabon, Ira Glass, John Updike, Chip Kidd, and others manages to make comics literary.
6. No.11: The Issue That Contained The Best Writing: T.C. Boyle! Joyce Carol Oates! Denis Johnson! All sit alongside great writing from the lesser known Tom Bissell, Samantha Hunt and David Means. Plus the bonus 'The Editing of The Making of McSweeney's Issue #11 DVD' is genius.

List 2. The Best Online Description of *McSweeney's*:

1. Good as Gold. As in 'McSweeney's™ is Proudly Canadian. Our meat snacks are a big favourite, made with a high quality of meat that tastes great and has the right texture.' Yes, it is referring to a different brand of McSweeney's, see: www.mcsweeneys.ca
2. No, number 1. Still has it right. Taste, texture, good as gold.

To date, I have been in the same room as Dave Eggers on three occasions. Once at a reading on London's Southbank, once at the Book Critics Circle Awards at City Lights and once in a bar in San Francisco, on that solo 2008 trip when I thought I'd move there the month after and go and work at 826 Valencia. I didn't, I moved to

Bristol. Well, they both have suspension bridges, right? I may be back in Wales now, but I am currently planning some state side visits. Next time, just maybe, I'll pluck up the courage to speak to him and demand a column, a beer, or a kiss. Until then, I'll get my happiness in beautiful *McSweeney's* form. Subscribed not prescribed.

THE RACONTEUR

AN ESSAY
ON THE MOST
FAMOUS POETRY READING
EVER TO OCCUR IN CALIFORNIA
AND ON THE MOST FAMOUS SINGLE POEM
EVER WRITTEN THERE

HOWL AND THE HOWLERS

GINSBERG'S POEM
FIFTY-PLUS YEARS LATER

Jack Foley

'The Beat Generation' was one of the most publicised, misunderstood, attacked, understood, deeply considered, cannibalised, ripped-off art movements of the twentieth century. Its influence extends from the adolescent troubled about sexuality and identity to the dry-as-dust scholar looking for history and significance in old books and papers. Whereas the 'hippies' seem somewhat passé, sentimental, and – worst of all – old, the even-older Beats (some of whom were also hippies) have passed into history as American artists of considerable importance. Like Elvis, Jack Kerouac is now forever young, intense and handsome – a symbol of American success – and only occasionally remembered as the middle-aged, fat, lonely man he became. He has in fact become exactly what he wished to be: a great American writer. But he has become more than that: an icon. If America has secular saints, he is surely one. But, like many prophets perhaps, he has become a saint of a religion he would have despised: his image is used to sell things; he is the American bourgeoisie raised to cosmic proportions.

From its inception, the Beat Generation was a testimony to the power of the fuzzy definition. Intensely meaningful – and with certain aspects continually but not always manifesting – 'Beat' has never been adequately defined. Had it been adequately defined, it might have been long dead as a movement. Though everyone would agree that something took place in the middle of the twentieth century, after the war, it would be difficult to find agreement about exactly what that something was. Was it a rebellion, as people often claimed? Kerouac announced, with some justice, that he was never a 'rebel'. In his late bitterness but with some irony still, he told Bruce Cook in The Beat Generation, 'The Beat Generation? – We were just a bunch of guys who were out trying to get laid.' He also wrote,

> The Beat Generation, that was a vision that we had, John Clellon Holmes and I, and Allen Ginsberg in an even wilder way, in the late Forties, of a generation of crazy, illuminated hipsters suddenly rising and roaming America, serious, curious, bumming and hitchhiking everywhere, ragged, beatific, beautiful in an ugly graceful new way.
>
> ('About the Beat Generation', 1957)

On October 7, 1955, a poetry reading was held at The Six Gallery, a cooperative art gallery in San Francisco. The featured readers were Allen Ginsberg (the organiser), Michael McClure (whose first reading it was), Gary Snyder, Philip Whalen, and Philip Lamantia. Jack Kerouac was visiting Ginsberg at the time and attended, though he did not read. Kenneth Rexroth was Master of Ceremonies.

Ann Charters writes in *The Beat Reader*, 'The "Six Poets at the Six Gallery" reading was the catalyst that dramatically revealed what Ginsberg later called the "natural affinity of modes of thought or literary style or planetary perspective" between the East Coast writers and the West Coast poets.' Both Jack Kerouac and Michael McClure wrote about the Six Gallery event, Kerouac in *The Dharma Bums* (1958) – in which he calls the Six Gallery the Gallery Six – and McClure in *Scratching the Beat Surface* (1982). The event soon became famous as the first public reading of 'Howl' (though Ginsberg read only the first section of the poem that night). Ginsberg's poem created a sensation. Kerouac collected money for wine and passed around gallon jugs of California Burgundy. When Ginsberg's turn came, writes Barry Miles, 'he read with a small, intense voice, but the alcohol and the emotional intensity of the poem quickly took over, and he was soon swaying to its powerful rhythm, chanting like a Jewish cantor, sustaining his long breath length, savouring the outrageous language. Kerouac began cheering him on, yelling "Go!" at the end of each line, and soon the audience joined in. Allen was completely transported. At each line he took a deep breath, glanced at the manuscript, then delivered it, arms outstretched, eyes gleaming, swaying from one foot to the other with the rhythm of the words.'

All descriptions of the Six Gallery event emphasize the transformative character of Ginsberg's reading. Michael McClure writes that '"Howl"... was Allen's metamorphosis from quiet, brilliant, burning bohemian scholar trapped by his flames and repressions to epic vocal bard.' Kerouac's communal wine-drinking gave the event a Bacchanalian, Dionysian quality. (Wine is of course associated with various religions, including Kerouac's own, Catholicism; in a 1958 letter to John Hollander, Ginsberg himself refers to 'Howl' as 'rather like a jazz mass.') Barry Miles too attests to both transformation and religious associations. These various elements coalesce into a single image: what the audience at the Six Gallery was witnessing was the metamorphosis of Allen Ginsberg, 'horn-rimmed intellectual hepcat with wild black hair' (in Kerouac's phrase), into Allen Ginsberg, 'epic vocal bard'.

Ann Charters remarks that Ginsberg 'found the audience so fervently sympathetic to his words that he discovered his unrecognised talents as a performance artist'; his 'predecessor as an incandescent performer of poetry was the Welsh poet Dylan Thomas, whose widely acclaimed reading tours of American cities in the early 1950... and his bestselling recordings had revolutionized the way his audiences thought of poetry.'

True enough, but Kerouac's and the audience's shouts of 'Go!' indicate that Ginsberg had taken on the persona not only of the rhapsodic poet but of the jazz musician. Though Ginsberg wasn't reading his poem to jazz accompaniment (as Ruth Weiss, Kenneth Rexroth and others were soon to do at The Cellar), his unaccompanied reading was alive with a sense of music – even with a sense of bebop: 'who poverty and tatters and hollow-eyed and high sat up smoking in the supernatural darkness of cold-water flats floating across the tops of cities contemplating jazz.'

In his notes to the LP album, *Allen Ginsberg Reads Howl and Other Poems* (1959), Ginsberg describes his poem as full of 'long saxophone-like chorus lines' and suggests that writing it was equivalent to the experience of a jazz musician improvising. Like the hipster, who, Norman Mailer wrote in 'The White Negro' (1957), 'absorbed the existentialist synapses of the Negro', Ginsberg's performance at the Six Gallery took on the aura of the hippest of public performers: in Mailer's formulation, 'for practical purposes [he] could be considered a white Negro.' Instead of being the observer of what Kerouac called in *On the Road* 'the happy, truehearted Negroes of America', Ginsberg became the authentic conveyer of their power. Like Neal Cassady – the 'secret hero of these poems' – the sensitive, gay, bespectacled, hustling, funny, lonely, fiercely intellectual, convivial, drug-taking ex-student of Lionel Trilling's stood before his audience as something equivalent to Charlie Parker. For one of the very few times in the twentieth century, poetry seemed *cool*.

And – most importantly – if Ginsberg could do it, so could we.

Kerouac's *Mexico City Blues* had already presented the jazz musician as analogous to the poet, but Kerouac was not yet widely known. (*On the Road* did not appear until 1957; *Mexico City Blues* was not published until 1959.) 'Howl' was written at a time when influential critics such as Arthur Mizener were saying, 'The age of Yeats is over; we are in the age of Auden' – which Mizener meant that Romanticism had been replaced by irony and *sotto voce*. Ginsberg sent 'Howl' to a critic even more distinguished than Mizener, his old Columbia mentor Lionel Trilling. Trilling was – as the poet knew he would be – horrified:

> I'm afraid I have to tell you that I don't like the poems at all. I hesitate before saying that they seem to me quite dull, for to say of a work which undertakes to be violent and shocking that it is dull is, I am aware, a well known and all too easy device. But perhaps you will believe that I am being sincere when I say they are dull. They are not like Whitman...

Poet John Hollander, writing in the *Partisan Review*, was even harsher:

> It is only fair to Allen Ginsberg... to remark on the utter lack of decorum of any kind in his dreadful little volume.

In 'The White Negro', Norman Mailer asserted that after the Second World War and the revelation of what went on in concentration camps 'one could hardly maintain the courage to be individual, to speak with one's own voice'; these years, he complained, are 'the years of conformity and depression. A stench of fear has come out of every pore of American life, and we suffer from a collective failure of nerve... The only courage, with rare exceptions... has been the isolated courage of isolated people':

> If the fate of twentieth century man is to live with death from adolescence to premature senescence, why then the only life-giving answer is to accept the terms of death, to live with death as immediate danger, to divorce oneself from society, to exist without roots, to set out on that uncharted journey into the rebellious imperatives of the self.

In such a climate, Ginsberg could appear not only as an immensely talented poet but as a harbinger of cultural change. 'Howl' too 'lives with death as immediate danger' and insists on 'the rebellious imperatives of the self'. The poet's LP liner notes indicate that writing 'Howl' was a kind of conversion experience, a personal transformation: 'I suddenly turned aside in San Francisco... to follow my romantic inspiration – Hebraic-Melvillian bardic breath.' The extraordinary thing about the event at the Six Gallery was that the audience could *witness* Ginsberg's transformation: they could actually see the poet become jazz musician. Ginsberg's powerful reading, 'arms outstretched, eyes gleaming,' was not only the presentation of a poem but a living emblem of the possibility of change. Through rhythm (the 'beat') it turned being 'beaten down' ('I saw the best minds of my generation destroyed by madness...') into, in Kerouac's French pun, *'béat'* – blessedness. The poet's longing for the visionary transforms him, through the jazz musician, into active, epic, Whitmanic, visionary bard. This transformation experience is at the absolute centre of 'Howl' and is in fact its primary subject. The 'Footnote to Howl,' completed after the Six Gallery reading, makes the transformation explicit:

> Holy! Holy! Holy! Holy! Holy! Holy! Holy! Holy! Holy! Holy!
> Holy! Holy! Holy! Holy! Holy!
> The world is holy! The soul is holy! The skin is holy! The nose
> is holy! The tongue and cock and hand and asshole holy!
> Everything is holy! everybody's holy! everywhere is holy!
> everyday is in eternity! Everyman's an angel!
> The bum's as holy as the seraphim!

'A human voice and body,' commented McClure, 'had been hurled against the harsh wall of America.'

And what of 'Howl' these days – more than 50 years after the poem was written? On October 7, 2005 – the opening night of 'Litquake,' San Francisco's city-wide celebration of literature – 'Howl Redux' was presented at the city's elegant Herbst Theater exactly 50 years after the Six Gallery event. The event was meant not only as a celebration but a mirroring of the Six Gallery event. Unfortunately, one was constantly reminded of the differences between the two events. The Six Gallery was an auto repair garage that had been converted into an art gallery. The building still stands. It was not a small space, but it boasted a kind of cavernous intimacy. You could see the people who were listening to you and the crowd was active – encouraging readers, making remarks. This was not the case with Herbst Theater, in which the audience – some of whom had paid $200 for the privilege of attending – was largely passive, as if it were attending a concert of classical music. There were 'refreshments' in the lobby, but certainly no one was passing around a jug of homemade 'Dago Red', as Jack Kerouac had done at the original reading. Michael McClure remarked, 'There are a lot more people here tonight' than there were at the Six Gallery. There were indeed about a thousand people in Herbst Hall's ample, packed space, though no one had to stand, as they had at the Six Gallery reading. Earlier in 1955, McClure writes in *Scratching the Beat Surface*, the Anarchist poet Robert Duncan had performed at the Six Gallery and 'had stripped off his clothes at the end of [his play, *Foust Foutu (Faust Fucked)*].' One could have the sense of doing something *illicit*, even 'subversive' at the Six Gallery. Not at Herbst Theater.

'Howl Redux' was subtitled 'Allen Ginsberg's "Howl" and Other San Francisco Revolutionary Writings.' Scarcely a month goes by in San Francisco without a newspaper article announcing that 'The Beat Goes On': literature, and particularly Beat literature, has become part of the city's tourist industry. San Francisco wants 'Howl' to be 'Redux', and so it isn't surprising that a genteel, officially-sponsored, city-wide event like Litquake should celebrate the 50th anniversary of Ginsberg's great, anarchic, thumb-nosing poem – a blast of language directed precisely *against* gentility, 'over-turning', Ginsberg wrote to Richard Eberhart in March 1956, 'any notion of propriety, moral "value", superficial "maturity", Trilling-esque sense of "civilization."' The poem celebrates those

who passed through universities with radiant cool eyes hallucinating Arkansas
  and Blake-light tragedy among the scholars of war,
who were expelled from the academies for crazy &
  publishing obscene odes on the windows of the skull,
who cowered in unshaven rooms in underwear, burning their money in
    wastebaskets and listening to the Terror through the wall,
who got busted in their pubic beards returning through Laredo with a belt
  of marijuana for New York,
who ate fire in paint hotels or drank turpentine in Paradise Alley, death, or
  purgatoried their torsos night after night
with dreams, with drugs, with waking nightmares, alcohol and cock and
  endless balls...

The event at Herbst Theater was unfortunately more like the embalming of 'Howl' than like its revivification. There was certainly no mention of 'drugs' – even though drugs (heroin and peyote in addition to marijuana) were an important aspect of the early work of both Lamantia and McClure, who were celebrated along with Ginsberg. Beat historian Ann Charters attended the first complete reading of 'Howl' in March, 1956 in Berkeley – the first attempt to 'repeat' the Six Gallery reading – and remarked to me in an interview that, while she was impressed with the poetry of Ginsberg, Whalen, Snyder, and McClure, she was 'unnerved by the drunken wildness of their friends in the audience and Robert LaVigne's drawings of Orlovsky [her date for the evening] making love with Ginsberg.' Robert LaVigne corrected Charters' remark – Ginsberg's partner in the drawings was not Peter Orlovsky but someone else – but wildness, nakedness, drunkenness, and eroticism were all aspects of what the Six Poets at the Six Gallery were doing. Like Ginsberg's poem, the event was meant to shock. It was certainly not meant to assure a city's bourgeoisie that Great Literature continued to be produced within city limits. The audience at Herbst Theater tittered when mention was made of U.S. Customs Officer Chester McPhee's opinion that 'Howl' was 'obscene', but none of the poem's genuine and deliberate obscenities – imagination's grenades hurled at propriety – were present in Herbst Hall. The people in Ginsberg's poem

> howled on their knees in the subway and were dragged off
> the roof waving genitals and manuscripts...
> let themselves be fucked in the ass by saintly motorcyclists,
> and screamed with joy...
> blew and were blown by those human seraphim, the sailors,
> caresses of
> Atlantic and Caribbean love...

No one was doing anything like that at Herbst Theater. Though we were shown film of Ginsberg reading from the first section of 'Howl' – which was all that was read at the Six Gallery – such passages were edited out of the footage. The 'secret hero' of the evening was definitely not 'N.C.... cocksman and Adonis of Denver' who 'sweetened the snatches of a million girls trembling in the sunset' and 'went out whoring through Colorado in myriad stolen night-cars.' At Litquake, all of the rough edges – where subversion happens – were carefully smoothed over. The organisers of Litquake undoubtedly meant well, but Jack Kerouac's Allen Ginsberg – 'Allen Ginsberg in an even wilder way' – was definitely not present. 'Howl' is a wonderfully subversive poem – and part of what it is subverting is 'literature', what Ginsberg called 'civilization'. *Tout le reste est littérature* (Verlaine) – but not 'Howl'. It maintains its power not through genteel public presentation but through the secret, quasi-illicit longings of generations of readers who believe that the poem speaks precisely, and uniquely, to them. For all its fame, 'Howl' is not a public poem – though it became a public poem in every possible way.

As Ginsberg himself understood, 'Howl' is fundamentally a 'guilty pleasure':

> I thought I wouldn't write a poem but just write what I wanted to without fear, let my imagination go, open secrecy, and scribble magic lines from my real mind – sum up my life – something I wouldn't be able to show anybody, writ for my own soul's ear and a few other golden ears. So the first line of Howl, ' saw the best minds etc,' the whole first section typed out madly in one afternoon, a huge sad comedy of wild phrasing, meaningless images for the beauty of abstract poetry of mind running along making awkward combinations like Charlie Chaplin's walk, long saxophone-like chorus lines I knew Kerouac would hear sound of – taking off from his own inspired prose line really a new poetry... Have I really been attacked for this sort of joy?
>
> (Notes to the LP, *Allen Ginsberg reads HOWL and Other Poems*)

But even a guilty pleasure can be a testimony to human freedom. 'Howl' is closer to the writings of the Marquis de Sade than it is to *The Waste Land*. It is not surprising that such a poem, like the writings of de Sade, should run afoul of the law, but it is certainly ironic that 'Howl' had to be defended not as a great blast of anarchic (even pornographic) freedom – which is what it is – but as an outstanding piece of 'literature', a monument to the 'civilization' that good liberals like Lionel Trilling were strenuously upholding. (The difference between Trilling and Kerouac is immediately apparent if you compare the titles of their novels: both titles invoke the metaphor of travel, but Trilling wrote *The Middle of the Journey*, with its quietly genteel reference to Dante; Kerouac wrote the more demotic – and memorable – *On the Road*.)

It's not that 'Howl' isn't 'literature' – of course it is – but it is not genteel literature; it is in some deep sense *illegal*, but it had to be defended as if it were *A Tale of Two Cities*. The people who attacked it were in a certain sense correct. Ginsberg (who did not attend the trial) is saying '*Yes*, I *am* being obscene – *and I don't care if you think so*.' Of course the book should not have been banned, but the terms in which it had to be defended were necessarily to some degree a betrayal of the very energy which gave the poem life. David Gates is surely correct when, in 'Welcoming "Howl" Into the Canon' (in *The Poem That Changed America: 'Howl' Fifty Years Later*, ed. Jason Shinder), he writes, 'Ginsberg *meant* the poem to be obscene':

> not merely offensive in its forbidden words describing forbidden acts but offensive to intellect, to common sense, to all our consensual realities, to all the boundaries we believe necessary to civilized life. This is not, at bottom, a poem holding up liberal, or libertarian, pieties against conservative pieties, although that's how it had to be sold to the judge and the public, and it's what Ginsberg himself sometimes seemed to argue when he put on his crusader-for-free-speech hat. It's a radically offensive poem, or used to be – offensive even to received notions of what poetry is, and it needs offended readers whose fear and outrage bring it most fully to life.

Ginsberg always insisted on 'Howl''s structure and tirelessly pointed it out: 'The Poem," he told Richard Eberhart, 'is really built like a brick shithouse.' But in fact the thrill of 'Howl' does not reside in its structure but in its astonishing and exhilarating approach to sheer chaos, to madness – its '*radical* offensiveness'.

City Lights' new *Howl on Trial: The Battle for Free Expression*, definitely wears the crusader-for-free-speech hat. But this too is an aspect of Ginsberg's poem – if not exactly of what he originally wrote, at least of the poem's tangled, intricate history.

The book begins with a brief introduction by Lawrence Ferlinghetti. The celebrated poet/publisher reminisces about his involvement with the publication of 'Howl' – 'the repressive, conformist, racist, homophobic world of the 1950s cried out for it' – and denounces 'this time of rampant materialism, militarism, nationalism, and omnivorous corporate monoculture eating up the world.' It's interesting to note that Ferlinghetti didn't really 'get' 'Howl' until he heard Ginsberg read it: 'Ginsberg handed me "Howl" with some hesitation, as if wondering whether I would know what to do with it. I didn't. But later that week when I heard him read it at the Six Gallery, I suddenly knew what had to be done.' (In a 1956 letter to Lucien Carr, Ginsberg himself notes that 'Howl' is 'very good read aloud cause it's got swing.' And Gregory Corso's review of the poem – included in *Howl on Trial* – asserts, '"Howl" is essentially a poem to be read aloud, but only by the Howler... any other Howler would screw it up...').

Ferlinghetti's remarks are followed by a useful chronology of 'Howl' and then by Nancy J. Peters' searing essay, 'Milestones of Literary Censorship'. 'And so it went,' she writes, 'American law continuing to be shaped by a small group of evangelistic zealots that claimed to represent everyone in the country.' The essay gives us a fascinating chronology, 'The Struggle for Free Expression', which begins in 1821 with John Cleland's *Fanny Hill: Memoirs of a Woman of Pleasure* and ends with the chilling assertion, 'Under present law, Allen Ginsberg's "Howl" could be subject to censorship once again if offered on City Lights' web site.' One of the dates mentioned in 'The Struggle for Free Expression' is 1978: *F.C.C. v. Pacifica Foundation*. The Court held that the F.C.C. could create time, place, and matter restrictions on literary and other material to be broadcast. For example, Ginsberg's 'Howl' was among the works restricted to the early morning hours when children would presumably be asleep.

This 28-year-old ruling continues to create problems for people attempting to broadcast literature on stations such as KPFA.

On October 3, 1957 Judge Clayton W. Horn issued his enlightened decision finding Lawrence Ferlinghetti not guilty of publishing and selling obscene writings. *Howl on Trial* includes passages from Judge Horn's decision. In part the decision reads,

> The theme of 'Howl' presents 'unorthodox and controversial ideas.' Coarse and vulgar language is used in treatment and sex acts are mentioned, but unless the book is entirely lacking in 'social importance', it cannot be held obscene... The book or material must be judged as a whole by its effect on the average adult in the community. If the material is objectionable only because of coarse and vulgar language which is not erotic or aphrodisiac in character it is not obscene... The People state that it is not necessary to use such words and that others would be more palatable to good taste. The answer is that life is not encased in one formula whereby everyone acts the same or conforms to a particular pattern. No two persons think alike; we were all made from the same mold but in different patterns. Would there be any freedom of press or speech if one must reduce his vocabulary to vapid innocuous euphemism?

Ginsberg's letters are enjoyable and interesting. Many of them are about money, which was a factor for both Ferlinghetti and Ginsberg. Ginsberg defends his work but occasionally has doubts about it too: 'The poems are actually sloppy enough written,' he admits, "ithout sloppiness made worse by typographical arrangement.' He generously credits Jack Kerouac for 'Howl''s technique: 'I realize how right you are, that was the first time I sat down to blow, it came out in your method, sounding like you, an imitation practically.' There are amusing moments, tech talk about poetry ('The technical problem raised and partially solved is the breakthrough begun by Whitman but never carried forward, from both iambic stultification and literary automatism, and unrhythmical shortline verse, which does not yet offer any kind of *base* cyclical flow for the build up of a powerful rhythm'), and the long, impassioned defence of his work to John Hollander. In fact, one could wish for even more letters.

Louis Ginsberg's 1956 letter to his son, for example, in which the father commends the son's 'wild, rhapsodic, explosive outpouring' but deplores his foul language: 'I still insist... there is no need for dirty, ugly, words, as they will entangle you unnecessarily in trouble. Try to cut them out...' Or Allen's 1955 letter to his previous mentor William Carlos Williams – a poet noted for his 'shortline verse':

> The key is in Jazz choruses to some extent; also to reliance on spontaneity & expressiveness which long line encourages; also to attention to interior unchecked logical mental stream. With a long line comes a return [to], (caused by) expressive human feeling, it's generally lacking in poetry now, which is inhuman. The release of emotion is one with rhythmical build-up of long line.

The excerpts from the trial testimony are fascinating and well edited, so that one has a sense of the progress of the trial. Judge Horn's statements are always balanced and interesting, and he emerges as a literate, intelligent man. 'It is obvious,' he states, 'that you are never going to get unanimous consent on anything that is involved in this case. That's the reason it is such a difficult question. That's the reason why the freedom of the press should be so stringently protected, so that no one segment of the country can censor to the injury of the rest, what they can read, see and hear and so forth. That is why this case is such an important one, why I am giving it such a lot of time and consideration.'

Notable writers – some of them now more or less forgotten –

come forth to praise Ginsberg's poem. Mark Schorer, who had written a book on Blake, speaks of 'The language of the street, which is absolutely essential to the aesthetic purpose of the work'; Kenneth Rexroth describes 'Howl' as 'prophetic literature': 'the theme is the denunciation of evil and a pointing out of the consequences and a call to repent and a pointing out of the way out... "Woe! Woe! Woe! The City of Jerusalem! The Syrian is about to come down or has already, and you are to do such and such a thing and you must repent and do thus and so."' He describes 'Howl' as a poem of 'extraordinarily high' merit and calls it 'probably the most remarkable single poem, published by a young man since the second war.'

Though *Howl on Trial* centres on a particular poem, it is less a book about poetry than it is about a poem's encounter with history – history in the particular form of a society the poem not only places in question but actually insults: 'Moloch the incomprehensible prison! Moloch the crossbone soulless jailhouse and Congress of sorrows! Moloch whose buildings are judgment! Moloch the vast stone of war! Moloch the stunned governments!' If such a book can emerge triumphant within the American judicial system, is Moloch as all embracing as he seems? The trial, as the editors of *Howl on Trial* know very well, gives reason for hope.

Howl on Trial opens with the assertion that 'Fifty years after the trial it seems impossible to believe that anyone could have ever doubted the literary merit of *Howl and Other Poems*.' That may be the way things appear to the talented people at 261 Columbus Avenue, but despite 'Howl''s many, many adherents – its 'howlers' – doubts about the 'literary merit' of Ginsberg's work continue to be voiced, most recently by New Formalist writers such as David Mason. I don't agree with the naysayers but have to admit that there is something deliberately annoying about Ginsberg's poem, something which all its success has never succeeded in covering over. The poem continues to sting. *Howl on Trial* ignores that fact in order to pursue other matters – matters of considerable importance, to be sure, even matters of considerable personal importance to Allen Ginsberg, for whom free speech and censorship were burning issues. Bill Morgan is surely right when, in the concluding chapter, he insists that 'The Censorship Battle Continues'. But in making its case *Howl on Trial* is not quite fair to the amazing, violent, tender, excessive, controversial poem City Lights published on November 1, 1956.

'Howl' may be, as Jason Shinder has it, 'the poem that changed America', but the event at Herbst Hall is an indication of how America can change 'Howl'. The poem is not only a thumbing of the nose at 'propriety, moral "value", superficial "maturity",' but the product of a tremendous longing for the visionary, for what Ginsberg calls in 'Model Texts: Inspirations Precursor to HOWL' the 'breakthru to unobstructed Spirit', a condition which will redeem the 'bad boy' aspect of his poem and give the writer access to another, more satisfying mode of 'respectability'. Ginsberg cites – and quotes from – Christopher Smart's 'Jubilate Agno', Shelley's 'Adonais' and 'Ode to the West Wind', Apollinaire's 'Zone', Kurt Schwitters' 'Priimiititiii', Mayakovsky's 'At the Top of My Voice', Lorca's Poet in New York, Hart Crane's 'Atlantis', William Carlos Williams' 'To Elsie' and of course Whitman's *Leaves of Grass*.

From this point of view, the outcast becomes the poet-saint, the sage. In effect, the poet is saying, 'I am not only not to be discarded, treated as dirt – beaten down, destroyed – I am at this moment better than anyone, and I can prove it by my words and by the precursor poets who come alive in the texture of my verse. I have transformed myself into the High Priest of your culture. Listen to the holiness of my utterance.'(In his 1956 letter to Richard Eberhart, Ginsberg wrote, 'I used to think I was mad to want to be a saint, but now what have I got to fear? People's opinions? Loss of a teaching job? I am living outside this contex.')

'Howl' is indeed the '*radically* offensive' document David Gates claims it to be, but it is also the announcement of the creation of a poet – and the poet is, precisely, the redemption of the pariah. Ginsberg remarked in 1976 that '"Howl" is really about my mother,' the formidable Naomi who died in the insane asylum and whose spirit animates his great poem, 'Kaddish' ('More Explanations Twenty Years After'). Naomi's was definitely a mind 'destroyed by madness', and she lurks behind the more public figure of Carl Solomon.

In an interview with Lawrence Grobel, published in *Endangered Species: Writers Talk About Their Craft, Their Visions, Their Lives*, Ginsberg remarks, '"Howl" was actually written with [my mother] in mind':

> 'Carl Solomon! I'm With You in Rockland' really is my mother and 'I'm with you in Pilgrim State Hospital', in the sense of a release of feeling, an acknowledgement and release of maternal tenderness, which though thwarted still exists intact with me, or in anyone, probably. Tenderness toward mother, the only mother I have after all, whatever condition she was in. So 'Howl' was actually an emotional reunion with my mother.

At the same time he remarks about his horror at actually seeing his mother:

> I sent her 'Howl' at Pilgrim State Hospital, where she was in her last months before her stroke. She hadn't recognized me about a half year before when I visited. She thought I was a spy, actually. It was very disturbing – I wept. It seemed like the farthest limit of dehumanisation and illness and madness, that she couldn't remember me.

The poet's letter to Eberhart insists that 'I am saying that what seems "mad" in America is our expression of natural ecstasy' but also admits to feelings of sympathy and identification with the rejected, mystical, individual even 'mad'. His ambivalent feelings about madness – cf. the hipster's exclamation, 'crazy' – are at the very centre of 'Howl'. The poem is an act of identification with the mother, but it is also an expression of the poet's horror at what his mother has become: trapped in the power of Moloch. 'Howl' is simultaneously mad (really mad, like Naomi) and – a poem, an 'expression of natural ecstasy'. The power of the piece is that it inhabits both worlds and will not exchange one for the other:

> Breakthroughs! over the river! flips and crucifixions!
> gone down the flood! Highs! Epiphanies! Despairs!
> Ten years' animal screams and suicides! Minds!
> New loves! Mad generations! down on the rocks
> of Time!

Jack Foley's landmark book *Visions &Affiliations: A California Literary Time Line: Poets and Poetry 1940-2005* is available now from Pantograph Press.

THE RACONTEUR

POETRY

MADISON TIME
L.A. RAIN

Tim Wells

The three of us had driven up from Los Angeles. Roddy and myself were to read. We didn't know it was an old folks' spread 'til we got there. They weren't ready for the Poetry Group yet and the organiser seemed somewhat surprised at our relative youth. It seems that up until then he'd had no competition for the affections of the ladies. I can't speak for Roddy but I'd no intention of giving him any. Roddy did his Wing Biddlebaum bit and smoked. I'd been looking forward to a drink at the bar, but there wasn't one so I killed time looking at the notice board instead.

The plugs were mainly dead women's belongings and burial plots. I'd have settled for a Whiskey Mac.

I heard music from down the corridor, and so far it had been the only sign of life being lived so I went to see what was happening.

Looking into a room I saw Fifty something year old Koreans circling the room in time, mostly, to music spun by an old, diskette type record player. There were two couples, and a dozen single women who had to dance alone. Their empty arms held onto partners they'd craved, never had, or lost.

There they were, shuffling around the room, alone, as the Korean boss lady barked:

'1 2 3 4,

1 2 3 4.'

They were preparing for an America that had died with JFK. Only no one had told them.

I put my face to the glass of the door and waved. Most just looked at their feet as they 1 2 3 4'ed around the room. One lone woman though, she looked back, smiled and then waved too.

I felt better; if no-one could Howard Keel through the song in their heart here at least was a soul whistling the refrain.

Next door the poets were solving the problems of the world. None of them was dancing.

L.A. RAIN

you can see the neon and never see the light
the footsteps of all those who can afford not to walk
readily washed away
men's feet in women's shoes

the footsteps of all those who can afford not to walk
water dancing hipshots across the oiled smear
men's feet in women's shoes
the hookers of Santa Monica Boulevard

water dancing hipshots across the oiled smear
water finds its own level
the hookers of Santa Monica Boulevard
the gutters full to bursting

water finds its own level
only cream and bastards float
the gutters full to bursting
fresh water gives life, this beats down

only cream and bastards float
waitresses course through the channels of Chinatown
fresh water gives life, this beats down
dirtiest rain I ever saw

waitresses course through the channels of Chinatown
readily washed away
dirtiest rain I ever saw
you can see the neon and never see the light

THE RACONTEUR

WRITERS' GRAVES

BILLY WILDER

Dylan Moore

© Dylan Moore

The Westwood Village Memorial Park Cemetery is famous as the last resting place of the interred remains of Marilyn Monroe. As such, it is one of the most popular celebrity grave pilgrimages in the world, rivalled only by the eclectic likes of Shakespeare and Princess Diana, Jim Morrison and Elvis, Mark Twain and Oscar Wilde. But this quiet cemetery, hidden away in this upmarket suburb of Los Angeles, is also the final resting place of many other stars of stage, screen and letters. Dean Martin, Truman Capote and Jack Lemmon – whose headstone reads simply 'Jack Lemmon in', comically indicating the ground – all have their final resting place here.

But in terms of memorable epitaphs, there is none better than Marilyn and Jack's director on *Some Like It Hot*, Billy Wilder, which uses a play on the film's famous last scene, in which Jerry (Lemmon) takes off his wig to reveal that he can't marry Osgood (Joe E. Brown) because 'I'm a man!' to which he gets the immortal reply, 'Well, nobody's perfect.'

It seems fitting that the director had the good humour to ally the comic line that cemented his place in movie history with his primary concern; despite his skills as an auteur, Billy Wilder considered himself, first and foremost, 'a writer'. Unlike more experimental contemporaries like Hitchcock and Welles, who were reinventing cinema with films like *Psycho* and *Citizen Kane*, Wilder was a storyteller. His conservative cinematography allowed for tightly scripted character-driven plots and in the process produced some of the most memorable films of Hollywood's Golden Age.

Even if you haven't seen the films, titles like *Sunset Boulevard* and *Double Indemnity* are redolent of an almost mythical era when the film industry seem to capture America in her mid twentieth-century pomp. *Indemnity* was his collaboration with Raymond Chandler and for many the apotheosis of film noir. *Sunset Boulevard*, as its title suggests, is about Hollywood itself. The main character, Joe Gillis, played by William Holden, is a screenwriter. He sums up his film-writing career with the remark, 'The last one I wrote was about Okies in the dustbowl. You'd never know, because when it reached the screen, the whole thing played on a torpedo boat.' When another character says, 'I'd always heard that you had some talent', he replies, 'that was last year. This year I'm trying to make a living.'

Other writers may have been more caustic in their criticism of the censorship laws, but few were as successful as Wilder in pushing the boundaries back. His films – *The Lost Weekend*, an adaptation of Charles R. Jackson's story about alcoholism, and *The Apartment* and *The Seven-Year Itch* about infidelity and adultery – defied the censors and put real-life issues on screen for the first time.

What Wilder realised about characters – and therefore about people in general – now glints in gold in the west coast sunlight. The inscription on his headstone reinforces the fact that far from being a throwaway remark the line is an insight into the human condition that all true writers know only too well: *Nobody's Perfect.*

That's all folks.

THE Raconteur

Beauty

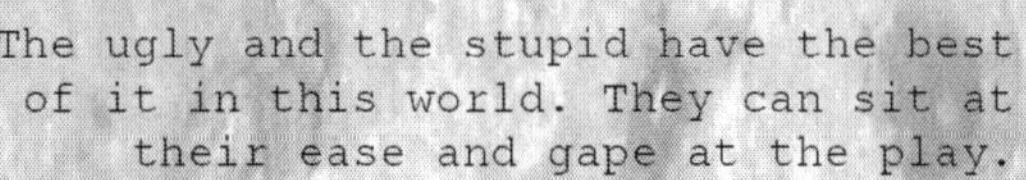

The ugly and the stupid have the best of it in this world. They can sit at their ease and gape at the play.

eauty is only skin
eep, but ugly goes
lean to the bone

A thing of beauty is a joy forever; its loveliness increases; it will never pass into nothingness

eauty is truth, truth
eauty, - that is all Ye
now on earth, and all ye
eed to know.

People are like stained-glass windows. They sparkle and shine when the sun is out, but when the darkness sets in, their true beauty is revealed only if there is a light from within.

It is better to be beautiful than to be good, but it is better to be good than to be ugly.

Beauty is unbearable
drives us to despair,
offering us for a minute
the glimpse of an
eternity that
we should like
to stretch out
over the
whole of time.

ove of beauty
s Taste. The
reation of
beauty is Art.

No object is so beautiful that, under certain conditions, it will not look ugly.

Beauty is not caused. It is.

CONTRIBUTORS

Russell Celyn Jones is a novelist and critic. His novels are: *The Ninth Wave*; *Ten Seconds From The Sun*; *Surface Tension*; *The Eros Hunter*; *An Interference of Light*; *Small Times*; *Soldiers and Innocents*. He has won a Society of Author's Award, a Welsh Arts Council Fiction Prize, David Higham Prize and the Weishanhu Award (China). He has been a Man Booker Prize Judge and is currently Professor of Creative Writing at Birkbeck College, University of London.

lloyd robson is a writer, broadcaster, maladjusted malcontent and loose gum for hire. He is author of *city & poems*; *edge territory*; *letter from sissi*; *cardiff cut*; *bbboing! & associated weirdness*; and *Oh Dad! A Search for Robert Mitchum*.

Bobby Sanabria – drummer, percussionist, composer, arranger, recording artist, producer, filmmaker, conductor, educator, multi-cultural warrior and multiple Grammy nominee – has performed with a veritable Who's Who in the world of jazz and Latin music, as well as with his own critically acclaimed ensembles.

Catherine Fletcher is a poet, an editor for *Rattapallax* magazine, and the Director of Poetry Programs at City Lore. Her work has appeared in *Poetry Wales*, *Urhalpool*, *Rattapallax* and other journals, and she has produced poetry events around New York City and abroad, most recently *Illuminated Verses: Poetries of the Islamic World*. She lives in New York.

Salena Godden hosts and produces The Book Club Boutique – Soho's hippest literary salon. She features regularly on the BBC's *The Verb* and *Bespoken Word* and is a poet-in-residence on Radio 4's *Saturday Live*. Her latest poetry collection *Under The Pier* was published by hip-indie imprint Nasty Little Press in 2011.

Rhian Edwards' first collection of poems *Clueless Dogs* will be published by Seren in February 2012. Rhian's pamphlet *Parade the Fib*, (tall-Lighthouse), was awarded the Poetry Book Society Choice for autumn 2008.

Taylor Glenn is an award-winning American comedienne, writer and actress based in the UK.

Tom Abbott lives in Bath. After growing up in Hertfordshire, it was the five years he spent living in Virginia as a teenager that had the most profound effect on his writing. He is represented by AP Watt literary agency, and his first novel, *To The Pines*, set in prohibition-era East Tennessee, has been delivered to publishing houses in both the UK and the USA. Whilst he keeps his fingers crossed hoping for a publishing deal, he has started work on a new novel, *Mark Me With An Anchor*, set in a tattoo parlour in modern-day Savannah, Georgia. He is 28 years old.

Jo Mazelis is a writer of short stories, non fiction and poetry. Her collection of stories *Diving Girls* (Parthian, 2002) was short-listed for The Commonwealth Best First Book and Welsh Book of the Year. Her second book, *Circle Games* (Parthian, 2005), was long-listed for Welsh Book of the Year.

Tamar Yoseloff was born in the US in 1965. Since moving to London in 1987, she has been the organiser of the Terrible Beauty reading series at the Troubadour Coffee House; Reviews Editor of *Poetry London* magazine; and from 2000 to 2007, Programme Coordinator for The Poetry School. She currently works as a freelance tutor in creative writing.

Tom Anderson grew up in Porthcawl, and was led into a writing career through journeys taken as a surfer. His debut travel memoir *Riding the Magic Carpet* told the story of a quest to visit South Africa and surf at the fabled 'J-Bay'; this was followed by *Chasing Dean*, a mixture between novel and travelogue set against the backdrop of the Atlantic hurricane season.

Yahia Lababidi, born 1973, is an internationally published writer of Egyptian-Lebanese origin. His first book was *Signposts to Elsewhere*. In 2007, his work was included in an encyclopedia of the World's Great Aphorists. Meantime, Lababidi's essays and poems have appeared in journals world-wide. His latest collection of essays is *Trial by Ink*.

Heathcote Williams – poet, playwright and actor, has made a significant contribution to many fields. He is best known for his extended poems on environmental subjects: *Whale Nation*, *Falling for a Dolphin*, *Sacred Elephant* and *Autogeddon*. His plays have also won acclaim, notably *AC/DC*, produced at London's Royal Court, and *Hancock's Last Half Hour*. As an actor he has been equally versatile – taking memorable roles in *Orlando*, *Wish You Were Here*, and Derek Jarman's *The Tempest*, in which he played Prospero.

David E. Oprava is an American writer who has been published in over one hundred journals online and in print. He has three full-length collections of poetry: *VS.* (Erbacce Press, 2008) *American Means* (American Mettle Books, 2009), and *sole* (Blackheath Books, 2010). He lives in the UK.

Graham Isaac is a writer of fiction, poetry, and music reviews who grew up in the Pacific Northwest. He holds an MA in Creative and Media Writing from University of Wales, Swansea, and his work has appeared in *Licton Springs Review*, *Jeopardy*, *Roundyhouse*, *Hoarse* and other publications. He currently lives and writes in Seattle.

Robert Lewis is from the Black Mountains, in the Brecon Beacons. *The Last Llanelli Train*, his first novel, was nominated for the 2006 Bollinger Everyman Wodehouse Prize for Comic Fiction and began the Robin Llewellyn Welsh noir trilogy. He concluded it with his latest book *The Bank of The Black Sheep* (Serpents Tail, 2010).

Joâo Morais is from Cardiff, and is about to start a PhD at the University there. He appeared in Parthian's recent anthology, *Nu2: Memorable Firsts*. He was a runner-up in the 2009 Rhys Davies Short Story Competition.

Dan Tyte is a writer based in Cardiff, Wales. He's written on subjects as diverse as Tim Burton movies, baby names and the Icelandic mayoral system, for men's magazines and newspapers. He used to interview rock stars in budget hotel rooms but got out before the beer got flat. He had a poem turned into a short film earlier this year and is currently writing his debut novel.

Mimi Thebo is an American author who lives and works in England. She has published seven books in the last ten years. Her work has been read on Radio Four, adapted for a Bafta-winning film by the BBC, translated into eight languages and illustrated in light against the Shell Building on London's South Bank.

Tim Wells has cultivated a laugh that's more like a caress. He walks properly. He does not slouch, shuffle or stumble about. He knows that wide, floating trousers are only good for wearing on a veranda with a cocktail in your hand. His latest collection, *Rougher Yet*, is published by Donut Press.

Jack Foley is a widely-published San Francisco poet and critic. Born in Neptune, New Jersey in 1940, raised in Port Chester, New York, and educated at Cornell University, Foley moved to California in 1963 to attend U. C. Berkeley. His new book, a mammoth encyclopaedia of Beat poetry, *Visions & Affiliations: A California Literary Time Line, Poets & Poetry*, is out now published by Pantograph Press.

Todd Zuniga is a Puschart Prize-nominated writer for his short fiction and an award-winning journalist. The founding editor of *Opium* magazine, the journal of literary humor for the deliriously captivated, Zuniga is also the co-creator and host of worldwide spoken word event *Literary Death Match*.

Images